THE ANGELIC CONFLICT

THE ANGELIC CONFLICT

Pastor Robert R. McLaughlin

Copyright © 2012 by Pastor Robert R. McLaughlin.

Library of Congress Control Number:		2012907363
ISBN:	Hardcover	978-1-4771-0219-0
	Softcover	978-1-4771-0218-3
	Ebook	978-1-4771-0220-6

All rights reserved. No part of this book may be reproduced or transmitted in any form or by any means, electronic or mechanical, including photocopying, recording, or by any information storage and retrieval system, without permission in writing from the copyright owner.

This book was printed in the United States of America.

To order additional copies of this book, contact:
Xlibris Corporation
1-888-795-4274
www.Xlibris.com
Orders@Xlibris.com
113122

Contents

Introduction ... 11
1. The Beginning ... 23
2. The Existence of Rational Creatures. ... 28
3. When and How the Angelic Conflict Began ... 36
4. After Satan's Fall, He Deceives the Whole World ... 46
5. Satanic Attacks During the Church Age ... 51
6. The Satanic Plan and Two Categories of Fallen Angels Under his Command. ... 73
7. The Courtroom Trial of the Angelic Conflict. ... 97
8. The Third Witness ... 114
9. The Strategic Victory of the Angelic Conflict ... 161
10. The Importance Of The Hypostatic Union ... 171
11. The Pseudo-Victory of Satan in The Original Fall of Man. ... 190
12. How God is Glorified in the Angelic Conflict. ... 224
13. Free Will in the Human Race Perpetuates the Angelic Conflict ... 244
14. The Angelic Conflict Observation and Opposition in Human History. ... 267
15. The Angelic Conflict in Human History Answers the Basic Questions About Life. ... 276
16. Operation Footstool ... 318

Glossary of Terms ... 337

SYMPATHY FOR THE DEVIL

Please allow me to introduce myself
I'm a man of wealth and taste
I've been around for a long, long year
Stole many a man's soul and faith

And I was 'round when Jesus Christ
Had his moment of doubt and pain
Made damn sure that Pilate
Washed his hands and sealed his fate

Pleased to meet you
Hope you guess my name
But what's puzzling you
Is the nature of my game

I stuck around St. Petersburg
When I saw it was a time for a change
Killed the Czar and his ministers
Anastasia screamed in vain

I rode a tank
Held a general's rank
When the Blitzkrieg raged
And the bodies stank

Pleased to meet you
Hope you guess my name, oh yeah
Ah, what's puzzling you
Is the nature of my game, oh yeah

I watched with glee
While your kings and queens
Fought for ten decades
For the gods they made

I shouted out,
"Who killed the Kennedy's?"
When after all
It was you and me

Let me please introduce myself
I'm a man of wealth and taste
And I laid traps for troubadours
Who get killed before they reached Bombay

Pleased to meet you
Hope you guessed my name, oh yeah
But what's puzzling you
Is the nature of my game,

Pleased to meet you
Hope you guessed my name, oh yeah
But what's confusing you
Is just the nature of my game

Just as every cop is a criminal
And all the sinners saints
As heads is tails
Just call me Lucifer
Cause I'm in need of some restraint

So if you meet me
Have some courtesy
Have some sympathy, have some taste
Use all your well-learned politesse
Or I'll lay your soul to waste,

Pleased to meet you
Hope you guessed my name,
But what's puzzling you
Is the nature of my game,

> Tell me baby, what's my name
> Tell me honey, can ya guess my name
> Tell me baby, what's my name
> I tell you one time, you're to blame

Although, this is a song that has many personal opinions to it, the concept I want you to note is how Satan does deceive the human race and tries to disguise his real intention. Ultimately, Isa 14:12-14 describes his intent, which we will note in this book. Being in a Rock band I use to actually sing this song being totally ignorant of its true meaning. I thank my Lord and Savoir for the deliverance from this deception and lies.

Introduction

The Angelic Conflict began before human history and is the reason for the creation of mankind. It is a conflict that is in full force today. This conflict explains the small personal problems in life as well as the major events that take place throughout all of human history. Although most individuals are ignorant of this conflict (including many Christians), the Angelic Conflict nevertheless does affect all aspects of our lives.

Author Karen Hancock put it this way:

> "The ultimate conspiracy, its true nature and parameters remain among the most carefully guarded secrets of all time. For the devil has deceived the whole world, as God tells us through the apostle John. Satan is the prince of the powers of the air, the ruler of the earth, the roaring lion prowling about seeking someone to devour. He is craftier than any creature, able to appear as an angel of light, with an indescribably beautiful voice. Far superior to man in intellect, he has blinded the minds of men, both Christians and non-Christians alike, persuading them that there is no God, that they are not sinners, that they do not need grace, that they can please God with their own works—that there is no devil, no hell, no unseen war at all." (see Rev 12:9; Rev 13:4; Eph 2:2; Joh 12:31; Mat 4:8-9; Eze 28:13-19; 2Co 11:3,14-15).

Most people, including many Christians, are unable to associate the events of their lives with the big picture, the Angelic Conflict itself. Like it or not, believe it or not, we are all a part of that conflict. One can hardly live in today's society and not come across the concept of good versus evil. Books, movies, video games, news, it is found everywhere, in a multitude of things that range from the abstract (evil as an unreasoning destructive force) to the personal (Satan against the servants of good or God Himself). It is a measure of Satan's genius that he uses all of these things to disguise, obscure, and pervert the truth.

It is through those means that this conflict is often trivialized, portrayed in comic book fashion, with Satan as a great monster. Drool glistens on his teeth as he rears up from the flames of his subterranean throne room to devour yet another hapless soul.

Most people have never seen such a monster in their lives, nor are they likely to. They know it does not exist, and therefore conclude that neither does Satan. Or perhaps they do believe such a thing exists, but it is down there in hell, out of the way, a place they certainly do not plan on going. In any case, it has little bearing on their workaday world. They leave the theater, or close the book having been amused, entertained, perhaps even somewhat frightened, but not enlightened. Rather, one more layer of deception has wrapped itself around their spiritual vision.

The shocking fact for many is that Satan is not a slimy, slobbering monster with terrifying teeth, red epidermis, a forked tail, and glowing eyes. Satan is also not confined to a subterranean inferno ruling over souls he has stolen from life to eternally torment in death. Satan has many titles, and the Bible says that he is the most beautiful creature ever to come from the hand of God. One of his titles, Lucifer, means "son of the morning." Satan was the guardian of the throne of God and persuaded at least a third of the angels to remain in rebellion against their perfect, righteous, and holy Creator. These two things alone would seem to testify to his personal appeal, beauty, intellect, and charisma. Satan still has free access to heaven when he is not roaming about the earth itself. (Eze 28:12-14, 17; Isa 14:12; Rev 12:4; Job 1:6, 7; Rev 12:10)

Many people, again even Christians, are also shocked to find out that Satan's greatest desire is not to destroy everything, nor to bring down a reign of darkness, fear, and terror as so many portrayals of him would have us believe. Satan intends to be like God, to rule in God's place, to be worshipped, loved, and praised as God is worshipped, loved, and praised (Isa 14:13,14; 2Th 2:4). If things go wrong in the nations and institutions he controls, it is far more likely the result of his inability to manage the sinful nature of man than his plan. Not that there are not things he wishes to destroy, there are many: he desires to destroy the Word of God, the reputation of the Lord Jesus Christ, the true memory of the Cross and what occurred there, as well as the Gospel.

Satan also desires to destroy any believer, particularly anyone who is advancing in God's plan for his or her life. Local churches proclaiming the Truth, nations that operate under Divine laws, the Jews, these are also on his list of things to destroy. Satan has as many plans to implement his desires of destruction as he does those to bring about his planned perfect world (see 2Co 11:3-4, 13-15; 1 Ti 4:1).

So how is it exactly that things have gotten to this point? The Bible teaches that before the creation of man, a conflict arose between God and His angels, when Satan attempted to ascend to the Mount of Heaven and wrest God's rulership away from Him. The resulting battle left the surface of the earth in what the Hebrew says (tohu wa bohu) was in ruins, at this point the earth was packed in ice. Presumably it was at this time that the trial occurred in which Satan and his cronies were found guilty and sentenced to the Lake of Fire.

> "Behold, the Lord lays the earth waste, devastates it, distorts its surface and scatters its inhabitants." (Isa 24:1)

> I looked on the earth, and behold, it was formless and void; And to the heavens, and they had no light. I looked on the mountains, and behold, they were quaking, And all the hills moved to and fro. I looked, and behold, there was no man, And all the birds of the heavens had fled. I looked, and behold, the fruitful land was a wilderness, And all its cities were pulled down Before the Lord, before His fierce anger." (Jer 4:23-26)

> "The earth was formless and void, and darkness was over the surface of the deep, and the Spirit of God was moving over the surface of the waters." (Gen 1:2)

The Hebrew phrase "tohuw waabohuw" is also used in Jer 4:23 to describe the results of a battle which verse 26 says occurred at a time when "there was no man" or in pre-history. Verse 26 adds that it was done by the Lord in "fierce anger."

> "Then He will also say to those on His left, 'Depart from Me, accursed ones, into the eternal fire which has been prepared for the devil and his angels;'" (Mat 25:41)

> "And the devil who deceived them was thrown into the lake of fire and brimstone, where the beast and the false prophet are also; and they will be tormented day and night forever and ever." (Rev 20:10)

Since Satan is obviously not yet in the Lake of Fire, the logical conclusion is that he appealed his sentence. We can speculate a number of grounds on which he is making this appeal, but one that seems to carry the most weight is an accusation against God's character that we hear often enough in life: How can a loving God cast His creatures into hell? To answer this appeal, God created man, a lower being, and set him in the great stadium of earth, an open theater for all the angels to observe.

1Co 4:9 uses the Greek word *theatron,* the place where public dramas were shown, it is where we get our English word for *theater*. Throughout all of human history, an audience of angels sees the character and nature of God shown to be infinitely loving and just and righteous. Through the genius of His plan, using the free will decisions of the original perfect man and woman, God arranged that all the rest of us would begin life condemned as sinners and rebels, condemned just as Satan is condemned.

> "For I do not want you, brethren, to be uninformed of this mystery—so that you will not be wise in your own estimation—that a partial hardening has happened to Israel until the fullness of the Gentiles has come in; and so all Israel

will be saved; just as it is written, 'The Deliverer will come from Zion, He will remove ungodliness from Jacob. This is My covenant with them, When I take away their sins.' From the standpoint of the gospel they are enemies for your sake, but from the standpoint of God's choice they are beloved for the sake of the fathers; for the gifts and the calling of God are irrevocable. For just as you once were disobedient to God, but now have been shown mercy because of their disobedience, so these also now have been disobedient, that because of the mercy shown to you they also may now be shown mercy. For God has shut up all in disobedience so that He may show mercy to all" (Rom 11:25-32).

God would take on the form of this lower being Himself, that had to be an incredible shock to all of the angelic creation. More shocking still, He would allow pitiful, sinful, stupid, gullible man to abuse and mock Him, and finally to nail Him to a Roman Cross in an attempt to destroy Him. In the end our Lord would bear the penalty for the sins of those same sinful, stupid, vicious people, and all the rest of us as well. In this He neutralized the claims His justice had against us, so that we could live with Him and fellowship with Him forever. There is no greater demonstration of love than this. This great show of self-sacrifice must show the angels what He was willing to do for them when they fell, though Scripture makes no direct mention of this.

"When you were dead in your transgressions and the uncircumcision of your flesh, He made you alive together with Him, having forgiven us all our transgressions, having canceled out the certificate of debt consisting of decrees against us, which was hostile to us; and He has taken it out of the way, having nailed it to the cross. When He had disarmed the rulers and authorities, He made a public display of them, having triumphed over them through Him." (Col 2:13-15)

"So then as through one transgression there resulted condemnation to all men, even so through one act of righteousness there resulted justification of life to all men." (Rom 5:18)

> "Truly, truly, I say to you, he who believes has eternal life. I am the bread of life. Your fathers ate the manna in the wilderness, and they died. This is the bread which comes down out of heaven, so that one may eat of it and not die. I am the living bread that came down out of heaven; if anyone eats of this bread, he will live forever; and the bread also which I will give for the life of the world is My flesh." (Joh 6:47-51)

The people who reject that love and the gift it has provided do not escape their state of condemnation.

> "For God so loved the world, that He gave His only begotten Son, that whoever believes in Him shall not perish, but have eternal life. For God did not send the Son into the world to judge the world, but that the world might be saved through Him. He who believes in Him is not judged; he who does not believe has been judged already, because he has not believed in the name of the only begotten Son of God." (Joh 3:16-18)

Eventually and eternally they will reap the consequences of their free will decisions against Him, just as Satan and his followers will one day reap theirs. All of it clearly demonstrates that God is indeed fair, just, and right, and that the fallen angels do deserve the sentence they have received. There is more though, for God is nothing if not thorough. Salvation from eternal condemnation is just the beginning of God's plan for those who believe and accept the gift. As He has delivered us from the power of sin in eternity, so He wishes to deliver us from its power in time. He wants to bless us in the devil's world, a world of sin, by giving us the privilege of testifying in this great trial as invisible heroes, witnesses for the prosecution. To that end, He has provided everything, all of the power and knowledge we need to be successful. We have only to take advantage of it, though that is a matter of choice. It is a matter of many choices made day after day after day all the way to the end of our lives. (Eph 1; Job 1-2; Job 42; 1Co 4:9; Heb 12:1)

It is naturally Satan's objective to see that we fail in this, his desire is to instead turn us into witnesses for the defense, to embarrass ourselves, our loved ones, and most of all, the One we claim to serve. Satan wants to deceive us and use us against each other, to confuse, scare, and neutralize us. Satan wants to get us distracted with inconsequential issues, making mountains out of molehills, wasting our lives as the Exodus generation wasted theirs, to have us too wandering in circles in the wilderness, ignorant, ineffectual, and ignominious. Above all he wants to keep us out of that Promised Land of blessing beyond imagination that is the province of the spiritually mature believer.

> "But the Spirit explicitly says that in later times some will fall away from the faith, paying attention to deceitful spirits and doctrines of demons." (1Ti 4:1)

> "What do I mean then? That a thing sacrificed to idols is anything, or that an idol is anything? No, but I say that the things which the Gentiles sacrifice, they sacrifice to demons and not to God; and I do not want you to become sharers in demons. You cannot drink the cup of the Lord and the cup of demons; you cannot partake of the table of the Lord and the table of demons."
> (1Co 10:19-21)

> "But before faith came, we were kept in custody under the law, being shut up to the faith which was later to be revealed."
> (Gal 3:23)

> "And someone came to Him and said, 'Teacher, what good thing shall I do that I may obtain eternal life?' And He said to him, 'Why are you asking Me about what is good? There is only One who is good; but if you wish to enter into life, keep the commandments.' Then he said to Him, 'Which ones?' And Jesus said, 'You shall not commit murder; You shall not commit adultery; You shall not steal; You shall not bear false witness; Honor your father and mother; and You shall love your neighbor as yourself.' The young man said to Him, 'All these things I have kept; what am I still lacking?' Jesus said to him, 'If you wish to be complete, go and sell your possessions and give to the poor, and you will have treasure in heaven; and come, follow Me.' But when the young man heard this

> statement, he went away grieving; for he was one who owned much property. And Jesus said to His disciples, 'Truly I say to you, it is hard for a rich man to enter the kingdom of heaven. Again I say to you, it is easier for a camel to go through the eye of a needle, than for a rich man to enter the kingdom of God.' When the disciples heard this, they were very astonished and said, 'Then who can be saved?' And looking at them Jesus said to them, 'With people this is impossible, but with God all things are possible.' Then Peter said to Him, 'Behold, we have left everything and followed You; what then will there be for us?' And Jesus said to them, 'Truly I say to you, that you who have followed Me, in the regeneration when the Son of Man will sit on His glorious throne, you also shall sit upon twelve thrones, judging the twelve tribes of Israel.'" (Mat 19:16-28)

> "Let no one in any way deceive you, for it will not come unless the apostasy comes first, and the man of lawlessness is revealed, the son of destruction, who opposes and exalts himself above every so-called god or object of worship, so that he takes his seat in the temple of God, displaying himself as being God." (2Th 2:3-4)

Because the Angelic Conflict is a trial, and because the human race is a witness in this trial, let us begin this doctrine by looking at some basic strategies that are used by lawyers in our judicial system. These strategies have some definite similarities with the Angelic Conflict. For example, one tactic is that of discrediting a witness. A lawyer will use other witnesses to introduce an opinion or testimony that is contrary to that of the person who is on trial. Satan and the kingdom of darkness have been using this tactic since the scene in the Garden of Eden, when Satan challenged the woman with the question: "Indeed has God said . . . ?" (Gen 3:1).

> "And even if our gospel is veiled, it is veiled to those who are perishing, in whose case the god of this world has blinded the minds of the unbelieving, that they might not see the light of the gospel of the glory of Christ, who is the image of God." (2Co 4:3-4)

This is one of the reasons why the apostle Paul wrote: "For He delivered us from the domain of darkness, and transferred us to the kingdom of His beloved Son."
(Col 1:13)

A second method or tactic used is that of looking for independent written evidence to contradict the one on trial. Throughout human history mankind has come up with all kinds of religions and false scientific evidence to try to discredit the Word of God. This contrary evidence is easily disputed with a thorough understanding of God's purpose, plan, and person.

A third strategy is to use other so-called expert witnesses to discredit the one on trial. Satan and his kingdom of darkness have used the so-called wisdom of men to discredit the wisdom of God.

> "For since in the wisdom of God the world through its wisdom did not come to know God, God was well-pleased through the foolishness of the message preached to save those who believe. For indeed Jews ask for signs, and Greeks search for wisdom; but we preach Christ crucified, to Jews a stumbling block, and to Gentiles foolishness, but to those who are the called, both Jews and Greeks, Christ the power of God and the wisdom of God. Because the foolishness of God is wiser than men, and the weakness of God is stronger than men." (1Co 1:21-25)

A fourth method or tactic is to disparage the witness by using prior statements in such a way as to make them appear inconsistent. This has been accomplished through discrediting the people of God for their sins and failures, as well as for their inconsistencies in fulfilling the plan of God for their life.

A fifth strategy or tactic is to show that the witness's testimony is prejudiced because of personal interest in the outcome of the trial. Satan tried to accomplish this with Job.

> "There was a man in the land of Uz, whose name was Job, and that man was blameless, upright, fearing God, and turning

away from evil. Now there was a day when the sons of God came to present themselves before the Lord, and Satan also came among them. And the Lord said to Satan, 'From where do you come?' Then Satan answered the Lord and said, 'From roaming about on the earth and walking around on it.' And the Lord said to Satan, 'Have you considered My servant Job? For there is no one like him on the earth, a blameless and upright man, fearing God and turning away from evil.' Then Satan answered the Lord, 'Does Job fear God for nothing? Hast Thou not made a hedge about him and his house and all that he has, on every side? Thou hast blessed the work of his hands, and his possessions have increased in the land. But put forth Thy hand now and touch all that he has; he will surely curse Thee to Thy face.' Then the Lord said to Satan, 'Behold, all that he has is in your power, only do not put forth your hand on him.' So Satan departed from the presence of the Lord. Again there was a day when the sons of God came to present themselves before the Lord, and Satan also came among them to present himself before the Lord. And the Lord said to Satan, 'Where have you come from?' Then Satan answered the Lord and said, 'From roaming about on the earth, and walking around on it.' And the Lord said to Satan, 'Have you considered My servant Job? For there is no one like him on the earth, a blameless and upright man fearing God and turning away from evil. And he still holds fast his integrity, although you incited Me against him, to ruin him without cause.' And Satan answered the Lord and said, 'Skin for skin! Yes, all that a man has he will give for his life. However, put forth Thy hand, now, and touch his bone and his flesh; he will curse Thee to Thy face.' So the Lord said to Satan, 'Behold, he is in your power, only spare his life.'" (Job 1:1-2:6)

So, the Angelic Conflict is a doctrine that needs to be completely understood by every believer in the Lord Jesus Christ. With that understanding comes the ability to answer important questions such as: "Why are we (the human race) here?" "Why is there salvation, and what are we (the human race) to do after salvation?" "Why is there suffering?" "Why is there sin and chaos?" "Why is the dispensation of the Church

Age so unique?" Those are just a few of the questions this book will answer.

If we are not well trained and equipped in spiritual matters, Satan will succeed against us. We must be humble enough to recognize our need. We must be humble enough to submit ourselves to the authority of our pastors and to God's Word itself, to study it as we study no other subject, burning it into our souls, and then using it in our lives. Man does not live by bread alone, says our Lord, but by the Word of God. As we eat physical food on a daily basis, so we should eat spiritual food as well. It is the key to temporal victory. For apart from the knowledge of the Word of God and the application of that knowledge to our lives, we will be left to wander among the rocks, whining and mewling about our misfortunes, always wondering why, never really understanding what is going on. Those who live life this way are the casualties in a war they do not even know they are fighting.

Chapter 1

The Beginning

The Angelic Conflict is the result of pre-historic creatures' being in opposition to God, beginning with the fall of Satan. It refers to two trials of Satan and the fallen angels, one in pre-historic times, the other during human history. It began with the rebellion of Satan manifested by the five "I wills" in Isa 14:12-14, and continued until all the angels had made a decision either for or against God.

> "How you have fallen from heaven, O star of the morning, son of the dawn! You have been cut down to the earth, You who have weakened the nations! But you said in your heart, 'I will ascend to heaven; I will raise my throne above the stars of God, And I will sit on the mount of assembly In the recesses of the north. I will ascend above the heights of the clouds; I will make myself like the Most High.'" (Isa 14:12-14)

The Angelic Conflict is a two-phase conflict in which the fallen angels are defiant against God, His elect angels, and believers in the Lord Jesus Christ. The first phase was completed in eternity past, and after that man was created. Man entered this spiritual conflict from the time that the woman ate of the tree of the knowledge of good and evil by the subtle suggestion of Satan. She partook of the forbidden tree and fallen mankind was thus handed a key role in this conflict. It is a conflict that will continue to exist until the second coming of Jesus Christ.

The Church Age, in which we now live, is therefore unique, it is the age of the glorified humanity of the Lord Jesus Christ. Jesus Christ, as the God-man, is glorified because of the work He accomplished on the Cross. This is the basis for understanding many of the important doctrines in the Word of God such as justification, which means an act of vindication. This is a judicial act of vindication, because we are born under condemnation, being spiritually dead. Therefore, justification is an official judicial act which occurs every time anyone believes in Christ. The justice of God acts on our behalf pronouncing us justified, which means having a relationship with God forever, having the perfect righteousness of God imputed to us. Justification means that God recognizes that He has given us His perfect righteousness.

There is also the doctrine of propitiation, which is the God-ward side of the work of Christ in salvation. God the Father is satisfied with the sacrificial ministry of our Lord on the Cross. Propitiation is the work of Christ on the Cross which deals with the integrity of God, His justice and righteousness. Propitiation means that our Lord satisfied God the Father. Hence, in propitiation the justice of God judges our sins, and the integrity of God is satisfied with that judgment. Propitiation frees the justice of God to immediately give anyone who believes in Christ the perfect righteousness of God. When God looks at any of us, he sees, not our fallen nature, but His perfect righteousness given to us. This is the down payment on our salvation. Then there is reconciliation, which refers to all the doctrines that make up the finished work of Christ on the Cross.

Following the work on the Cross, Jesus Christ in His humanity was seated at the right hand of God the Father in His resurrection body (His deity was always glorified and everywhere present). However, right now a member of the human race has been glorified and that is the Lord Jesus Christ. Ever since His work on the Cross when He totally disarmed Satan and the fallen angels, He has been in the place of glorified humanity.

> "And when you were dead in your transgressions and the uncircumcision of your flesh, He made you alive together with Him, having forgiven us all our transgressions, having canceled out the certificate of debt consisting of decrees against us and which was hostile to us; and He has taken it out of the way, having nailed it to the cross. When He had disarmed the rulers and authorities, He made a public display of them, having triumphed over them through Him." (Col 2:13-15)

When Jesus Christ defeated Satan by His work on the Cross, the Angelic Conflict shifted gears. Until that time it was the intent of Satan and the fallen angels to frustrate the incarnation of the Lord Jesus Christ and to try to stop His birth. Thank God they did not succeed regarding this scheme since the Lord Jesus Christ, because of the Cross, is now in glorified form. The attack is now made upon every believer in time, and that means you are in a conflict that is invisible and has greatly intensified in all areas of our lives. We have an enemy described in detail in Ephesians chapter 6, where the apostle Paul points out the spiritual armor that every believer must learn and put on to be able to combat the schemes of the devil and to participate effectively in this conflict.

> "Put on the full armor of God, that you may be able to stand firm against the schemes of the devil. For our struggle is not against flesh and blood, but against the rulers, against the powers, against the world forces of this darkness, against the spiritual forces of wickedness in the heavenly places. Therefore, take up the full armor of God that you may be able to resist in the evil day, and having done everything, to stand firm. Stand firm therefore, having girded your loins with truth, and having put on the breastplate of righteousness, and having shod your feet with the preparation of the gospel of peace; in addition to all, taking up the shield of faith with which you will be able to extinguish all the flaming missiles of the evil one. And take the helmet of salvation, and the sword of the Spirit, which is the word of God. With all prayer and petition pray at all times in the Spirit, and with this in view, be on

> the alert with all perseverance and petition for all the saints, and pray on my behalf, that utterance may be given to me in the opening of my mouth, to make known with boldness the mystery of the gospel, for which I am an ambassador in chains; that in proclaiming it I may speak boldly, as I ought to speak." (Eph 6:11-20)

The New Testament actually uses warfare as the basis for illustrating this great spiritual conflict in which we find ourselves. Long ago in eternity past God knew every need we would ever have in this intensified stage of the Angelic Conflict. He knew that we would live in a very difficult period of our own national history as well as in the spiritual history of mankind. He knew all about the attacks that would be made, all the chaos and the different political movements which are anti-doctrinal, anti-establishment, anti-client nation. He knew that there would be much confusion with regard to the Gospel.

This would come about from those who would choose the satanic view and follow ecstatic and emotional criteria rather than Bible doctrine as their way of life. God knew that we would have to face personal, national, and financial crises. God also knew that Satan would try, and succeed in many cases, in causing divisions in the local churches. Satan knows the importance of sowing discord in the local assemblies so that the local assembly will not be filled with leaders who have unity and one purpose which is to glorify the Lord Jesus Christ. This is why we encounter many forms of pressure even in the local churches. These difficulties are identified for us in the Word of God and must be taught and revealed by the pastor-teacher who teaches the mystery doctrine of the Church Age as well as the problem-solving devices which must be utilized accordingly.

The word *mystery* refers to the doctrine for the great power experiment of the Church Age, called *the mystery* because it was never revealed in Old Testament times. The problem-solving devices include the rebound technique, the filling of the Spirit, the faith-rest drill, grace orientation, doctrinal orientation, a personal sense of destiny, personal love for God the Father, impersonal love for all mankind, sharing the happiness of God, and occupation with Christ as the priority solution to life.

Everything in the Church Age, except salvation, is vitally different from any other previous dispensation. However, provisions for every believer in this dispensation of the Church Age are phenomenal. In this book I will identify who the true enemy is as Eph 6:12 teaches, and also reveal the solution to every problem that we would ever face. My hope and prayer is that you consider the information in this book to be a vital part of your spiritual life.

Chapter 2

The Existence of Rational Creatures.

The Scripture teaches us that there are only two categories of rational creatures. First of all, there is the pre-historic category called Angels as given in Psa 8:4-6; Heb 2:6-7; 2Pe 2:11. This category of rational creatures is the superior category, created superior to mankind. Angels were created in eternity past, before the creation of the human race or in pre-historic times. It is important to note that angels are created beings, as stated in the Bible.

> "Praise Him, all His angels; Praise Him, all His hosts! . . . Let them praise the name of the Lord, For He commanded and they were created." (Psa 148:2,5)

The second category of rational creatures, I should say sometimes rational creatures, is the historical category called human beings, mankind, or man. By rational I mean that they have a soul, a complete soul essence, not that they always behave rationally! We all have our irrational moments! The historical category is called simply man, but it refers to both man and woman. So angels are created beings, according to Psa 148:5, and while they are superior to us by creation we do have some things in common. One thing is the soul structure, the souls of both the angels and humans are similar.

So some facts so far:

1. Angels are superior to humans, and Satan is the most brilliant creature who has ever been created. He is the most attractive, the most personable, he has the greatest personality that has ever existed in a creature.
2. He is called *heylel* in the Hebrew, he is also known as *Lucifer* taken from the Latin language. Whether we call him Satan, Heylel, the Devil or Lucifer, at one time he was the highest of all rational creatures.
3. Satan was a cherub angel and at that particular time the cherub was the highest and most superior form of angelic life.

Satan was the greatest of the cherubim. For those of you who have done a study on the doctrine of angelology, you know that today the seraphim, those with six wings, are the highest ranking angels, above the cherubim. Here is where the elect angels fit into the Angelic Conflict and the doctrine of angelic observation. The point is that the elect angels and the fallen angels both observe the human race in human history! The question that you should have is "why?". The answer is the most difficult thing in the world to teach or to write about i.e. the subject of Satanology or the Angelic Conflict. The reason for this is that the devil does not like to be exposed. When the average person thinks of the devil or Satan, they think of a creature with red epidermis carrying a trident, having a long tail with green eyes and fangs protruding from his mouth. However, that is far from the truth. As mentioned, the devil is the most beautiful and intelligent creature that was fashioned from the hand of our Creator. Perhaps one of the most shocking things you will learn is the fact that the devil is not interested in getting people to sin, he is vitally interested however in getting people to perform human good.

By human good I mean the good that people do that is credited to them, rather than to the Creator. These people are living under the power of the human nature (flesh), and man will usually applaud them. This is why Paul warned in 2Co 2:11 "that no advantage be taken of us by Satan." Satan and his followers are actively interested in putting down any believer anywhere who knows Bible doctrine and produces divine good, which glorifies the Creator.

Another fact that most are surprised to learn is that Satan is not interested in immorality. Immorality is embarrassing to him because he is the ruler of the world. In 2Co 4:4 we read that Satan is the god of this world, capable of blinding and deceiving mankind. As the greatest creature ever created, immorality is an insult to his leadership! Satan's plan is to guide people toward producing as much human good as possible thus infiltrating the plan of God with this human good. The only way he can do so is to persuade believers to perform human good, and he cannot do this if a believer has real knowledge of the Word of God.

Satan's desire is to keep all people (believers and unbelievers) ignorant of Bible doctrine and therefore suckers for human good, thus cleaning up the Devil's world. Every time people participate in a works program, it does not bring glory to the Creator! The act of performing good deeds appeals to a deep inner lust for approbation. Satan plays on that basic human desire we all have which is to be recognized. It is a form of power lust and gives us a sense of feeling good about what we accomplished. This is called human good and it appeals to the old sin nature. As far as most believers are concerned, performing human good is the only contact the devil will ever have with them. They will have spent numerous hours, and in some cases large portions of a lifetime, performing acts of human good to help the devil clean up his world. The government, education system, social programs, as well as several religious organizations are included in Satan's plan to deceive the human race. The fact is that the presence of evil in this world is not necessarily due to Satan's intention to have it so, but rather his inability to control the human race. This is why God's plan for the human race is not to clean up the devil's world.

Imagine a loving God that offers salvation and then puts forth a plan whereby this believer now has to leap into the muck and filth of an evil system that only God can wipe clean. Worse yet, the burden of the clean-up would be placed upon the believer. This believer, by the way, has an old sin nature that actually wants to wallow in the muck and filth. Does that sound like the plan God has for you after salvation? Actually the plan God has for all believers is to gain knowledge of Bible doctrine or Truth. For the believer there is a verse which describes this very accurately:

> "He desires all men to be saved and to come to the (epignosis) knowledge of the truth." (1 Ti 2:4)

By *gnosis* I mean metabolizing the Word of God as *gnosis* or *knowledge*. Then the knowledge is converted into wisdom when you begin to apply or live in the knowledge, that is *epignosis*. Once that occurs you then begin to mature as a born-again believer. The only foundation that can elevate a believer to maturity is knowledge of Bible doctrine which is the Truth that sets you free.

As you mature in the spiritual realm, the devil and his kingdom, through his cosmic system, will give you an increasing amount of attention because you constitute the greatest threat to his cosmic system. We have all seen the weirdo who says "pray for me, the devil is after me." These are usually the individuals that no one likes, and wherever they go people avoid them. The devil gets blamed for a lot of things for which he should not be blamed, just as there are many things for which he should be blamed but he is not. Most people are totally ignorant of the devices and schemes of Satan.

> Satan is very personable, he has the greatest personality that has ever existed in a creature. Looking back to the Garden of Eden we are reminded that Adam was created perfect, but he fell and now anyone who believes in the Lord Jesus Christ actually becomes greater than Adam. The reason believers become greater than Adam is because they now have the very righteousness of God and of our Lord Jesus Christ. In his fallen state the difference between the perfection of Adam in the Garden of Eden and the perfection we enjoy as believers is the fact that we have received a nature that cannot sin. Adam, even though he was created perfectly, did not receive this same nature (1Jo 3:9; 4:16; 1Pe 1:23, 2Pe 1:4).

The key word is in 1Pe 1:23, the word *seed*. *We* have all received a seed or a nature that cannot sin. What happens if we sin? We are not sinning as a new creature in Christ but as an old creature in our flesh. This is why the apostle Paul says in Rom 7:17 "So now no longer am I the one doing it (sin)." Paul says again in Rom 7:20, "But if I'm doing the very thing that I do not wish, I am no longer the one doing it, but the sin nature which dwells in me."

The point is that Adam was created perfect, he then sinned against God and a higher category of humans came into existence called *the children of God*. The same thing was true in the angelic realm. Lucifer, also known as Satan, the son of the morning, the anointed cherub, was created perfect and was the highest-ranking angel. At that time the cherub was the highest form of angel. Just like Adam was created perfect in the beginning, so shall anyone who follows God become greater than Adam.

There are angels that were awarded a higher rank than Satan after his fall, namely the Seraphim, angels with six wings. Because of the character and nature of God, we can conclude that just as members of the human race are rewarded for their faithfulness to the Lord Jesus Christ, so too the angels were given rewards for living in something similar to our Pre-designed Plan of God. There is a difference among the angels just as there is a difference among humans (1Co 15:40-42). God has never and will never coerce angelic or human volition to make choices, so there is a special group of angels who in eternity past made the right possible grace decisions for our Lord and Savior Jesus Christ. They stayed to serve the Lord Jesus Christ in the extension of the Angelic Conflict.

As physical beings angels are quite different from humans. Angels were apparently created out of light and are able to move through space at will. Currently, angels remain invisible, but they have been here since long before mankind and have had time to conduct a thorough investigation of the human race. Angels are rational and superior pre-historic creatures, and they existed in the universe before man for an unknown period of time. This is very important to understand. Is there some life on other planets? Or is this something invisible in the sky or in the atmosphere in the heavens? The answer according to the Word of God is yes, there are angelic creatures in the atmosphere and in space.

The atmosphere around the earth is controlled by the prince and the powers of the air as we are told in Eph 6:12, planet Earth is currently under the authority of Satan for the duration of his appeal. Television, movies, and the Internet often show creatures from other planets, but we get the Truth from the Word of God. There are indeed other creatures in the stellar systems. This universe is currently the battleground between those who chose for God and those who are fallen angels. In certain situations, humans are entered into this conflict as witnesses for God in the Supreme Court of Heaven. This is revealed for us in Job 1:6 and Job 2:6. As you can see the atmosphere is filled with these invisible creatures. We see Job called as a witness as a lower creation, in front of these superior invisible creatures.

Angels are intelligent creatures that can defy time, and have existed in the universe for an unknown period of time since long before the creation of man on planet Earth. They witnessed Adam, Job, Abraham, Moses, David, and Solomon face to face, and yes even the Lord Jesus Christ face to face! Julius Caesar, Aristotle, Shakespeare, and Hitler were all on display for the angelic community, and seeing them each day with their human traits and flaws, angels know more about the human race than we do. They know more about you than you do! This is extremely important because the doctrine of the Angelic Conflict is established in this way. The elect and fallen angels observe the human race in their success or failure as witnesses in the Angelic Conflict, either glorifying the Lord Jesus Christ or falling for the plans and deceptions of Satan as the god of this world.

Before the scripture was completed angels often became visible to members of the human race. In fact the dispensation of Israel, or the dispensation of the Law, was characterized by the appearance of angels in the world, and the universe around was filled with them.

There are untold numbers of angels, and many details concerning them have been a source of controversy over the centuries, but few of these have ever been resolved. Not all angels look the same, some are described as very beautiful and some are not. Apparently they are all male, although there may be some passages in the Scripture that could possibly be interpreted as referring to female angels. If there were any female angels, however, they are not clearly revealed in the Word of God.

So angels appear to have only one gender among their multitude, which points to all angels being created equal. This may explain in part some of the events of Genesis 6 which we will cover later in this book. The best we can do on the composition of angels is to say that they seem to have a body, one which is quite different from our bodies. While our body is tangible theirs is intangible. Angelic bodies appear to be composed of light and since light has content it should make a definite form. These forms could easily become invisible or visible. Wings are often attributed to them, but not all angels have the same number of wings. Eze 1:6 reveals four on some angels, while seraphim have six (Isa 6:2; Eze 1:11; Rev 4:8). Angels may differ in beauty and strength as compared to others and those created super angels are called cherubim.

Cherubim is plural from the Hebrew. A cherub therefore is not a little baby with wings, he happens to be the most beautiful and the most magnificent creature designed by the hand of God! Some of the cherubim are actually named for us, either with names or titles. The leader of the elect angels is called Michael, the leader of the fallen angels is called Lucifer or some say the devil. These two angels apparently are among the most beautiful of all creatures. Lucifer is described in terms that exceed any regarding the Biblical description of a creature. In Eze 28:14-15 no one is more beautiful or more personable than Satan. Of course that eliminates the usual representation of Satan with red epidermis, slanted green eyes etc. Knowing something of the tremendous pride which the scriptures attribute to him, Satan apparently is not at all flattered by that earlier image of him. He thinks more highly of himself than he ought to.

Gabriel is another cherub angel who has a responsibility that far exceeds the power of any person in the human race. Gabriel is the one who keeps cruel dictators or rulers from getting totally out of control and remaining that way, unless it is a part of God's plan. Gabriel delivered a vital message to Daniel in Dan 10:13. Gabriel is speaking in that passage, showing that nothing in history escapes angelic observation, and that there is no major event in history that is not a part of the Angelic Conflict.

> "But the prince of the kingdom of Persia was withstanding me for twenty-one days; then behold, Michael, one of the chief princes, came to help me, for I had been left there with the kings of Persia." (Dan 10:13)

From the fall of man to the Second Advent of Christ, angels were, are, and will be involved. At the Second Advent angels will follow the Lord Jesus Christ (Mat 25:31). Angels will be involved in war spoken of in Rev 12:7, and fallen angels will be removed from planet Earth during the Millennium in Rev 20:1-3. References to angels in the book of Revelation are more abundant than in any other book in the Bible. The conflict will be entering its last days before the fallen angels are removed from the earth. Therefore the intensity of the conflict is portrayed clearly in the book of Revelation. The 12th chapter of Revelation teaches how Satan seeks to destroy the Jews. Satan has always tried to destroy them. In fact, when he is not trying to destroy them directly he attacks them in subtle ways and is responsible for all anti-Semitism. He has many times lit the fire of rumors that the Jews are the reason for the troubles of the world. It is from his position in the Angelic Conflict that he establishes battalions of teachers who teach false doctrine to unbelievers. Satan also has promoted the push of false doctrine into the soul of believers.

CHAPTER 3

When and How the Angelic Conflict Began

To establish the fact that angels have existed since long before mankind was created we need look no further than Genesis.

> "In the beginning God created the heavens and the earth. Now the earth became formless and void, darkness was over the surface of the deep, and the Spirit of God was hovering over the waters" (Gen 1:1-2).

Notice that *the earth became* (not was) *formless and void* (tohuw waabohuw in the Hebrew). In the original language there is a gap between Gen 1:1 and Gen 1:2. This space, or gap, is actually a time period for which we do not have exact facts and figures, it could have been two million years or two months. This same phrase *formless and void, tohuw waabohuw,* is in other passages such as Isa 24:1 and Jer 4:23-26.

> "Behold, the Lord lays the earth waste, devastates it, distorts its surface, and scatters its inhabitants." (Isa 24:1)

> "I looked on the earth, and behold it was formless and void." (Jer 4:23)

Jeremiah goes on to describe hills and mountains being moved, man and beast being scattered about, as if the Lord were angry and were wiping the slate clean and starting on a fresh canvas of earth. This was the beginning of the conflict. It is here that we see God prepare the earth for the coming of mankind in the last words of Gen 1:2, "The Spirit of God moved over the waters." At this point it is God granting Satan his appeal trial.

So we know for sure that the earth was here in one form or another long before the human race was put upon it. We may venture a guess that Satan and his fallen legion had full run of this sphere before Adam took it over. One of Satan's first and great victories was when Adam fell and he (Satan) was given reign once again to wallow in his arrogant attempt to duplicate God.

In the second chapter we briefly touched on the make-up and components of the angelic bodies. But we must now look deeper into the leader of the fallen legion. We will call him Lucifer and, as we know, he possesses many titles. We see in Eze 28:11-19 that he held great authority and power in his heavenly realm. We also see his desire for greater power and how he began to simmer into arrogance, which then boiled over into a rebellious attitude. We must see him as he really is, the most attractive, beautiful, and astounding creature of all creatures molded from the divine hand of God.

> "The word of the Lord came to me: 'Son of man, take up a lament concerning the King of Tyre and say to him: 'This is what the Sovereign Lord says: You were the model of perfection, full of wisdom and perfect in beauty.'" (Eze 28:11-12)

The King of Tyre was one of the few individuals possessed by Satan, just as the serpent in the garden and Judas Iscariot who betrayed our Lord were also possessed. The Lord is speaking to Satan who is within the soul of this king, calling him "the model of perfection." This is a serious statement. To have the seal of God's perfection is a status of the highest caliber. Scripture also refers to him in the realm of genius and perfect beauty, meaning the most attractive of all creatures, an overt beauty that no human possesses. Satan has the most superb voice matched by his sterling personality, this is a being who could successfully sell snow in Alaska.

> "You were in Eden, the garden of God; every precious stone was your covering: The ruby, the topaz, and the diamond; the beryl, the onyx and the jasper; the lapis lazuli, the turquoise and the emerald; And the gold, the workmanship of your settings and sockets was in you. On the day you were created they were prepared." (Eze 28:13)

These adorning jewels suggest his great importance and the glory of his appearance. In the garden his name was *nahash*, translated *the shining one*. The apostle Paul states that he is disguised as an angel of light in 2Co 11:14. Satan was the sum of total perfection in his position in heaven. At some point he became not only bored with his perfect environment and lofty position, but he became enthralled with his own beauty and power. This is common among humans as well, a desire to be recognized, a lust for more power. We call this approbation lust, and it starts with a thought of malcontentment with our position or where we have been placed within the plan of God. Maybe a thought that we can be the ultimate authority, possibly do a better job than those above us. This type of thought leads to the arrogant thought process of self-importance and a pre-occupation with self. This then sets the mind to wondering why we do not have more or we may even begin to demand a better standard for ourselves. This chain of thinking will lead to an arrogant ambition, inordinate ambition. Inordinate ambition most times leads to inordinate competition, striving to out-do or to out-shine those around us and especially those in authority over us. Remember, Satan was the leader of all angels in the beginning, the anointed cherub or the Messiah's angel, so he had no competition around him.

Satan did not seek to compete because none compared, he looked *above* seeking to compete and compare with the ultimate authority. This all began with one arrogant thought and led to a chain of events called the Angelic Conflict! Arrogant thought became rebellious action long before mankind even existed.

It was between Gen 1:1 and 1:2 that the first rebellion and conspiracy went into action. This is why an arrogant man can be intelligent yet appear so dumb at times, and a beautiful woman can be viewed as ugly when she thinks too highly of herself. Arrogance is truly a gruesome and debilitating sin. Adam displayed the same sin in a perfect environment and chose to rebel. You are truly fooled when you mistake beauty, wealth, or power for a form of happiness. Happiness is contentment deep within your soul that is developed by a close relationship with God and has nothing to do with environment or circumstances. Arrogance is certain to destroy beauty and also certain to corrupt power, we see this all around us in the world in which we live today. When an arrogant person develops a plan to rebel or to overthrow authority the individual will always seek to gain strength by adding to their ranks.

Satan was the father of rebellion as we see in Rev 12:4, when he took a third of the angels with him on his quest to "be like the most high." But arrogance will not take a step back. It will not recognize when it is wrong. Arrogance cannot face failure. Satan and his army are well aware that this conflict has a distinct end to it, just as definite and clear as the beginning was. These fallen angels struggle against the end result daily! When two demon-possessed men became violent and shouted to our Lord, "What do You want with us, Son of God? Have You come here to torture us before the appointed time?" (Mat 8:28-29), we see that they are clear on the outcome, clear and angry, but still in full rebellion. Satan was created a powerful and superior adult being with flawless abilities and exceptional features, dwelling in an atmosphere of the highest intellect and perfection. Satan had everything any ordinary human would desire, but he was not satisfied. For those reading this that believe that they would have remained happy and faithful in such an environment, you are allowing your own pride and arrogance to fool you. We all would fail in Satan's or Adam's place, do not fool yourself because you certainly are not fooling anyone else.

Satan was essentially in the second place of authority within the entire universe; however, he basically felt that this was not enough! His power and intelligence go beyond human comprehension. He realized his own beauty and greatness and he became filled with pride and arrogance. Satan's position noted in Eze 28:13 highlights the precious stones and gems appointed to him. These precious stones were a significant sign of his authority and importance in the grand scheme of the universe. These precious stones are mentioned 3 times as recorded in the Bible:

1) In the high priest's breastplate as a manifestation of divine grace (Exo 28:17-20; 39:10-13).
2) In the New Jerusalem, which reflects the glory of God (Rev 21:18-21).
3) As the covering of this great angel, which signifies the highest of all creations (Eze 28:13).

No distinction could be placed upon any creature more exalting than the one imposed by these covering stones. The "workmanship of your settings and sockets" refers to the fact that he did not need an instrument to praise and glorify God, he was given a built-in crown of praise to praise his Creator. Satan's voice is like that of a breathtaking pipe organ, he truly does not even need a voice because his being is an exceptional instrument of praise. Take note of the last phrase in Eze 28:13, "On the day you were created they were prepared." This phrase points to Satan as a created creature from the hand of God. In the next verse we pass from Satan's royalty into his priestly dignity.

> "You were the anointed cherub (The highest rank of angel) who covers and I placed you there. You were on the holy mountain of God (third heaven); You walked in the midst of the stones of fire." (Eze 28:14)

This is a personal anointing by God. The anointing indicates that God put Satan in the specific position of being the Messiah's angel. We see Satan in the throne room of God as well as having set foot upon the Holy Mountain of God and having scaled the midst of the Stones of Fire. Satan's presence on the Holy Mountain would indicate his power and enjoyment of the full privileges that come with the rank of Cherubic Angel. This insinuates that he has been within arm's length of the Throne of God.

In Exo 4:27 and Psa 2:6, the Holy Mountain of God is a place of His presence in visible glory, where God's High Priest would stand before Him to minister. Cherubim were angels designated for the protection and defense of the throne. Therefore we can deduce that this highest-ranking guardian and privileged angel turned from his duty and attacked that which he was assigned to protect. The protector of the Holiness became the enemy of the Throne. There is a principle here for those in authority to note: do not be surprised when those under your authority who are assigned to protect and honor your position turn on you and begin to attack or discredit you. When someone under your authority begins such an assault, realize that their father the devil was the first to launch such a conspiracy.

The statement "their father" has valid ground as clearly displayed in 1Jo 3:10 where Christians under the thinking of Satan are called students (teknons) or sons of the devil. It is interesting that God placed Lucifer in such a dominant position although God knew he would rebel!

> "You were blameless in your ways from the day you were created, until unrighteousness was found in you." (Eze 28:15)

Calling the devil the father of sin, the father of lies, or even the father of rebellion is really quite appropriate. He was the first sinner of all of God's creatures. His lust for more power took him down the path toward the first sin. He was implacable, unsatisfied with his perfect position in a divine environment.

> "By the abundance of your trade you were internally filled with violence. Your heart (system of thinking) was lifted up because of your beauty; you corrupted your wisdom (distorted it) by reason of your splendor (breathtaking beauty). I cast you to the ground; I put you before kings, that they may see you (future)." (Eze 28:16-17)

The scripture notes that Satan's pride stems from his conceited attitude. Pride is a blatant sin associated with several wicked relatives such as conceit and arrogance. In 1Ti 3:6 Paul warns Timothy not to put men in positions of authority too soon, "lest he become conceited and fall into the condemnation incurred by the devil." Satan with his vast knowledge, power, and intellect can easily design a plan to undermine authority and implement a hostile take-over.

The phrase *the abundance of your trade* refers to his genius abilities to manipulate and plan subtle attacks or even straightforward, full-on military assaults. It is no surprise that he took along an army of angels with him. And it should be no surprise that he erodes belief in the Word of God, or even has the ability to dilute and misquote Scripture and to confuse Christians, leading them astray. Satan was able to organize and gain the confidence of one third of the angels while still operating within the perimeters of heaven. Do you truly believe that he does not have a plan or a multitude of schemes to deceive human beings who dwell on a corrupt planet?

Satan had the ability to promote the greatest rebellion in a perfect environment. Imagine how much easier it is for him on a planet in disarray, a planet over which he has a supreme level of authority. We have no idea what promises Satan made to his would-be allies that would tempt them to leave a loving Creator and to rebel with him. It is interesting to note that the word *trade* in the Hebrew is *rekullah* and is also translated slander or gossip against someone's reputation. It speaks of peddling something for the sake of personal gain. This type of word works perfectly as a description for what Satan did to light the fire of conspiracy under his fellow angelic creatures. When you hear of conspiracies in this world always take into consideration the first one who developed the plan, Satan!

In Eze 28:17-18 we see Satan saying "Mirror mirror on the wall, who is the fairest of them all?" And he knew the answer long before he put forth the question. When pride reaches this type of zenith, it has a blinding effect upon the one contaminated by it.

> "By the multitude of your iniquities, in the unrighteousness of your trade (conspiracy) you profaned your sanctuaries (Satan's first fall). Therefore I have brought fire from the midst of you; It has consumed you, and I have turned you to ashes (the second fall occurs during the Tribulation period) on the earth in the eyes of all who see you. All who know you among the peoples are appalled at you: You have become terrified, and you will be no more." (Eze 28:18-19)

This will all take place before the Millennial Reign of Christ and after it as well. It is obvious that these verses point out the immediate future and the final judgment of God on this mighty angel. There are more in-depth descriptions within the Bible. In these few verses God records the origin, the estate, and the character as well as the sin of the greatest of angels. God has put Satan's arrogance and blind pride on display for our benefit, for our learning experience. We are to witness the devastating effects of pride and arrogance from the Scripture. A good way to view the subtle difference between pride and arrogance is to remember that arrogance is the thought process and pride is the follow-up or the action. They are close relatives and in many cases operate in conjunction with one another.

> "Respect for the Lord is to hate evil; Pride and arrogance and the evil way, and the perverted mouth, I hate." (Pro 8:13)

> "Thus I will punish the world for its evil, and the wicked for their iniquity; I will also put an end to the arrogance of the proud." (Isa 13:11)

God did not create Satan as an arrogant, pride-filled demon. God created Satan as a perfect angelic creature with free will. It is the creature who takes his free will and operates independently from what God intended. It is the creature who strays from the thoughts and words of the Creator. As we approach the end of this chapter there are several principles that need to be noted:

1. Through the degenerating power of sin, Satan, like Adam, became an entirely different being. This was done with their own free will. As part of God's divine blessings humans as well as angels must be given choice and a free will to reject or to accept what they deem fit.
2. When God creates a being to fulfill a certain purpose, that purpose must be a perfect fulfillment of a divine pattern or plan that was laid out in eternity past. God will provide what is needed to fulfill His plan, this is called logistical grace. And we have problem-solving devices within the Word of God as well as the availability of divine power to follow His plan.
3. This is why we need to identify the purpose for which Satan was created and to evaluate the qualities which were his in view of that purpose. As we have noted, his purpose was to operate as the highest-ranking angel and to protect the Throne of God.

4. By his sin he lost his original holiness and heavenly position, still retaining his wisdom and beauty. He has turned his surpassing abilities into ways of evil. His wisdom and his understanding have been perverted to the level of lies, deceptions, snares, and conspiracies.
5. Satan's office was originally to protect the Throne of God and to forbid the approach of evil or any unrighteousness. However, most of God's creatures (human and angel) reject the plan of God and rely on their own plans and schemes. That is why every time a believer says no to God this individual is acting like a child of Satan.
6. The original sin of Satan was independence from God and self-exaltation. We tend to look at sin as immorality and not view it as independent thought and action. Independence from God can be the most destructive sin in a person's life.
7. Satan was said to have been upon the Holy Mountain of God an anointed Cherub, referring to a position of being a High Priest of his realm.
8. Satan was considered the highest-ranking of all angels and would be considered a leader or king over all other creatures.
9. Finally, he was created perfect in all his ways and apparently was in this condition for a long period of time.

All of this took place before his fall and before the creation of mankind. The analogy between Satan's office of priest and king, created perfect in all his ways, and the position our Lord took, is very interesting. Satan abused his power like a crooked politician and corrupted the high office given to him. So God created Adam to function as a prophet, priest, and king within his earthly domain. Under God's supervision Adam was the ruler over all he surveyed.

"Then God said 'Let Us make man in Our own image, according to Our likeness; And let him rule over the fish of the sea and over the birds of the sky and over the cattle and over all the earth, and over every creeping thing that creeps upon the earth.'" (Gen 1:26)

Adam was to function as a prophet in the sense of teaching the Word of God to Ishah (Eve) as well as to perform his worship toward God as a believer priest. But as we all know, as it is well documented, Adam fell.

Perhaps this is where the saying, "If you want something done right, you've got to do it yourself!" was derived. So after the failure of Adam, the Lord Jesus Christ came forth from the divine Godhead to become a member of the human race and to fulfill all three functions of prophet, priest, and king. Christ has already been exercising His gift of prophet and priest, but not that of King, at least not yet on planet Earth. Had our Lord come down and first established His kingdom and taken His rightful place as the King of Kings, without going to the Cross first, it would have been utter destruction for all of us!

We are all sinners in a hopeless situation without the work on the Cross. It would have been a blistering trip into the lake of fire for all mankind. It was therefore necessary to first put away the iniquity of those who would be saved. In God's pre-designed plan, His modus operandi, our Lord Jesus Christ had to come down to sacrifice Himself first, before He could return to claim the power from the hands of Satan and then cast him into prison. In His perfect plan, the Lord will return purity and order to creation in His perfect time.

> "But when the fullness of the time came, God sent forth His Son, born of a woman . . ." (Gal 4:4)

> "Therefore, He had to be made like His brethren in all things, so that He might become a merciful and faithful high priest in things pertaining to God, to make propitiation for the sins of the people." (Heb 2:17)

> "Since then the children share in the flesh and blood (humanity), He himself likewise also partook of the same, through death He might render powerless him who had the power of death, that is, the devil." (Heb 2:14)

> "And He laid hold of the dragon, the serpent of old, who is the devil and Satan, and bound him for a thousand years." (Rev 20:2)

The government that Christ will take upon His shoulders appears identical to that which was once committed to Satan. But the original order of things will begin to be restored in Christ's Millennial Kingdom.

Chapter 4

After Satan's Fall, He Deceives the Whole World

In Isa 14 there is a presentation very similar to that in Eze 28 but with a little different twist. We will again touch on Satan's arrogance and pride as he steps out of God's plan and becomes independent with his own plan. We can then see the fall of Satan, not one but three falls, and how he divides and deceives the nations.

"How you have fallen from heaven, O star of the morning, son of the dawn! You have been cut down to the earth, You who have weakened the nations! But you said in your heart, 'I will ascend to heaven; I will raise my throne above the stars of God, And I will sit on the mount of assembly In the recesses of the north. I will ascend above the heights of the clouds; I will make myself like the Most High.' Nevertheless you will be thrust down to Sheol, To the recesses of the pit. Those who see you will gaze at you, They will ponder over you, saying, 'Is this the man who made the earth tremble, Who shook kingdoms, Who made the world like a wilderness
And overthrew its cities, Who did not allow his prisoners to go home?'" (Isa 14:12-17)

The fall that is referenced here is the second fall of Satan where he is being cast out of heaven during the Tribulation. His first fall took place in eternity past, perhaps billions of years before man ever existed. Note that in Eze 28:15 "You were blameless in your ways from the day you were created, until unrighteousness was found in you." It is in the middle of the Tribulation that Satan has his second fall when he is cast out of heaven.

> "And the great dragon was thrown down, the serpent of old who is called the devil and Satan, who deceives the whole world; he was thrown down to the earth, and his angels were thrown down with him." (Rev 12:9)

This is not to insinuate that Satan does not have access to heaven right now as we dwell here on planet Earth. Satan has full access to both heaven and earth. It is after the second fall during the Tribulation that he cannot return to heaven. At the climax of the Millennial Reign of Jesus Christ, at the end of time, occurs the third and final fall of this troublesome angelic creature.

> "And the devil who deceived them was thrown into the lake of fire and brimstone, where the beast and the false prophet are also; and they will be tormented day and night forever and ever." (Rev 20:10)

In Isa 14:12-17 we start out with the second fall, then look back to the first fall, and finally we see Satan have his final demise. The Lord Jesus Christ prophesied in Luk 10:18, "I was watching Satan fall from heaven like lightning." This takes place historically in Rev 12:7-9.

It is also interesting to note that the name *Satan* in the Greek is *Satanas* which means to slander, gossip, malign, and accuse. Put that together with his frequent trips to and from heaven and you can understand what he speaks of when he goes before God to give an account on the human race. We will touch on this subject later in this book. We have also noted that the title *Heylel* is used to describe Lucifer in verses like Isa

14:12. This label or title *Lucifer* is derived from a Latin word meaning light-bearer, or shining one, translucent and stimulating. As we have seen, Satan has the most stimulating personality of any created being.

The Bible describes two creatures who throw off light in an attractive manner. One is *Heylel* and the other is the Hebrew word for a serpent which is *nachash,* this is the same serpent we see in Genesis 3. Both Satan and the serpent are described as shining, and this shining is a form of magnetism and beauty. The serpent of our day and age may not appear magnetic to you, but this one unique serpent in the Garden of Eden was definitely attractive enough to draw the woman away from the plan of God. 2Co 11:14-15 portrays Satan and his angels transforming or appearing righteous as angels of light.

So there can be little doubt that angels of both categories, fallen and elect, have the ability to emanate light. Fallen angels are those in the army of Satan, those that followed the arrogant one. Satan has ministers, evangelists, and teachers woven into the human race that spread false doctrine and distort Truth as the serpent did to the woman in the garden. Most people do not even realize that they are simply pawns in a universal chess game. They may even spread a gospel, but it is not the Gospel of Christ. They may speak on a holy spirit but not the Holy Spirit of God, and when they preach on Jesus it is not the Jesus of the scriptures.

> "But I am afraid, lest as the serpent deceived Eve by his craftiness, your minds should be led astray from the simplicity and purity of devotion to Christ. For if one comes and preaches another Jesus whom we have not preached, or you receive a different spirit which you have not received, or a different gospel which you have not accepted, you bear this beautifully." (2Co 11:3-4)

Paul was teaching believers of that time but also forewarning of things to come related to Satan's false prophets and leaders. Always check your facts concerning your spiritual intake. The personality of the pastor does not matter, it is his content that is the issue! Sweet personalities and kind words will come and go like a warm summer breeze keeping you feeling comfortable, but it is the content of the material taught that holds the structure of your soul together. Truth should be the subject, not a nice guy or a cozy feeling. In fact, the serpent in the garden appeared attractive, kind, and obviously made the woman feel very comfortable. Some ministers may have the glamorous appeal, a shining Hollywood glow, but they give you almost no substance to sustain your spiritual diet or perhaps even worse, lead you away from Truth which is what Paul was really attempting to suggest. When training to recognize a counterfeit you must know the genuine article thoroughly. A good counterfeit is very close to the original. If you have the criteria of the Word of God in your heart you will not be fooled by sweet personalities.

Isa 14:12 clearly states that the devil has weakened the nations. This is again a clear indication that the mind of Satan is far superior to the most genius mind of any man on planet Earth. We are no match when it comes to the cunning wit of the fallen demon rulers of this planet. Only one mind is the ultimate genius, only one mind has no equal, and that is the mind of Christ. As shown in 1Co 2:16, Phi 2:5, that mind is the thoughts, actions, and full record of our Lord Jesus Christ. And we are freely offered this divine thought process and guidelines, yet many simply say NO THANKS!

It is the arrogance that is deep within the human DNA that thinks he or she cannot be deceived. In Rev 12:9; 13:14; 18:23 and Rev 19:20, Satan is said to deceive the whole world. Read in Rev 20:3 how just before the Millennial Reign a Seraph Angel is said to throw Satan into the abyss and seal it shut so that he can no longer deceive the nations.

The word "nations", also used in Isa 14:12, refers to one of God's Divine Institutions, the fourth Divine Institution which is nationalism. God's order for the preservation of the human race is nationalism. This is the principle whereby a nation benefits from acting independently rather than collectively. One of the first great attacks on this institution occurred at the tower of Babel, the organization of the first United Nations structure. God Himself destroyed their collective and He divided the nations three ways: first by race, secondly by dividing them geographically, and thirdly He divided them linguistically. There will be increased efforts made for a one-world government, a one-world order, before the end times. The devastating effects on the Church will be that the teachings and belief in our Lord Jesus Christ will be diminished to an attitude of just believing in a god, any god, not the God. We see this attitude in full swing already. It is the mantra of "Let's all just get along, the facts and Truth of the Gospel aren't as important as the fact that we believe in something greater then ourselves." This is an important tool for Satan and he has honed it into a powerful force. Satan does not care if you believe in a god, it is all the same as long as you are a good person who believes in some form of spirituality. What Satan does not want is for you to believe in the God, and in His Son the Lord Jesus Christ. If you already believe in Him then Satan's goal is to distract you from that relationship. How powerful and yet subtle are the tricks of the kingdom of darkness. Many earthly events will become clear to us when we become students of the Word of God. The spotlight of truth will shine on the satanic plots and schemes around human history.

CHAPTER 5

Satanic Attacks During the Church Age

Here is a simple question: Why would the most charming, stimulating, intelligent, and beautiful creature ever created by God be cast down from heaven? The answer is given in the Book of Isaiah:

> "How you have fallen from heaven, O star of the morning, son of the dawn! You have been cut down to the earth, You who have weakened the nations! But you said in your heart, 'I will ascend to heaven; I will raise my throne above the stars of God, and I will sit on the mount of assembly In the recesses of the north. I will ascend above the heights of the clouds; I will make myself like the Most High.'" (Isa 14:12-14)

These are the five "I wills" of Satan and within these scriptures of Isaiah are found the first sin from the Lord's creatures: Independence! So there is the answer to the question posed above: the first sin, committed perhaps billions of years before mankind was put upon planet Earth, was a rebellious act known as independence from God. This act began with Satan becoming self-reliant, which led to his thinking much too highly of himself and this eventually resulted in the sin of independence. Choosing your will over God's will points back to the father of the first revolt. This attitude is the root of all sins, standing against the will of God, saying NO to His plan, His guidelines, and His words. Rom 7:13

calls it "exceeding sinful" and this is in reference to the thought, not the action. Anything done outside the will of God becomes a form of evil, and this is why deeds of the flesh will be judged. Human works are said to be evil, not necessarily sin. Works that are not divine good will burn up like wood, hay, and straw at the Judgment Seat of Christ (1Co 3:12-15).

Satan wanted the highest heavenly position, to be exalted to the throne above the stars (angels). The stars refer to angels as noted in several passages in scripture such as Job 38:7, Jud 13. Sitting upon the mount of the assembly (Isa 14:13) is in reference to ruling over the government of the earth. Satan's arrogance is swelling with each 'I will' he spews forth, he is on a rapid course to becoming the Messiah in his own mind.

In Isa 14:14 clouds are used to represent the divine presence of God or His glory. A study of the Exodus generation shows the glory of God or a representation of Jehovah in a cloud, such as Exo 16:10, or a passage such as Psa 104:3 that states that Jehovah rides upon a cloud. So this is a blatant grab for the glory which belongs to God alone. Satan's arrogant statement speaks for itself: "I will make myself like the Most High."

In spite of the universal impression that God and Satan are in complete contrast, there are several outward qualities that are similar. The Lord Jesus Christ bears a parallel title as noted in Rev 22:16 i.e. "the bright morning star." Satan has been deemed "shining star." The Lord Jesus Christ is called the last Adam, directing us toward the fact that Christ had to fulfill the role of Adam. The Lord Jesus Christ had to fulfill or become the successor to the fallen angel as well as to fallen man. God created both Satan and Adam perfect, created them in perfect environments, and yet the Lord Jesus Christ had to arrive on the scene to complete the job and clean up the mess, making Him the true Savior for all created creatures. Satan just attempts to make himself a type of savior or ruler.

Independence appears to be a good thing, promoted in the world as a sense of strength and freedom. Independent thinking is taught and pushed throughout our nation. When it comes to standing on your own two feet and being independent of outside influence, it is a sign of a strong and mature individual. However, the independence that is a cancer to the soul and leads to sin is the separation of your will from God's will, the separation of your plan now in opposition to God's plan. This independence is what turns good works into evil works. Our human mind and weak imagination cannot fathom the depth of the crisis that took place in eternity past when the gifts and plans of a loving and generous God were laid out for a perfectly created being and the response was, "NO!" It was also accompanied by the devious attitude of "I will rise above You and do it my way, get the results that fulfill my desires." At that moment when the first repudiation of God occurred in heaven it was the first anti-God thought. The majority of the world cannot understand that people who reject God and appear as strong individuals, who do things their own way, are in fact sinning like Satan. What other conclusion do we draw after a study on the original sin of independence? If there is a protocol, a set guideline to do a task, and you ignore it and put in place your own, have you truly followed the instructions given to you? Can you really expect the results that the designer had planned?

So the first attitude of rebellion, the first thought in a series of thoughts that set up the action for a rebellion, is this: "I will do it my way." Plainly and simply put, it was the attitude of "I know better." In an overview of rebellion and/or independence, is not apathy regarding authority, and instruction from that authority, the first step into independence that leads to the path of rebellion toward that authority? In Joh 8:44 our Lord said to the religious leaders, "You are of your father the devil, and you want to do the desires of your father. He was a murderer from the beginning, and does not stand in the truth, because there is no truth in him. Whenever he speaks a lie, he speaks from his own nature; for he is a liar, and the father of lies."

Our Lord states emphatically that he is not only the father of lies but a murderer from the beginning! This reveals the depth and seriousness of the rejection of God's plan and the rebellion that followed. All these disclosures are various ways of describing one sin, all pointing toward Satan's inordinate desire to be like God, more accurately to be higher than his Creator. This displays a clear displeasure with his purpose and assignment in life, followed by actions of an unholy self-promotion and an assault upon the Divine Throne of God.

The shocking item within this lesson of satanic rebellion is that we see this attitude toward God in unbelievers and believers every day! We are designed to have a relationship with God, a loving, devoted rapport right now and throughout eternity. As He is the true Father of all beings, angelic and human, we are to obey and trust in Him, to have an understanding of Him and communication with Him. Yet sadly most people (believers and unbelievers) are so wrapped up in the world and what they want for themselves that they have no time or desire for God in their so-called busy lives.

> "And He died for all, so that they who live might no longer live for themselves, but for Him who died and rose again on their behalf." (2Co 5:15)

> "Or do you not know that your body is a temple of the Holy Spirit who is in you, whom you have from God, and that you are not your own?" (1Co 6:19)

Unmistakable verses like these (also see 1Co 6:20 and Rom 6:19) put a clear spotlight on what our relationship and attitude toward God is to resemble, yet most people will say NO! This is very similar to the same attitude of Satan in a time before mankind came into existence. We are told to glorify God in Mat 5:16 and the majority have said NO to that as well. There is very little difference between a believer that has no time or makes no effort to have a relationship and commitment to the Lord, and what Satan did. No matter how intelligent and skilled you are, there is no promotion unless God promotes you! Anything you accomplish for your eventual credit, through human vigor and strength or your clever wit, is simply a deed of the flesh i.e. wood, hay, and straw to be torched in the end. If we truly desire to glorify God then we must realize that His grace will not be satisfied until He can take some members of the human race, who by original position are lower than the angels, and lift them up to an eternal citizenship in the highest realm.

> "You have made him for a little while lower than the angels; You have crowned him with glory and honor, and have appointed

> him over the works of your hands; you have put all things in subjection under his feet. For in subjecting all things to him, He left nothing that is not subject to him. But now we do not yet see all things subjected to him." (Heb 2:7-8)

Satan is infuriated that puny humans could one day rise above him and be in such lofty positions. Even his demon empire realizes that they do not hold the special privileges that Christian believers obtain once they become born again and saved. Believers are given position as well as assets that angels have never, nor will ever, receive. The night before our Lord went to face His death He spoke of a union within Himself and believers:

> " . . . that they may all be one; even as You, Father, are in Me and I in You, that they [believers] also may be in Us [Trinity], so that the world may believe that You sent Me." (Joh 17:21)

Our Lord Jesus Christ goes on with this prayer in verse 22 stating that the glory Christ received is given to us and we are one with the Father, Son, and the Holy Spirit (Trinity). It is interesting to see that God knew and prepared for this present conflict perhaps millions or billions of years in advance as noted in this next line of scripture.

> "Father, I desire that they also, whom You have given Me, be with Me where I am, so that they may see My glory which You have given Me, for You loved Me before the foundation of the world." (Joh 17:24)

Before the earth was formed, God had resolved all issues in the upcoming Angelic Conflict. Satan has no right to lay claim to such an honored citizenship that is bestowed on believers, we are in fact citizens of heaven! (Phi 3:20) This is an eternal passport into divine royalty and power beyond any angelic dominance. This passport is irrevocable, never expires, a gift of a family crest within the highest dynasty of any universe, it is privilege and power beyond human imagination. No position or redemption offered to Satan would have ever put him in such possession of this type of title. His self-seeking intention revealed in Isaiah 14 was an outrage to God's perfect plan. God describes His reprobate in Rom 1:25 as those who "exchanged the truth of God for a lie, and worshipped and served the creature rather than the Creator, who is blessed forever, Amen."

> "They exchanged the glory of the incorruptible God for an image in the form of corruptible man and of birds and four footed animals and crawling creatures." (Rom 1:23)

The kingdom of darkness promotes evolution because they want humans to believe that they were derived from the animal kingdom. Many people will buy the lie that we evolved from an ape-like creature and not a Royal creation, higher than any angelic creature. When research is done, and we must follow only accurate and in-depth research, the results always reveal glaring disparities between the human being and any species within the animal kingdom. Evolution theories are full of mistakes, human error, hoaxes, and cover-ups that have been allowed to bleed into the text books and fact sheets of schools and universities throughout the world.

It is one of Satan's most celebrated victories over most of mankind. They have always been known as evolution theories, not facts, never lose sight of that subtle difference. Evolution is a philosophy masquerading as a science.

Satan has no problem with mankind's having a belief in a higher power, a god or divine being in some realm, because that is what he considers himself to be! It is the issue of our Lord and Savior Jesus Christ and the work on the Cross that is the thorn in his side, his true nemesis in this invisible battle. If he can lead you down the road of atheism and devoted thoughts of evolution, that is great for him, an easy victory with very little effort. The best way to undermine the Creator is to sow seeds of doubt into the created. But he also directs people toward the road of belief in other gods, be it idol worship or another savior other than Jesus Christ. The full-on frontal assault does not work often in heated warfare with cluttered battlefields. Camouflage or guerrilla tactics are best suited to nibble at the opponent and weaken him physically and mentally over a long period of time. One of the best examples is the war that took place in South East Asia known as the Vietnam Conflict. It was an extended nightmare of mental and physical assaults, some may call it a war of attrition. Boxers often deal with this when facing another fighter of equal skill and technique inside the squared circle. The boxer with the best conditioning will outlast the other, slowly pecking away until his opponent collapses or quits in his corner. Never lose sight of the fact that Satan has been around since the dawn of time and has observed and examined human behavior and weakness to the point that he is the highest-trained professor of human psychology and human behavior. Satan is head and shoulders above the human race in any degree program derived from a worldly university. When it comes to believers he simply re-directs efforts with varied angles of attack, perhaps keeping them busy earning wealth in the world or distracted with family matters.

Satan will install a false teacher in a believer's life who uses murky doctrines and half-truths to ensure the futility of their attempts to live the Christian way of life. This is a creature who stood up against God and said, "I will raise myself above You!" We cannot think for a moment that the human race at this point in history can match wits with him or stab fear into his heart. In fact, in Isa 14:13, "will raise" is the hiphil imperfect of the verb *rum* which is the causative stem, and he is saying, "I will cause myself to rule." Can you as a flesh and blood, flawed creature say that to your Creator and then make a real attempt at this outrageous claim? Realize who and what the human race is dealing with, and realize that his methods and schemes go back to a time before human beings walked the earth, and that his power and intellect surpass anything in the human realm. Then take into consideration that God, being the author of fair play, the only superb and Divine Judge, has given Satan the monarchy of power over this earth, to exhibit his testimony that he will be like the Most High. Satan is said to be the prince of the power of the air in Eph 2:2. As we have seen, in 2Co 4:4 he is labeled the god of this world!

This is God's will for Satan to have his turn at superior power and authority, a term in office in the role of a ruler. Unfortunately for Satan he is witnessing a terrible reflection peering back upon him in this rulership role, as God has allowed human beings a free will as well, and in using it they have the ability to be the ruler over their own lives, making their own positive or negative decisions. Not even Satan can force the human race to turn out like he wants! The chaos in this world is an embarrassment to Satan's rule! However, thanks to many ignorant, well-meaning Christians, who are performing human good instead of living in God's plan for their lives, Satan is having some assistance ruling this world.

The first original sin began with independence, but when we delve deeper into an inspection of the original sin we can clearly see that it was a thought, the content within Satan's heart (system of thinking) and soul. Most people truly do not understand sin, to them it will always be an issue of immorality or a deliberate overt gesture that they consider to be sin. Immorality and some overt gestures or actions are sin, if a spiritual believer occasionally falls in such areas, and it does not mean that they are "fallen from God's grace," or any less a Christian than the nice moral guy sitting next to them in church. Someone who appears moral is not necessarily a spiritual giant or mature believer compared to the believer recently fallen into an overt sin visible to others.

In simple terms, morality is not spirituality! Many unbelievers are moral, kind, and good members of society, but they will end up in the lake of fire if they do not become believers in the Lord Jesus Christ. People are entrenched with the outward appearance more than they realize. God looks at the heart where only He sees the truth within His creatures' souls. When a believer begins to reach different levels of spiritual maturity this will automatically have some overt consequence on lifestyle or result in dismissing immoral behaviors and negative attitudes, but it is God at work in their life, not anything that they accomplished in their flesh.

To believe that spiritual maturity will rid someone of all problems, flaws, and weakness is to say that here on planet Earth in the flesh we have the ability to reach perfection. This is utter nonsense! A quick study on David (a man after God's own heart) will nullify any thoughts about such nonsense. It would appear that Satan was not only created perfect but certainly mature, and yet over time he fell into a vicious series of sins. He is the first sinner to be exact. Some of the worst sins have to do with thought and sins of the tongue, not immorality. Mental attitude sins and how you use that tongue to speak of others can certainly turn you into a monster.

Almost any person with a shred of common sense can remain moral for long periods within a life span, and yet never reach a level of spiritual maturity or perhaps not even be born again and saved. This is very important to understand. In fact, if you can understand this perspective it will straighten out your life in a fantastic way! If not, you can be part of the crowd that spends their lives trying to be moral and self-righteous, nit-picking and judging others. You will amount to nothing in the Pre-designed Plan of God, and you will struggle with envious, jealous thoughts and sins like gossip, as well as a heart filled with pride because you are so outwardly good. The reason Christians get away with this disgusting behavior is because everyone witnesses the outside of these so-called spiritual giants, and the church or those in their periphery are so impressed that they buy into the façade. People may even seek out the morally perfect believer for advice or to be a leader, which inflates the hidden sin of pride and arrogance to higher levels.

In most churches people are evaluated on the basis of obvious sins, what can be seen or even heard through gossip. So overt sins become a basis for condemnation; meanwhile, hidden sins such as arrogance, judging, and sins of the tongue along with several other gross sins are ignored. As stated in Isa 14:13 it all comes from within the heart, the right lobe, which is our thinking pattern. "But you said in your heart" is a clear statement of where sin came from. "I will" is another statement that clarifies the beginning step toward the sins of independence, arrogance, and rebellion against God. Satan's initial grab for power and glory was in the angelic realm, conquering and dividing the angels to be the supreme ruler on his own. He needed to start a conspiracy in order to gain the ground required to develop faithful followers. He planted seeds of doubt and unrest within God's congregation, trying to set forth the belief that God is unfair and unjust.

We have noted that the Biblical reference to clouds refers to a divine presence, be it the Lord returning on them in Mat 24:30 or Rev 1:7, or a cloud as a sign of the presence of God in the Old Testament. So in his arrogance Satan wants to ascend above the clouds (Isa 14:14) but the truth of the matter is that he does not have the required eternal compatibility with God on any level. His desire to function as God is an exercise in frustration and failure. Satan is so taken with himself that he truly believes that his efforts and aptitude are enough to equal God or possibly surpass the Creator! His power lust was first aimed at ruling over angels: "I will raise my throne above the stars," and then the third "I will" is his ambition to rule the earth: "I will sit on the mount of assembly in the recesses of the north." It was Satan's will to rule the earth and over the angels upon the earth as well as in heaven, mankind is not even in view yet. Satan has neither the character nor the personality to control all types of creatures and bring them into a harmonious eternity. This is where he fails.

All of Satan's systems working together will not bring about a unified race. He wants the glory but lacks the ability, and that same spirit is manifested everywhere in the human race. People seek out glory, but they have neither the ability nor sense of responsibility to gain any glory. This is true in business, in churches, within the military, in athletics, and in social life. In every phase of life you can find people who are unstable, off balance and trying for the glory in which only God can operate. God is the one who designed and works within divine principles and divine structure. All other creatures are simply created and lack divine superiority and power that the Creator alone possesses. God's power and character run so deep and so unfaltering that neither angelic nor human creatures will ever truly be able to understand it. The grace of God is far beyond our ability to fathom! (Rom 11:33) Man can do nothing in the weakness of his flesh or his own talents to glorify God. It is one of the grand schemes of the kingdom of darkness to promote creature credit, which is accomplished by human works that lead to self-righteousness and legalism. Satan is the greatest creature ever created, so he is for creatures getting all the credit—creature credit instead of Creator credit. Satan would love to have the world with all the prosperity of the Millennium, just without the Creator getting the credit!

Man does not deserve or even more importantly earn a thing. It is by the grace of God that we are saved, so no one can boast. Yet Satan will promote works and human effort for salvation and then push more works and deeds on the human race after salvation. This attack is directed upon one of God's divine principles, the grace principle. God does all the work, we simply have to be positive or operate in faith toward our Father.

If Satan is able to distract man with works programs and creature credit then he has successfully promoted himself as the greatest creature in the universe! Here is Satan using his talents and ability, all blessings from God, in an attempt to supersede God in function as well as in person. Mankind operates the same way, man glorifies man instead of God. This is an age-old principle of human talent or success as the issue, and this goes on within doctrinal ministries and Christian churches as well as out in the world.

The glorification of a person due to talent or effort on his or her part was the initial sin of independence that Satan began before mankind came to be. There are many Christian publications loaded with plenty of hot air on how to become a better believer or how to work toward a goal in the spiritual life, be it salvation or spiritual growth. When success comes to a believer, the individual is surrounded with adoring people asking, "What's the secret to your success?" That is when the oddball replies come out that they fasted for 30 days or sat in a swamp and spoke with God through nature, always a gimmick or something they did to achieve the goal. Any true victory rests entirely upon the shoulders of our Lord Jesus Christ. Our lives, as part of the Angelic Conflict, are about who and what God is, not who and what a creature is or can accomplish. We simply clutter up God's work and get directly in His way when our human effort is involved. In fact, God will step aside because He is a perfect gentleman who allows us to do as we please. For any true victory or accomplishment, it is God doing all the work, anything else accomplishes nothing at all.

Satan's fifth I will: "I will make myself like the Most High." Satan wished for the attributes of God and the essence of God, but the very nature of his sin frustrates that possibility, he cannot reproduce any part of the character of God. So Satan with the assistance of his demon army has set a course to duplicate that which they believe they can of God. It is a cheap imitation, a shameful counterfeit. Satan can also claim the title of first counterfeiter known to mankind. What infuriates Satan is that lowly people have the ability to be imitators of God by becoming positive believers and following the guideline of being filled with the Holy Spirit. In Gal 5:16 we read for believers to "Walk by means of the Holy Spirit." Simply put, Jesus Christ is God and believers are able to be imitators of Christ. Eph 5:1 tells us to be "imitators of God, as beloved children." And in Gal 4:19 we see that Christ is being formed in us. Satan is not able to have any of this power from the Trinity. This leaves him with disdain and a teeth-grinding anger toward the human race. Outside of the Gospel there is nothing Satan hates as much as spirituality by grace. The problem is that most believers do not even understand spirituality by grace, largely due to the fact that true Bible doctrine is missing in this generation and real doctrinal teachers have always been in the minority throughout most of human history. This is why Satan has many easy victories in the area of teaching morality over spirituality. Only the filling of the Holy Spirit can produce fruit in a Christian life. When believers discover true doctrinal principles and realize how to be filled with the Holy Spirit it is like a direct hit onto the kingdom of darkness' side of the battlefield.

Even Satan can operate in morality. Remember that Satan is the master of the art of counterfeit and has the ability to have a god-like capacity. Satan wants the title of Most High because it refers to the possessor of heaven and earth. Gen 14:18-19 illustrates this title: "Blessed be Abram of God Most High, possessor of heaven and earth."

> "And Abram said to the king of Sodom, 'I have sworn to the Lord God Most High, possessor of heaven and earth.'" (Gen 14:22)

Satan is too clever to think that he could ever truly become the Most High, because Jehovah the self-existent One is irreplaceable and cannot be accurately replicated, but the title "possessor of heaven and earth" is definitely a goal Satan believes he can achieve. However, God will not share His glory with anyone! Authority in heavenly and earthly realms is what Satan wants to wrest from the Lord, and he will manipulate, lie, and cheat his way to a victory until his last day in this conflict. God is absolute and clear on authority and a chain of command, He states His view in many scriptures:

> "I am the Lord, that is My name: I will not give My glory to another, nor My praise to graven images." (Isa 42:8)

The Angelic Conflict

> "Thus says the Lord, the King of Israel and his Redeemer, the Lord of hosts, 'I am the first and I am the last, and there is no God besides Me.'" (Isa 44:6)

The essential evil character of sin is the unwillingness on the part of the creature to abide in the precise position in which he has been placed by the Creator. This is why pursuing the goal to be like God is what Satan recommended to Adam and Eve, that they too could be as gods. His desire is to displace God as the sovereign of the universe and to run it himself. The objective of the five "I wills" was to take over the function of God.

> "For God knows that in the day you eat from it your eyes will be opened, and you will be like God, knowing good and evil." (Gen 3:5)

This quote from Genesis is a crystal clear reflection of Satan's supreme ambition. As noted, Satan cannot even run this world much less a whole universe. Satan is smart and powerful but lacks God's consistent power and faithfulness. Satan's ideal man during the Tribulation period will declare himself to be God, sitting in the temple of God as highlighted in 2Th 2:4. Any being assuming the position to run a whole universe has got to be faithful and loyal to those under his authority, God is all that and much more, Satan is not! Satan will whisper of loyalty in your ear and turn around to kick you to the ground before the whisper is completed from his persuasive lips. Satan's love is a self-love, his sense of loyalty goes as far as what he desires. Satan made a deal with Judas Iscariot, actually indwelling him, and when trouble came upon Judas where was Satan to bail him out? Satan probably gave Judas the rope on which he hung himself. Once someone sells out to the kingdom of darkness they have had it. A fine example is drug addiction and those who indulge in this destructive behavior. The drugs are not faithful to a person, in the long run the drugs will hang those that use them. You need the drug but it does not need you. It is interesting to note that drug addiction and demon possession have similar characteristics.

> "Now the deeds of the flesh are evident, which are: immorality, impurity, sensuality, idolatry, sorcery (pharmakeia is the

Greek word giving us the English word pharmacy) . . ." (Gal 5:19-20)

In fact, drug addiction can lead to demon possession. There is no consistency in a person's life when they depend on a drug. This is true with Satan, no consistency, as he cannot provide and does not love or even help, because he lacks the character to do any of these things. Satan wants the glory but lacks the ability to get it and still attempts to provide it for himself. The analogy between Satan and addiction is very real. Drug addiction will make you pay constantly for the thrill, and it will hook you into a strong desire, a need that can plague a person and bring misery. There are always strings attached with Satan as well, and his path leads to a cheap, temporary thrill but in the end it is death. Satan never picks up the tab. He shows no grace to a fallen creature. When he cannot use you any longer he will discard you and move on. Satan appears to offer you a great time but you will pay and pay in the future, no free ride with the kingdom of darkness.

When the Lord Jesus Christ walked the earth Satan offered him the kingdoms of the world, and our Lord turned him down flat. As a believer—if and when the kingdom of darkness is making an offer that you know is not from your Father—this would be the time to imitate Jesus Christ. Satan will always try to give you what you want as long as it is not in the Pre-designed Plan of God. It is believers and unbelievers who chase the promises of this world, and ignore the will of God, that end up suckers in the end. Satan offers nothing for free and gives nothing from the goodness of his heart, instead it is always calculated and very costly. As believers grow they learn more about grace and this constructs a wall of fire around the soul to protect them from Satan's cruel plans. This can cause Satan great distress and pain in his efforts at getting into a believer's life. Satan has a low tolerance for pain, so this wall of fire is a great deterrent to satanic attacks. The grace of God is not only at the Cross of Jesus Christ but filtered into every day and every minute of a believer's life.

What price did Satan pay, where is his offering of grace and forgiveness to a fallen creature that he wants to worship him? Heaven depends on God's character, not Satan's character. The Lord is more than willing to pay any price for His children. Looking at the work of the Cross is the most spectacular display of suffering and love, one that we can never fully grasp. Pain, humiliation, and separation from God were never issues for the Lord Jesus Christ, He was always very prepared to pay the price for us to enter His flawless realm in heaven. Believers have Heaven prepared for them, a place of perfection beyond man's wildest dreams. Satan has a lake of fire prepared for him and his followers, a place of torment beyond imagination. This lake of fire was prepared for the devil and his angels as shown in Mat 25:41.

Satan's character is perfectly illustrated in eternity, just like fire Satan will do one thing well and that is to cause pain to those engulfed in it. So there is no grace with the devil, the only one who has the ability to offer grace is the Father in Heaven. God is the one who pays the tab in full. Everything is done and complete through Him, there is no authority on earth or the universe to compare with him. When we think of the counterfeit work of Satan, it is interesting to look at scriptures that warn of false teachers and phony leaders that are manipulated by demon influence.

> "For such men are false apostles, deceitful workers, disguising themselves as apostles of Christ." (2Co 11:13)

> "Therefore it is not surprising if his (Satan's) servants also disguise themselves as servants of righteousness; whose end shall be according to their deeds." (2Co 11:15)

These verses speak of disguises and of those that transform themselves into apostles of Christ, servants or ministers of righteousness. These are what can be called agents of the great deceiver and they teach people how to be what they call righteous. The imitation of doctrinal teachers is another method of attack in the counterfeiting of God. In order for a false teacher to present a message that appears doctrinal they cling to a form of godliness to cover up the lies with subtle hypocrisy. This form of counterfeit teaching from the kingdom of darkness is laced with Truth so that it can easily fall back on some Biblical verse or principle from Christianity. They promote good works and righteousness under a disguise of attractive features or compassionate words. This type of leader is usually respected in the community and accepted with open arms in our society.

The kingdom of darkness will assist such preachers of false doctrine by keeping up a pristine public appearance, helping them stay clear of scrutiny. These are the teachers and leaders of the church that are sincere and have a body of teachings that represent human viewpoint more than divine viewpoint. They will preach and teach what the angels of light have revealed to them, giving them the energy that will appeal to worldly views. It should be noted that these types of ministers do not even realize that they are pawns in Satan's own chess match here on earth. Most do not even have a clue about the filling of the Holy Spirit or they believe it to be an emotional wave that comes upon them. A natural man does not accept the things of the Spirit of God, "For they are foolishness to him, and he cannot understand them, because they are spiritually discerned." (1Co 2:14)

They will gladly preach of righteousness but know little of the doctrine of grace. They will appear as great humanitarians at times, always willing to go the extra mile for a brother, helping to do good in the devil's world. To show the clear difference between preaching on grace and preaching on righteousness, one must understand that preaching on righteousness is directed at reformation of the natural man, while teaching grace aims at regeneration of man through the power of God. Teaching this type of righteousness omits the power of God, the knowledge of grace, and all that accompanies it.

This counterfeit teaching allows Satan to use the strategy of forcing a secondary truth, which blinds people from the real Truth of grace. The secondary truth is a layer of factual doctrine but is covered up with incorrect teaching. A great example to further explain this comes from 2Co 7:10, "For godly sorrow produces repentance leading to salvation." This is a completely true statement; however, it is not saying that someone must feel sorrow for a sin they committed in order to be saved. You cannot put the cart before the horse! It is not God's will that you make yourself holy, but that holiness be the result of the doctrine in your soul by the filling of the Holy Spirit. Salvation for eternal life is always the gift of God, for faith alone in Christ alone. Satan is a master at taking deep, doctrinal principles and twisting and bending them to suit his battle plan. A believer that tries to reform his flesh to become saved or to show his spiritual growth represents the pinnacle of a human works program. The kingdom of darkness will use tongues, physical health, life after death, morality, unfulfilled prophecy, the baptism of the Spirit and many Biblical subjects, all fine within the right perspective, but in a way to lead believers away from Truth. Satan can use this secondary truth principle in many realms across many subjects, and it is just layer upon layer of deception wrapped in a piece of Truth. Satan can blind the eyes of almost any human being, it is not a difficult task for such a great genius. When we focus on secondary things we miss the primary things that will guide us to the knowledge God has intended for us. Very much the same trick a magician will use to deceive an audience.

> "You blind guides who strain at a gnat and swallow a camel!"
> (Mat 23:24)

This is a fitting verse for this deception. These false teachers can have systems of doctrinal teachings which include every truth of the scriptures except one, the Truth of the real person and work of our Lord Jesus Christ!

Satan will allow Christ to be worshipped, providing that believers remain ignorant of the power of God and the resulting glorification of God, therefore elevating secondary truths while ignoring the power of God. This system also appeals to the flesh. Both believers and unbelievers are drawn to it, because they are naturally-minded and cannot understand how to be filled with the Holy Spirit.

> "(They are) holding to a form of godliness, although they have
> denied its power; Avoid such men as these." (2Ti 3:5)

All of this information points to why Satan is in favor of programs to clean up his world, including Christian programs! Satan is all for making the world a better place to live, it is part of his camouflaged attack upon God's authority. Most believers are so busy cleaning up the world and working on making the old man, their flesh, more presentable, that they never learn of the subtle deceptions right in front of them. We cannot rinse off our flesh and present it to our Lord on a clean platter, it is an insult to His work and simply impossible to accomplish.

The principles we have covered in this chapter should begin to clear up the deceptions and confusion that are entrenched in many Christian churches within our world. The following principles are the overview and lessons to take with you as you move to the next chapter:

1. The major purpose of the 5 "I wills" is to promote Satan's efforts to be like the Most High. It is not to promote an effort to be the opposite of God as the world presumes.
2. Satan's key strategies in trying to be like the Most High are to influence man through false doctrines, to teach people to improve on self, to work on making their human nature more attractive, and to take the focus off of the new creature created by God. Our Lord spoke on the worthlessness of self-reformation in Mat 12:43-45.
3. The presence of gross evil in the world is not due to Satan's intention to have it so. Rather, it indicates Satan's inability to be like the Most High! It is Satan and his legions that desire to clean up the world and consider this their residence. The Lord Jesus Christ makes it clear that His kingdom is not of this world in Joh 18:36.
4. Satan's ambition to be like God has led him to take on more than he can handle.
5. Satan deceives the world and even the Christian church into thinking that he is totally the opposite of God. This makes his deception successful because outwardly he has some god-like qualities, yet inwardly he has no similarities to God.
6. Satan desires worship from mankind. So much so that during the Tribulation period he will demand worship from the people of the earth or they will pay the penalty of death.
7. Any plans to clean up the world and make it a better place to live complements Satan's evil goals and policies aimed at being like God! That is why there is little opposition to different types of improvement programs, be it for mankind or the environment.
8. All the counterfeit programs Satan has simply reveal his desire to be like the Most High.

9. In other words Satan has watched what God does and tries to counterfeit the Lord every chance he gets. This is why religion is his counterfeit and therefore Satan has:

   i. Counterfeit Gospel—2Co 11:3-4.
   ii. Counterfeit Ministers—2Co 11:13-15.
   iii. Counterfeit Doctrine—1Ti 4:1.
   iv. Counterfeit Communion Table—1Co 10:19-21.
   v. Counterfeit Spirituality—Gal 3:2-3.
   vi. Counterfeit Righteousness—Mat 23:13-36.
   vii. Counterfeit Power & Dynamics (miracles, tongues, healing)—2Th 2:8-10. viii)
   viii. Counterfeit Systems of Gods—2Th 2:3-4

It is interesting to note that in his third fall at the end of the Millennium Satan will be thrown into the lake of fire. His freedom to rebel against his Creator is taken away, and it is his final chapter. This too is what the final judgment will be like for the world, free will and volition will no longer be within reach when that final moment arrives. This is for all of eternity as indicated in Rev 20:10 and Mat 25:41. Those that reject the Lord Jesus Christ will keep Satan company, along with the fallen angels. Satan will have no power to escape or to release anyone from the final fate. It is true that Satan's run at being the ultimate authority will have weakened the world and caused all to fear him as noted in earlier passages of Isaiah, and this will be on display for the world to see.

The world is the battlefield, the theater, of the Angelic Conflict, an invisible warfare that will be revealed in God's divine timing. The Lord will return and be the rightful heir to the Throne, because the work will be done and the glory will belong to God alone.

> "I glorified You on the earth, having accomplished the work which You have given Me to do." (Joh 17:4)

Satan could be recognized as a prime minister for God, a powerful ruler over the earth, but in the end he will be a beaten creature, imprisoned for all eternity. Before Satan there was only one will in the entire universe, that will was God's. When the end finally comes and the world has witnessed the Lord's triumphant return, again there will be only the will of God. The free will of God's creatures constitutes the difference between eternity and time, in eternity past and in eternity future God has the only will. This does not mean we will be robots in Heaven. In fact, we will be free to enjoy our relationship with God and with others more than ever! What it does mean is that our old nature, the nature of rebellion against God's will, will no longer exist, only our new nature is taken to Heaven. Without our nature of rebellion we will be free to enjoy all the pleasures at God's right hand forever, in Psa 16:11, without even the ability to fall away from our Redeemer!

Satan was originally given the ability to enjoy all that Heaven offered, at the right hand of God. But when Satan began to operate in free will *against* the will of his Creator, we can see the monstrosity that began the whole conflict and this is especially evil for several reasons:

1. There was no previous example of sin and rebellion. This was the start of the anti-authority movement, even worse since it was the first rebellion against God!
2. Satan was created perfect, physically and mentally. He lacked for nothing; however, like many of God's creatures he was ungrateful and therefore started the first conspiracy.
3. Satan's sin is especially monstrous because he was the greatest creature created by God, and with his superior intellect and understanding he was well aware of God's goodness and love toward all creatures.
4. He was in the highest position of angelic authority, above all angels, and had many privileges, and still that was not enough.
5. Satan's sins are drenched in arrogant revolt against a God who let him become intimate and enjoy fellowship by His side.

There are certain things that took place and will take place due to this calculated revolution that Satan masterminded:

1. Satan's position and privileges are banished forever as noted in verse 12: "How you have fallen from heaven," says God to the one who so strongly desired to ascend to heaven.

2. The corruption of Satan's character. Remember that he was known as the "star of the morning, son of the dawn." He is now the adversary and opponent of God.
3. There is also the perversion of power. This power was designed for God's glory and the good of His creatures. Satan turned his God-given power against the Throne of God and used it to corrupt creatures and to weaken the nations.
4. However there is also the retention of dignity. Though he was cast down from his exalted position he was allowed to retain some of his great dignity. Remember that even a powerful angel like Michael the archangel did not dare pronounce anything against him as noted in Jud 9.
5. Satan is destined for the pit, to be thrust down to Sheol to the recesses of the pit as mentioned in Isa 14:15 and Rev 20.

One final question that should be asked is why a holy and righteous God, who is all knowing and all powerful, would allow this angelic fall? This fall introduced sin into the universe, affecting angels as well as human beings, not to mention its affect upon the Trinity. To answer this we simply need to realize that God is perfect. His plans are perfect from conception to completion. God's character and nature are always lined up with what is right and good. He is the perfect Judge above all other judges. He is the superb and loving Father even during a time of discipline. His ways are just and right. When you have a Father who is known as the righteous and perfect Judge as well as being the best Father, then there should be a feeling of safety and trust that He is in control and will take care of the outcome because He knows best.

Perhaps he allowed the angels to rebel in order that He might give an explicit example of the wretchedness and degeneration of sin and rebellion. God could have offered this test for angelic creatures to have a choice to serve Him or to wreak havoc out on their own. The old saying of setting someone free, and if they come back then they truly loved you, may help explain this aspect of the Angelic Conflict. This may have been the only way God could have shown true grace to His creatures, preserving some angels and in the redemption of unworthy, sinful man who fell because of Satan. In man God will magnify His grace forever before the angels. Leaving this chapter we put into view the following passage to assist with this age-old question:

> "But God, being rich in mercy, because of His great love with which He loved us, even when we were dead in our transgressions, made us alive together with Christ (by grace you have been saved), and raised us up with Him, and seated us with Him in the heavenly places in Christ Jesus, so that in the ages to come He might show the surpassing riches of His grace in kindness toward us in Christ Jesus. For by grace you have been saved through faith; and that not of yourselves, it is the gift of God; not as a result of works, so that no one may boast." (Eph 2:4-9)

CHAPTER 6

The Satanic Plan and Two Categories of Fallen Angels Under his Command.

In order to fully describe the history and difference between angels it would be best to give a clear view of the conflict and the multifaceted operations within this invisible battlefield. The first set of angels in need of more precise description are the non-operational angels which are under two categories. The first can be viewed in Genesis chapter 6, angels who infiltrated the human race and are now incarcerated underneath the ground in a place called Tartarus (a compartment in Hades).

These are the angels who cohabitated with the women and brought forth a race of super-creatures that were half-angel and half-human. The scriptures call them Nephilim, but in mythology you may have heard of Greek Gods such as Hercules, Zeus, or Casper. Well, the Bible points out that these mighty men were physically superior and intellectually advanced beyond any human being. They were god-like in size, strength, and appearance and were treated as deity by most people of that era.

> "The Nephilim were on the earth in those days, and also afterward when the sons of God (angels) had sex with the daughters of men, and they bore children to them. Those were the mighty men who were of old, men of renown." (Gen 6:4)

The second category of non-operational angels is not allowed out of the abyss until the Tribulation, these angels are of the first demon assault army of angels. These cruel creatures incarcerated in the abyss have transgressed the boundaries of the human race and are best referred to as demons rather than angels. There is a demon king among them called Abaddon who will have a severe impact during the Tribulation period. This supreme demon leader is considered Satan's right-hand man and will be furious and battle-ready when he is released. Abaddon is mentioned once in the New Testament and six times in the Old Testament. If you can recall the previous chapters there was a mention of demon possession and how the Lord removed the unclean spirits who indwelt a man. These demons asked not to be sent to the abyss because it is a maximum-security lockdown for fallen angels in time.

> "And Jesus asked him, 'What is your name?' and he said, 'Legion'; for many demons had entered him. And they were entreating Him (Jesus) not to command them to depart into the abyss." (Luk 8:30-31)

These demons are an organized military force, as the title *legion* points out and may have been in excess of 1000 indwelling this human being. They knew that they had violated rules of the conflict, and they also seem well aware that the abyss was a miserable and inescapable fate that was to be avoided at all costs! This prison is the fourth compartment within Hades reserved for angelic creatures that have violated the rules of engagement within this invisible warfare. It is translated as a bottomless pit in Revelation.

> "And the fifth angel sounded and I saw a star (Satan) from heaven which had fallen to the earth; and the key of the bottomless pit (the deepest place inside the earth, the abyss) was given to him." (Rev 9:1)

> "They (demons) have as king over them, the angel of the abyss; his name in Hebrew is Abaddon, and in the Greek he has the name Apollyon." (Rev 9:11)

Several other passages are worth seeking out and studying to clarify the abyss and the lock-down upon these fallen angels (see Rev 20:1-3). The abyss is related to visible warfare taking place in the Tribulation period. We are currently in the invisible phase of this conflict, known as the Church Age, and it requires believers to step up into military action and become invisible heroes. This is accomplished with positive choices for the plan of God, a dedication to Bible doctrine, as well as a clear view on events and circumstances surrounding the devil's world.

There is a point in human history when the invisible becomes visible and all will be revealed, so we will see visible heroes such as Moses and Elijah and the 144,000 Jewish evangelists. After the Rapture of the Church occurs there will be a radical change in God's plan. During the Tribulation, physical attacks will be allowed upon the human race for a period of 5 months. This brutal assault will be led by such demon angels as Abaddon because Satan will have released his three legions of fallen angels. Once again we will see the rules of engagement within this warfare as restrictions will apply to these attacks. Only those who are involved in Satan's world system will be attacked. Believers who have turned positive toward the Truth of the Scriptures will have what is known as a wall of fire surrounding them.

Another restriction will be that these demons will not be able to kill all those that they attack, their victims will surely suffer and perhaps even want to die but it will not happen. Very few will be permitted to die at this point in history! This devastating time of tribulation in human history could take place three and a half years from today as the Bible has made it clear that everything is complete, that the stage is set for the end times to ignite. During this attack upon humans we will see crisis evangelism at its peak. God has used and will use a crisis to direct unbelievers to the opportunity for salvation by recognizing the only savior, our Lord Jesus Christ.

The reality of the demon armies being released from the abyss and the invisible warfare becoming visible may seem overwhelming to a believer and impossible to the unbeliever, but it is backed up by Scripture and even human history itself is slowly revealing the signs of our own demise. According to the Bible it will be a time of wrath in 1Th 5:9 and Rev 6:16-17. It is called a time of judgment in Rev 14:7, Rev 15:4, a time of indignation in Isa 26:20-21 as well as a time of punishment in Isa 24:20-21. It is referred to as a trial in Rev 3:10, a time of trouble in Jer

30:7, and a time of destruction in Joe 1:15. This is a very serious series of events and these are very difficult times falling upon the human race. Only the believers of today, in the Church Age, are spared and removed before this critical set of events takes place.

In the passage of Rev 9:1 you can see that Satan is the star that has fallen, this is in the middle of the Tribulation and God has given him the key to unlock the abyss. The abyss is a seemingly endless hole that is inescapable, but it will be opened and the Greek gods of mythology will once again have a dominant role upon the face of this earth. Just as in the days of Noah they will reign in a visible capacity for a period of time. Satan and his army will show a display of fury and angelic power that has never been witnessed by any human being in history.

> "For this reason, rejoice, O heavens and you who dwell in them. Woe to the earth and the sea, because the devil has come down to you, having great wrath, knowing that he has only a short time." (Rev 12:12)

In Rev 12:7-8 we can see the war in heaven as Michael and his angels battle Satan's army. The intensity of the attacks upon the believers and unbelievers left behind after the Rapture will lead many to seek suicide and they will find no relief! As previously noted, death and suicide will not be permitted to occur. Satan will have no mercy upon his own followers, the people of the earth who remained faithful to his cosmic system. He is a brutal dictator that only focuses on his goals, his victory. The devil has no love or compassion for others, especially for mankind. Satan turns his demon shock troops on any and all human servants at this point of the conflict. His use for obedient humans will have come to an end, and his satanic frustration will boil over at this last stand and spill onto everything and everyone around him. This is very similar to the boss who uses his employees to advance his own career. The workers that are dedicated and have made him look good day in and day out, working as unto the Lord, are simply tossed aside, their careers crushed as the self-serving boss advances. Satan is the worst boss, he has no capacity to be a leader or to take on the authority role. He is the callous boss who steps on those underneath him to gain a higher salary or a better position, not thinking about families or children that may be affected or any destruction left behind.

The students or followers of the cosmic system become the same, cold and calculating, as they devise ways to improve self and gather more unto themselves. They are poor lovers and selfish friends, because they are self-serving and arrogant like their father the devil. This includes believers who function within the devil's world, the ones with no time for God or thoughts of spiritual growth. It is tragic to see that so many of God's people prefer the cosmic system and the frantic pursuit for all that resides in it over the pursuit of eternal things.

Once Satan is cast out of heaven he sheds all hypocrisy, all self-righteousness and shows his true colors. His pettiness, implacability, and vindictiveness come to the surface, which are the manifestations of his colossal vanity and relentless arrogance! The phenomenon in the end will be arrogance torturing arrogance, arrogance destroying arrogance. Arrogance always has a destructive path and devastates anyone within its periphery. There is no thought or hesitation once Satan gets his hands on the key to the abyss. He releases the demon army that he knows will torment and attack the people left upon the earth. His ruthless attitude will become painfully apparent, he will use that which God gave him to mount an attempt to destroy the human race. He has no reservation as the ruler to thrash those over whom he has ruled. Satan has despised man from the beginning, it should be no shock that he launches an assault upon the whole race.

Most people, believers or unbelievers, will ask "why me?" I do not follow the devil, I am independent from Satan. You may think you are independent from Satan but it is from God that you are independent! People that live outside the will of God live directly inside the will of the kingdom of darkness. Those that are wrapped up in the world system, grabbing at all the world has to offer with no time for God, are certainly employees on Satan's payroll. People are blinded and fooled by the sparkling, yet hollow promises within the world, promises like working more hours to earn a new house, or focusing on the celebrity or politician so they will guide your life in a better direction.

Depositing this kind of stock in the world is withdrawing your stock from our Lord. What type of effort or search have you been involved in concerning God? There is no independence from both God and Satan. This is an arrogant and foolish notion that the world promotes, and Satan rules this world. There are very few who think they are following Satan but their stubborn independence makes it clear who their leader is. No one is an original thinker, even if they think they are, everyone is either living in the viewpoint of God or the viewpoint of Satan and his world system.

> "And you will seek Me and find Me when you search for Me with all of your heart." (Jer 29:13)

> "You shall love the Lord your God with all of your heart, and with all of your soul, and with all of your mind, and with all of your strength." (Mar 12:30)

In Mat 7:7 we are told to knock and it shall be opened for us, yet very few even approach anything to do with the Lord Jesus Christ, the general public no longer even uses our Lord's name in celebrating Christmas! A believer that has been duped into focusing on this world has not lost his salvation, but has definitely become a slave to the grind, so to speak, a servant of Satan. Believers that remain out of fellowship slowly become numb to the things of God and actually gain worldly knowledge as they lose Godly wisdom. The mental attitude sins such as pride and arrogance always lower an I.Q., making those that operate in such sins appear stupid.

With God, favoritism is not an issue as it is with man. God recognizes sin for sin, no distinctions as to one being worse than another. The division we see in God's judgment is believer and unbeliever. The sin of unbelief is a singular sin and this is a clear-cut, final verdict. At the time of the Rapture all believers will be removed from what is to come, any that believe in Christ as Savior after that point will stay on earth to witness the demon attacks. In Rev 9:2 Satan unlocks the stronghold and smoke rises like a furnace. The demons have been sealed in two compartments that are grotesque, and they will be infuriated, prepared to punish and destroy mankind. This is not the time to be a believer that is left behind.

The two areas in Hades as noted earlier are Tartarus and the abyss, both are described as a place of darkness. "Angels who did not keep their own domain, but abandoned their proper abode, He has kept in eternal bonds under thick darkness for the judgment of the great day" (Jud 1:6). The smoke explains several verses related to demon prisons within Hades, it also describes the chains or bonds that hold the demons in place.

> "For if God Himself did not spare the angels when they sinned, but He incarcerated them in Tartarus with chains of darkness, keeping them for judgment . . ." (2Pe 2:4)

The black clouds or mist come from the Greek word *zophos* which is the same word used in many scriptures. Then we can see a description of the demon army in Rev 9:3, as locusts come forth and have power given to them as scorpions of the earth have power. Bear in mind that the Bible must be interpreted in the time when it was written. The scorpions and locusts are analogous to something resembling their identity or power. The function of the locust and the scorpion were the best descriptions the writer had to make an accurate account of the demon army. Actually the Bible uses this analogy of locusts to explain the swarm of an army or a plague illustrating a great attack in more than just this verse. The Greek word for locusts is *akrides* and is also used to display the destruction of Nineveh (Nah 3:16).

These demons that are currently in solitary confinement will invade the earth with such destructive powers that they will wipe away crops and trees! This demon army has a leader and functions in military order, just like literal locusts they will devour the countryside when they sweep down upon it. Locusts travel in large numbers, flying in such tight formation that they cause day to turn into night as they swarm and seek their feast. Real locusts also pitch camp in military style, and can occupy a space of 60 square miles as they invade an area. They stop at nothing and can pass through small openings in walls, under doors, smash through windows and smother anything with their mass. Their wings make a distinct noise as they fly and a frightening sound as they approach. Just imagine the angelic locusts: if literal locusts can cause such damage then demon locusts will wreak havoc like never seen before.

This attack is permitted by the grace of God during the Tribulation. When referring to the scorpion analogy we can visualize the poisonous sting of their tail. This sting can cause a numbing, near-death pain, causing tortured victims to lose the ability to speak as they shake and tremble. Some may die but most are destined to suffering with no reprieve! This is a warning judgment from God and yes, it is from His grace. Grace precedes judgment in God's perfect timing. This may be considered a last appeal, as God offers salvation one last time before He deems the battle to be complete. As God is the perfect judge He never destroys without an opportunity for repentance.

Noah is a perfect example of God's long-suffering attitude toward stubborn creatures. His open offer to become born again and saved is available until the last second of the last minute within the last hour before judgment is rendered. The illustration of 120 years of God's allowing Noah to preach His Word and to build the ark is one of the best examples of God's grace and patience. Noah was eloquent and an outstanding evangelist and still the negative volition toward the Word of God was so widespread that once the flood arrived, only Noah's family was permitted upon the ark. This was a universal negativity toward God much like we have today. The point is that God is going to use the wrath of angels to praise Him just as He uses the wrath of man to praise Him.

> "For the wrath of man shall praise Thee." (Psa 76:10)

The first demon army does have restrictions. It is to focus on the torment and torture, not to seek and destroy humans. After several months of attacks the opportunity to be saved and the opportunity for believers to get out of the cosmic system will be interrupted by a full-on military assault. The second wave of the demon attacks has orders to seek and destroy, it will be a bloody finale when the second army comes into the battle plan.

> "They were told not to hurt the grass of the earth, nor any green thing, nor any tree, but only the men who do not have the seal of God on their foreheads. And they were not permitted to kill anyone, but to torment for five months; and their torment was like the torment of a scorpion when it stings a man." (Rev 9:4-5)

Pain and adversity can be good motivators, giving some of us strength. However, the majority of people do not respond positively to painful situations and difficult trials. Pain and suffering will either leave a person better or worse, but few, if any, remain the same after a bitter experience. A major disaster is a life-altering period for any human being. No one comes out of a severe tragedy the same as they entered. For some it becomes a reason to be negative, bitter, and angry, a reason to lack trust and to judge people. For others it is an opportunity to grow and to change, to learn something new. Some people become positive, have that change of heart that turns their life around, while others will wallow in pity and become arrogant and resentful.

When you realize that these scriptures speak to all mankind, perhaps the next opportunity to make a positive change in your thinking should be before the disaster strikes.

> "It is appointed for men to die once and after this comes judgment." (Heb 9:27)

> "Behold I am coming quickly, and My reward is with Me, to render to every man according to what he has done." (Rev 22:12)

And yet there will be people who still reject the Lord Jesus Christ after this demon attack, they go even further towards the negative than before the assault! My personal opinion is that after thousands of years in the lake of fire, unbelievers would still reject Christ. The fact is that some people will become more bitter and angry after a painful event or a difficult period. The fall of Satan and his angels is proof enough to show that some creatures are never completely happy, never satisfied and will always have an evil agenda deep within their souls. When Satan is released from captivity the first thing he does is head straight back to the battlefield of revolution once again! He does not repent, does not seek a more sensitive, compassionate approach to the conflict that he started. In fact Satan's revolt escalates after the release.

The old sin nature within all of God's fallen creatures does not get better in time like a fine wine, instead it gets bitter over time when left unchecked. Those in the lake of fire will have an old sin nature that rages outward like the flames they dwell in as highlighted in Eph 4:22. Those that have fallen out of fellowship with God need to apply a rebound technique, which is simply to acknowledge or name and cite the sin. This is what the Bible calls washing clean.

> "Blessed are those who wash their robes, so that they may have the right to the tree of life, and may enter by the gates into the city." (Rev 22:14)

This is clearly stated in 1Jo 1:9, to simply confess and God forgives. This task takes no merit for the believer and puts the believer back into God's plan. For the unbeliever it is simply a one-time decision to believe in the Lord and Savior Jesus Christ. But arrogance prevents believers and unbelievers from following His plan, again it is independence from God!

> "Outside are the dogs and the sorcerers and the immoral persons and the murderers and the idolaters, and everyone who loves and practices lying." (Rev 22:15)

So when this second demon army leaps into action, nothing is safe, not trees, not grass, and certainly not mankind. These demons have such a deep-seated hatred for the Lord that nothing is sacred and anything that came from the hand of God is a target. These fallen creatures are extremely powerful and prone to violence. Killing a human is like shooting fish in a barrel for a demon angel.

In the current state of the conflict demons are only allowed to influence and possess a human. Divine permission is only given in such supernatural areas of murder by angelic creatures, or possession by a demon, if the killing perpetuates the Angelic Conflict. It clearly states in Rev 9:4 that only a certain group of people will not be harmed, those that have the seal of God. Not all believers after the Rapture have this seal. This is a strict reference to those that have become faithful servants of the Lord, those carrying out the will of God. Rev 7:1-4 specifies an elite group of believers that have a wall of fire surrounding them.

> "Do not harm the earth or the sea or the trees, until we have sealed the bond-servants of our God on their foreheads." And I heard the number of those who were sealed, one hundred and forty-four thousand sealed from every tribe of the sons of Israel. (Rev 7:3-4)

The term bond-servant is the Greek work *doulos* which means those believers who are slaves or servants to God. Many cosmic believers will not only suffer, but will face death upon the second attack from the evil armies. This is very similar to today in that believers that are positive toward the Word of God have a wall of fire that protects them from demon influence. A negative believer cannot be possessed but can be influenced by the kingdom of darkness. Unbelievers can be attacked by a demon possession if Satan needs to use that unbeliever. A fair warning to believers is that if you want to avoid being mugged by a demon get into the Truth of Bible doctrine and find the time for God within your busy life! The last place anyone wants to be handed over to is into the hands of Satan, especially in this final phase of combat. The believers that are sealed will be the positive ones who lay claim to the Lord Jesus Christ.

> Nevertheless, the firm foundation of God stands, having this seal, "The Lord knows those who are His," and, "Everyone who names the name of the Lord is to abstain from wickedness." (2 Ti 2:19)

The basic principle here is that any time a person says no to God they are saying yes to Satan. In the end, the wages of serving the kingdom of darkness are always pain and misery! Satan offers confusion, then torture, and finally death to his subordinates. The believer that is indoctrinated in the cosmic system has refused the protection of God now and during the tortures to come.

The Greek word for torture is *basanizo,* meaning to apply torture during questioning, inflict grievous pain, and torment mentally and physically. There will be 5 months of this allowed, and then the second army is released to commence on a death sweep! Those that are left alive will be used by Satan in one form or another. Satan's frustration and rage will be at such a fever pitch before the Second Advent of Christ that he will destroy that which he wanted to rule over. The kingdom he laid claim to will crumble from his own angry hands just before our Lord Jesus Christ comes back to clean up the mess. As He always does He will step in to right the wrongs, making everything seamless and pure. The pressure of the leadership role coupled with the realization that in the end he can do nothing to change the outcome causes Satan to do what any arrogant creature would do, explode!

When Christ returns the world will be in shambles, man fighting against man, demon fighting against man, destruction on every corner. Satan's kingdom will be divided and near ruins. Many believers will become involved in the cosmic system in the Tribulation and their attitude toward death changes drastically. As mentioned earlier, suicide will not be an option as death will elude the tortured ones, as made clear in Rev 9:6. The Bible is completely against suicide as mentioned in Psa 31:15, but this will be a divine barrier put into place to prevent death for a period of time. Believers that become entrenched with worldly viewpoint lose faith and forget that this earthly life is temporary and not designed to give true peace and happiness. This line of thinking comes from too much cosmic viewpoint and a lack of divine viewpoint. There are scores of people who claim to believe in Jesus Christ but cannot cope with adversity as it is today. To look ahead and wonder what they will do under such attacks is frightening. These types of believers do not have the good sense to start reversing their bad decisions in this current time, much less during a time when pain and confusion will be running rampant. There is great truth to the saying that you are a product of your own decisions. Be it a good or bad outcome, you lay the foundation with your choices in life first. Good decisions in the Biblical sense can lead to blessing and prosperity, bad decisions are certain to leave you at the doorstep of adversity. To survive life's adversities it takes a knowledge and thought process that only God can instill in you. Only when a believer is in fellowship and learning the Word of God can he then go apply the proper principles, executing the plan of God and fulfilling the mandates of Bible doctrine that will guide him through any adversity. The decisions we make today do affect us tomorrow, that is an inevitable fact of life. If your decisions determine where you go in life now, then how much more important will positive decisions be when the

Tribulation period arrives and a veil is lifted to reveal angelic creatures and a warfare that was invisible?

Keep in mind, believers and unbelievers will be targeted and toyed with by brutal, demonic angels. This is the last stop on this train of human life, the last opportunity to become born again and saved before the Millennial Reign begins. At that point there will be a baptism of fire upon the earth and it will remove all unbelievers. It may be difficult to comprehend, but there will be a majority who will still reject the Lord after this demon assault is complete! This all comes down to free will, our own volition, no one will have an excuse or reason other than their own stubborn mentality. To realize that many believers will still be bitter and negative toward God after withstanding such attacks is mind-boggling as well. God always provides grace, He always offers a solution before the problem arises. The difficulty that His creatures have involves the sins of arrogance, pride, and anger.

These types of sins take deep root in the soul and thinking patterns of people who dwell in them. They become mentally as well as emotionally altered and distorted, turned away from Truth and a relationship with God. Many that operate within these mental attitude sins consistently become delusional and impossible to reach in communication. There is not a problem that God cannot solve or an adversity that He cannot lift you out of or give you the ability to navigate through. God is the answer; it is just that most people reject Him at some level, perhaps by not being available to hear the Word of God, or perhaps by not metabolizing what they have heard or by refusing to apply what they have learned. If a believer has rejected the Word of God which is the negative perception of Bible doctrine, then obviously that individual will have to endure whatever the adversity is. However, they can rebound and begin to recover and allow their volition to line up with God's will. Locked-in arrogance and the skills that go with that arrogance can actually blot out Truth you may have had in your soul.

Anytime believers are involved in the cosmic system they are in reversionism, which means a series of steps away from the plan of God. This becomes total pre-occupation with self which in turn leads to a black-out of the soul concerning spiritual truths. Arrogance cannot endure torture because it is a state of tension which increases vulnerability to pain. The humility a relationship with God provides has capacity for life and prosperity and also provides the ability to withstand pain and adversity.

> "And in those days (referring to future days of the Tribulation) men will seek death (believers and unbelievers) and will not find it; they will long to die, and death flees from them." (Rev 9:6)

Nothing is more defeating than for a person who wants die to have to remain alive in a miserable situation. Arrogance will seek the easy way out, humility can stand in the gap during a time of pressure. Those that operate in the cosmic system are similar to Satan, they will make bad decisions from a place of weakness instead of good decisions from a position of strength. When you make a decision while entangled in your old sin nature you are weak and at the mercy of your circumstances.

We will witness Satan attempt to rule the world with violence and wrath instead of subtle tricks and deceptions. This final assault is when all the rules are tossed aside and the kingdom of darkness is given a period to come on the scene in a most destructive manner. The descriptions of the demon assault platoons continue in Rev 9:7-9 as they march forward like a victorious army conquering a country.

> "The appearance of the locusts was like horses prepared for battle; and on their heads appeared to be crowns like gold, and their faces were like the faces of men." (Rev 9:7)

This is like a cavalry with great mobility and firepower. The crowns are like gold which suggests a military insignia upon their heads. They also appear as men, or similar to men, which was mentioned in Genesis chapter 6. This appearance, which had not been seen since the book of Genesis, is significant because it is the visible form of fallen angelic creatures displaying their superior powers to the human race. From the points of human history between Genesis and Revelation they have been undetected and hidden from human view. The demon army may present itself as victorious but this, like all things that Satan represents, is false. Even their crowns are not real gold, but like gold—imitation only. The only combat victory they can claim is against members of the human race who were already under Satan's authority.

This is not much of a victory, conquering weak, negative human beings who have made one bad decision after another. Basically the master defeating his own slaves is what transpires. Verse 8 of this scripture in Revelation elaborates more on their power but also notes their beauty. Just as with the demon rulers of Genesis there is a magnetism or attractiveness about their presence.

> "They had hair like the hair of women, and their teeth were like the teeth of lions." (Rev 9:8)

Remember that the Bible was written in ancient times and there are phrases and words that were used to interpret different events and traits that may not make sense in today's society. The reference to long hair was an expression of beauty for women in the old world. It was also a form of covering and respect for the authority in her life (see 1Co 11:7,9,10).

These verses display the chain of authority in a marriage as well as how the elect angels respond positively to the believers of the earth who follow God's divine order and authority. 1Co 11:7-14 goes into detail on the respect and divine order God has set in place. This same order is what the devil's world has twisted and corrupted over the many years since mankind's conception. The Greek word for covering is *peribolaion* and it refers to the fact that her long hair is a sign that she is under authority. So we can see the double meanings of the long hair being a sign of beauty and a show of respect for a woman. We can also read in 1Co 11:14 that long hair is a sign of dishonor for the man. Other than a few Old Testament men like Samson, long hair on the man was a sign of shame or even a display of disrespect for authority, which suits these fallen angels who are affiliated with the demon army.

Beauty and glamour do not have to be related to arrogance, but in the case of Satan and his legion it is! Remember when we looked at Eze 28:12-17 we noted the beauty and seal of approval Satan had from God. His demon army is made up of perfect creatures in the areas of beauty and strength. Beauty and charm in an arrogant body can lead to a very dangerous creature. Beauty and certain qualities of strength like physique or intelligence are tools of entrapment for weak people and those that are easily led astray. King David warned his son about the deceitful woman who uses her beauty to lure a man.

> "Do not desire her beauty in your heart, nor let her catch you with her eyelids." (Pro 6:25)

David's wife Bathsheba also taught Solomon the same lesson in Pro 31:30, "Charm is deceitful and beauty is vain, but a woman who respects the Lord, she shall be praised." So basically beauty can be a trap if it is used by an arrogant person, and it can be the root of great pride and an attitude of self-importance much like Satan had with the five "I wills". One sign of a narrow-minded, petty society is that it elevates beauty and rejects Truth.

When we examine the "teeth like a lion" statement describing the demon army in Revelation 9:8, it has the connotation of destruction. It indicates that behind the façade of beauty is the ruthless desire to destroy. This is the most deceptive army that mankind will have ever witnessed.

There is another illusion that Satan has woven into the web of deception covering mankind, that the human race should be looking upward for the final attack. That perhaps an alien invasion will occur bringing about the end times. This is the exact opposite of what the Bible is teaching in this section of Revelation. The truth is that the attack will come from the depths of Hades below us.

One last principle about beauty is that it can either be a source of great distraction or wonderful appreciation. It takes humility to appreciate beauty and humility to have great beauty. Humility is the key factor in having the capacity for true love as well. Beauty can lead to arrogance and can be destructive for those that worship it and those that are blessed with it. The knowledge of what lies behind the beauty is important. Beauty is very blinding and misleading for many people and they cannot go much deeper than outward appearance; therefore, they are the ones who are so easily deceived.

Rev 9:9 tells us that the armor the demon army will have will be impenetrable from human weapons. This scripture describes it as breastplates of iron. In the ancient world iron was the highest quality choice for military hardware. Only fellowship with God will be a shield against the demon attacks, the one true weapon that is superior to any demon powers is the wall of fire that God can provide. These demon assault soldiers will strike fear into the hearts of men long before they make contact as we see by the last line of scripture in verse 9. The sound of their wings was like the sound of chariots, of many horses rushing to battle. Fear is a great weapon in battle because it drains the opponent of any composure and throws him into an emotionally filled state of mind. Emotion cannot think, it does not operate in common sense, it is reckless. Applying the Word of God to a stressful situation can be drowned out by emotional thoughts. Emotion is designed by God for responding to certain situations, such as love, the loss of a family member, or appreciating some form of art or entertainment.

Emotion needs to be controlled and not constantly unleashed to make everyday decisions, and it is especially not designed for leading you into the great battles of life. When emotions are linked up with a rational thought process and a doctrinal foundation you will make great decisions even in the heat of battle. The greatest equalizer you can have in combat is Bible doctrine circulating in your soul. Your free will and your volition are the most powerful weapons you have in any situation in life, God gave this to you and put no strings upon it. Our free will was given to help resolve the Angelic Conflict, but we are never forced to use it by God, as stated earlier in this book. God is the perfect gentleman. Up until the Tribulation period we have God the Holy Spirit as a restrainer of physical abuse from Satan's army. He does not allow the full force of demon creatures to be unleashed until the end of the battle. We see in 2Th 2:1-12 that there is a restraint put upon Satan and his soldiers.

> "And you know what restrains him (Satan) now, so that in his time he may be revealed. For the mystery of the lawless one is already at work; only He (Holy Spirit) who now restrains him will do so until he is taken out of the way." (2Th 2:6-7)

Again we see the grace of God (the Holy Spirit) restraining the kingdom of darkness and keeping them all at bay until the right moment in time.

> "And then that lawless one will be revealed whom the Lord will slay with the breath of His mouth and bring to an end by the appearance of His coming." (2Th 2:8)

2Th 2:10-11 goes into the wicked deceptions for those who perish, because they did not receive Truth and did not become saved. More specifically, 2Th 2:11 clearly states that God will send a deluding influence so that they believe what is false. And the final judgment is stated as plain as the daylight in verse 12, that they all may be judged who did not believe the Truth! Today we have the deceptions and mental pressure of the kingdom of darkness along with an old sin nature deep within our structure to battle with on a daily basis, but in this last combative stand of Satan we will deal with a physical assault which was not even seen in the antediluvian civilization. Those in the cosmic system will not only be witnessing a first in human history but will be unwilling participants in it! Demons like Apollo and Zeus were seen in ancient history and were worshipped by many people. Today we are inculcated by doctrines of demons teaching false scriptures, but we are not under the physical dominance that will occur in the Tribulation. The spiritual warfare we are entangled in today has many titles besides false doctrines and worldly viewpoints: legalism, antinomianism, asceticism, rationalism, humanism, and communism, as well as socialism, which are all part of Satan's battle plan in current history.

In the middle of the Tribulation period these worldly viewpoints will mean little or nothing because the battle plan will encompass the physical and audible and be much more gruesome than any of us could envision. The authority and power given to Satan in eternity past are allowed as part of God's justice to be fully unleashed for 5 months, most likely occurring in that last year of the Tribulation. God knew that this would be the last chance for man to repent and He knew that it would take a brutal attack to emphasize the importance of being born again and saved and the need for many unbelievers to finally wake up.

The leader of one of the most vicious demon regiments as we noted is Abaddon (Apollyon), and that name also is used as a description of a place of destruction (Hades) in the Old Testament in Job 26:6, in addition to another personification of Abaddon in Job 28:22. In Rev 9:11 we have seen him described as a king and leader under Satan's rule. His very name is a synonym for Sheol or Hades.

> "Sheol and Abaddon (lie open) before the Lord, how much more the hearts of men!" (Pro 15:11)

> "Sheol and Abaddon are never satisfied, nor are the eyes of men ever satisfied." (Pro 27:20)

He is like a demon prince and his name, much like Satan's, may just be a title within the Bible, not a true name. The Greek god Apollo has a very similar name or title, and next to Zeus it appears that Apollo was a powerful leader in ancient times. He was the demon god of light and was definitely involved in the attack noted in Genesis 6. Apollo was the god of the sun and lucidity or intellectuality. He was widely revered and feared by other gods as well as being very influential during that time before the flood. This Apollo of the Old Testament quite possibly could be the same one we see in Rev 9:11. Apollo also was a name or title called Phoebus meaning bright or pure, associated with the title of sun god. He was also known for death and terror, which lines up with another meaning in the Greek for Apollyon i.e. exterminator. So in Hebrew it notes destruction and in Greek it means exterminator, very interesting similarities! Next to Satan it seems he is a leader of highest rank among many angelic creatures.

The only other high-ranking demon creature we see is Beelzebub who very well may be equal to Abaddon. Beelzebub is in charge of covert warfare, a prince of deceit over the human race. This demon leader is responsible for most of the Christian servants that operate in the false doctrines and deceptive techniques like fake healings and speaking in tongues. Apollyon appears to be more of a combative-style military leader, whereas Beelzebub is involved in getting humans credit for feats of healings, signs and wonders that they perform, supposedly in the name of God.

Regarding the gift of tongues, there is no one that has had that gift since 70 A.D., and no one has it currently in our day and age. Eggastromuthos is a word that describes demon possession, specifically a person who is indwelt by a demon who reproduces the gift of tongues as it occurred on the day of Pentecost and for forty days thereafter. Miracle workers today are mostly confused people who operate within a sphere of emotional nonsense that they truly believe to be a form of faith or worship. However, there are some over whom Beelzebub has direct influence.

Any spiritual leader that promotes this is simply a pawn in Satan's chess match. Beelzebub is like the CIA, or an undercover agent within the Angelic Conflict. He always has people and connections to work through that appear legitimate and point away from the kingdom of darkness. Beelzebub has his own internal organization within the Angelic Conflict that is working on the miracle aspect of the false doctrines that Satan spearheads. Miracles such as healings have not been done by people since 70 A.D. either. This is not to say that prayer done in the right format and under God's divine guidance will not bring forth a miracle because it can, but not by the hand of any man. The true power in this Church Age we live in is derived from His Word and its application. Jesus Christ did not heal everyone on the earth during His earthly ministry. In fact His divine powers and healings were used to allow those in His periphery to see that He was the Messiah and to give credibility to His message and later on to messengers like Paul and Peter who were ordained by Christ. Even the Pharisees knew that throughout human history Satan would use miracles to deceive the human race.

> "Then a demon-possessed man who was blind and mute was brought to Jesus, and He healed him, so that the mute man spoke and saw. All the crowds were amazed, and were saying, 'This man cannot be the Son of David, can he?'" (Mat 12:22-23)

Beelzebul or as some say Beelzebub is a title that is given to this demon secret service agent, who basically has the power to cause illness and to quickly remove it as well.

> "But when the Pharisees heard it, they said, 'This man casts out demons only by Beelzebul the ruler of the demons.'" (Mat 12:24)

In the area of human illness we see a healing power from a demon, because the demon was the one causing it in the first place! Now it would appear that a person being used by the kingdom of darkness could perform a healing, because behind the invisible realm it is Beelzebub ordering the removal of the very demon influence that he had put on the person. The three categories of illness most common to human beings are psychosomatic (illness within the mind), physiological (illness of the body), and what we now know as demon-induced illness (possibly a form of both). The arrogant thinking of the Pharisees immediately points to Jesus Christ as a pawn under the command of this wicked demon. This system of healings and miracles gives the church leader or person performing these acts great human credibility. It then becomes easy for a following to develop and for those that become enamored to listen to the teaching and false doctrines put forth after that point. This deception works upon believers as well, getting them to go astray from the real issue of Jesus Christ and the work on the Cross.

There is an interesting piece of American history that speaks upon the subject of tyranny and the destructive role the government or leadership can take on, and this happens when arrogance initiates authority over others. First look at our next verse, Rev 9:12, "The first woe is past; behold, two woes are still to come after these things."

The following is from the Declaration of Independence of our original 13 states:

"When in the course of human events it becomes necessary for one people to dissolve the political bond which has connected them with another and to assume among powers of the earth the separate and equal station to which the laws of nature and nature's God entitled them a decent respect to the opinions of mankind requires that they should declare the cause which impels them to separation. We hold these truths to be self evident that all men are created equal. That they are endowed by their creator with certain unalienable rights. That among these are life, liberty and the pursuit of happiness. That to secure these rights, governments are instituted among men, deriving their just powers from the consent of the governed. That whenever any form of government becomes destructive to these ends, it is the right of the people to alter or abolish it, and to institute government, laying its foundation on such principles and organizations, its powers in such form as to them seem most likely to affect their safety and happiness. Prudence indeed will dictate that government long established should not be changed for light and transient causes. And accordingly all experience has shown that mankind are most disposed to suffer while evils are sufferable then to right themselves by abolishing the forms to which they have become accustomed. But when a long train of abuses and usurpations pursuing invariably the same object evinces a design to reduce them under absolute desperatism, it is their right, it is their duty to throw off such government and provide new guards for their future security. Such has been the patience, sufferance, of these colonies and such is not the necessity which constrains them to alter their former system of government. The history of the present king of Great Britain is a history of repeated injuries and usurpations. All having in direct object the establishment of absolute tyranny over these states. To prove this let the facts be submitted to a candid world."

Then what followed were about 20 grievances which the colonies had at this point in our young history.

"We have warned them from time to time of the attempts by their legislature to extend unwarranted jurisdiction over us. We have reminded them of the circumstances of our immigration and settlement here. We have appealed to their native justice and we have conjured them by the ties of our common kindred to disavow these usurpations which would inevitably interrupt our connections and correspondence. They too have been deaf to the voice of justice. We must therefore acquiesce in the necessity which denounces our separation and hold them as we hold the rest of mankind, enemies at war, friends in peace. We therefore the representatives of the United States of America in general congress assembled appealing to the supreme judge of the world for rectitude of our intentions due in the name and by the authority of the people in these good colonies solemnly publish and declare that these United states or United colonies are and of the right to be free and independent states. That they have our absolves of all allegiance to the British crown and that all political connections between them and the state of great Britain is and ought to be totally dissolved. And that as free and independent states they have the full power to levy war, conclude peace contract alliances, establish commerce and to do all other acts and things which independent states may of right to do. And for the support of this declaration, with a firm reliance on the protection of divine providence we mutually pledge our lives, our fortunes, our sacred honor."

One of my ancestors signed that document, John Adams, and that is the basis for one of our national holidays, the Fourth of July. The believers that have to endure the Tribulation attacks will not have a declaration to fall back on, and much like that adolescent set of colonies we now call America they will have to stand firm when the attacks arrive on their shores.

Before departing this chapter it is important to note another holding cell under the Euphrates River which will become pertinent upon the sounding of the sixth trumpet as we can see noted in Rev 9:13-21. This is the third battalion and is led by four demon generals that are certainly as ruthless as Abaddon. In verse 13 we see the sounding of the sixth angel and this is a signal for the release as noted in the next verse.

> "One saying to the sixth angel who had the trumpet, 'Release the four angels who are bound at the great river Euphrates.'" (Rev 9:14)

In the next verse it is said that they will kill a third of mankind. And it goes on to state that the number of the demon warlords on horseback are two hundred million, and it describes them in full armor using fire and brimstone as weapons of destruction.

> "The rest of mankind, who were not killed by these plagues, did not repent of the works of their hands, so as not to worship demons, and the idols of gold and of silver and of brass and of stone and of wood, which can neither see nor hear nor walk; and they did not repent of their murders nor of their sorceries nor of their immorality nor of their thefts." (Rev 9:20-21)

So much for the first category of angels, the non-operational angels, at this time. The second category are called functional or operational angels, demons who operate today. The operational army is directed and led by Satan himself. We have seen how the operational angels today use covert and deceptive warfare in the Church Age. Operational angels are also the ones we see that have access to the heavens and levels of the atmosphere (Rev 12:9). These are the angels who are our adversaries in the Church Age, in Eph 6:12. These angels also battle against Michael and the elect angels in Rev 12:7-8 and then attack the earth, along with the newly released forces of the kingdom of darkness.

During this series of events in Rev 12 the attack upon the Jewish population will ensue as Satan makes a final run at wiping out this race. As mentioned previously in this book, Anti-Semitism is one of the greatest systems of evil from Satan. The fact that Satan has already been sentenced and then attacks the earth like this reveals the existence of an appeal trial going on right now!

The kingdom of darkness, as this chapter has clearly displayed, has structure and organization, and it is also covered in Eph 6:12. "For our warfare is not against blood and flesh (people's old sin nature), but against the rulers (high-ranking demons,) against the powers (demon authority), against the world forces of this darkness (Satan's ambassadors in the cosmic system), against the spiritual forces of wickedness in heavenly places (demons within our atmosphere and the ones having access to heaven)." In the Church Age, the battle is a deceptive, invisible one, while in the future it will be a visible, violent conflict. However, both reveal the strategies of Satan against the human race, in a desperate attempt to win his appeal. The battle lines are drawn and the descriptions of angelic creatures and events are precisely and powerfully displayed for us in our indispensable weapon, the Word of God.

Chapter 7.

The Courtroom Trial of the Angelic Conflict.

The fact that we do not truly have a name for our enemy, only a title, should give us a clue as to what type of deceptive creature we are encountering. We simply know the antagonist in this conflict under titles like the devil or Satan. Even the name Lucifer, which is derived from a Latin name, is not fully accurate. We know the name Heylel means shining one or star of the morning.

The interesting name in the Greek is Diabolos (where we get devil) which refers to an adversary in the legal realm, an opposing attorney, and a slanderer. When we see the name or title of the devil in the Hebrew (SaaTaan), it refers to an attorney who uses slander to find loopholes in the law. Both of these terms point to an adversary in one form or another, which is quite accurate in all aspects of the definition of Satan. During the course of human history Satan is involved in a trial and acts as a shady attorney who is always badgering his witnesses, always looking for a loophole. It is often noted that he is the accuser of the brethren, in passages such as Rev 12:10, Zec 3:1. The first chapter of the book of Job definitely highlights the court case in full swing.

The book of Job was most likely the first written book of the Bible. It appears to be a sign of what was really going on when mankind was put upon planet Earth. God has a purpose and a reason for every detail and nothing is done randomly or out of order. The first book inspired to be written from the Holy Spirit shows Satan presenting his case against God as unjust, unfair, and not what He claims to be, namely a loving and forgiving Creator. The book of Job also states that Satan was walking about on the earth that was turned over to him after man's rebellion against God. God gave this principle under the inspiration of God the Holy Spirit as a major statement of the Angelic Conflict! Do not overlook the subtle details of such things because you will lose your spiritual focus of what is really going on in any given situation. As long as believers make positive decisions toward doctrine, the god of this world, Satan, will put pressure on them and will also seek to prosecute believers in the Supreme Courtroom of Heaven. Satan as a relentless prosecutor in the court of heaven is a major doctrine throughout the Bible. The object and focus every time Satan struts into the Supreme Court of Heaven is on the believer. This is because after salvation the believer continues to use his volition to commit certain forms of evil or sins. Many believers do not even acknowledge that they sin, and this attitude is in direct opposition to what the Word of God teaches.

> "If we say [assert] that we have no sin nature, we are deceiving ourselves and the truth (doctrine) is not in us. If we acknowledge [name and cite] our sins, He is faithful and righteous, with the result that He forgives us our sins [known sins] and purifies us from all unrighteousness [unknown sins]. If we say that we have not sinned, we make Him a liar, and His word (Bible doctrine) does not reside in us." (1Jo 1:8-10)

The simple solution to wipe away sin and get back in fellowship is to acknowledge it. In the Church Age, demons provide the accusations for Satan, like messengers or better yet tattletales. Just as Beelzebub has his specialty, so too there are demons that are experts at investigative research and detailed analysis of human beings. You can bet that Satan has his files and a specialized group of fallen angels who use satanic scrutiny and deceptions to keep a record of the sins and failures of each believer. Satan does not go to the courtroom without a briefcase full of

The Angelic Conflict

facts and information, especially concerning the lack of the use of the Problem-Solving Devices, ultimately focusing in on the Faith Rest Drill and trusting in the character and nature of God. Satan and the kingdom of darkness will certainly focus in on the believer who is taking positive steps in the plan of God, much like he did with Job. The first chapter of Job is the example of what a positive believer can expect Satan to say and do when he steps into the Supreme Court of Heaven with the believer's file in his hand. The believer need not worry because he will have the best defense attorney in the universe, the Lord Jesus Christ, as his divine attorney at law with the perfect record in and out of the courtroom!

> "Then he showed me Joshua the high priest standing before the angel of the Lord, and Satan standing at his right hand to accuse him. And the Lord said to Satan, 'The Lord rebuke you, Satan! Indeed, the Lord who has chosen Jerusalem rebuke you! Is this not a brand plucked from the fire?' Now Joshua was clothed with filthy garments and standing before the angel. And he spoke and said to those who were standing before him saying, 'Remove the filthy garments from him.' Again He said to him, 'See, I have taken your iniquity away from you and will clothe you with festal robes.' Then I said, 'Let them put a clean turban on his head.' So they put a clean turban on his head and clothed him with garments, while the angel of the Lord was standing by." (Zec 3:1-5)

The moment you became born again you received eternal life from the author of eternal life and the great defender of it for all time. He represents you personally and passionately each and every time the accusations begin to fly. When Satan and the kingdom of darkness make their brutal attack, our defense attorney Jesus Christ has as the basis of His defense, the doctrine of propitiation. This refers to the fact that the work He accomplished upon the Cross satisfied the essence of God, receiving the approval of God the Father. Propitiation is the God-ward side of the work of Christ in salvation, God the Father was satisfied with the sacrificial ministry of our Lord on the Cross. Propitiation is the work of Christ on the Cross which deals with the integrity of God, and the work of Christ on the Cross satisfied God the Father. In propitiation the justice of God judges our sins and the integrity of God is satisfied with that judgment. Propitiation frees the justice of God to immediately give anyone who believes in Christ the perfect righteousness of God, imputed to believers as the down payment on our salvation.

> "When Jesus therefore had received the sour wine, He said, 'It is finished!' And He bowed His head, and gave up His spirit."
> (Joh 19:30)

The phrase "It is finished" is the perfect passive indicative of teleo. In the perfect tense it means that salvation is completed and the results go on forever. In the passive voice it means that salvation has received fulfillment. The indicative mood means the reality of salvation. Our Lord said one word "Tetelestai" meaning "finished." It means to bring to an end, to complete, to accomplish, to fulfill, and to perform. Salvation is totally completed. Notice that Jesus is still alive when He says this. Salvation was completed by our Lord's spiritual death. Physical death has nothing to do with salvation. The phrase "He bowed his head" means that He deliberately did so. The aorist active participle of the Greek word klino actually says, "having bowed His head." It is a deliberate act on His part in order for something to be fulfilled. He has to get His head forward so that when the spear pierces His side out will come blood clots and serum. Jesus did not bleed to death. He dismissed His spirit. He died by His own volition. His work was accomplished and He dismissed His spirit, but before He did He bowed His head forward. Only John records that.

The apostle John also explains that we (believers) have an advocate (the Lord) who is righteous.

> "My little children, I am writing these things to you that you may not sin. And if anyone sins, we have an Advocate with the Father, Jesus Christ the righteous; and He Himself is the propitiation for our sins; and not for ours only, but also for those of the whole world."
> (1Jo 2:1-2)

The basis for a believer's defense is the work of Christ upon the Cross, it was complete and finished when the Lord said "Tetelestai." He bowed

His head and gave up His spirit after stating emphatically that it (the work that God the Father demanded for the judgment of sin, known to man as efficacious grace) is finished! This is definite and complete as noted in John 19:30. The bill was paid for in full. All sins were dealt with once and for all, and God the Father was completely satisfied. The point is that sins are no longer the issue in a believer's life and you can guarantee Satan hates that result. The New Testament says that a believer's sins are remembered no more and have been removed from God's sight.

> "For I will be merciful to their iniquities, and I will remember their sins no more." (Heb 8:12)

Let us then review the Greek word *tetelestai*, the intensive perfect tense of *teleo*, translated "finished in the past with the result that it stands finished forever." It refers to a present state resulting from a past action. The present state is that salvation is available, the past action is that Jesus Christ was judged for our sins. The intensive perfect is saying in a strong way that something is. So we know it is finished in the past with the result that it stands finished forever. The passive voice also represents Jesus Christ as being acted upon by God the Father, whose omnipotence imputed all our sins to Jesus Christ and judged every one of them. The Justice of the Father judged every sin in the history of the human race. Then the love of God the Father offered salvation to anyone who would believe. So, Jesus Christ received the action of the verb, being judged for the sins of the human race. Jesus Christ completed that action on the Cross while He was still alive. The indicative mood of the verb *teleo* is declarative as a dogmatic statement of Bible doctrine. In Rom 5:8 it states that Christ is the substitute for us. So we can attest to the fact that this scripture in Joh 19:30 is crystal clear on the completed work upon the Cross. It is not left half done nor is it a vague statement in the original scriptures. No human can take credit for the work upon the Cross, no one can add to it or take away from it. There is zero human merit added to the finished work on the Cross at any point in time. This is clearly a free gift of salvation when we have faith alone in Christ alone. To have eternal life is a decision based upon faith in Christ as Lord and Savior. It is a non-meritorious decision to believe in Jesus Christ, whose substitutionary spiritual death on the Cross provided all the efficacious work for salvation.

God's policy of grace concerning salvation or any of His gifts never includes human works or human efforts of any kind. As humans, we tend to get in God's way. Any church or spiritual leader that adds something like baptism, walking down an aisle, or repenting from your sins to gain salvation is simply rejecting the work done upon the Cross. In Phi 3:18 even believers become an enemy of the Cross when they add to or take away from the work our Lord did.

> "For many walk, of whom I often told you, and now tell you even weeping, that they are enemies of the cross of Christ, whose end is destruction, whose god is their appetite, and whose glory is in their shame, who set their minds on earthly things." (Phi 3:18-19)

There is a law of double jeopardy here on earth that holds true within the heavens as well. It plainly shows that once a crime is judged it cannot be brought to trial again. At a restaurant, if you pay the bill at the table, you do not go up to the cashier and pay for the meal a second time! Yet, in the devil's world, that simple principle is twisted and made to be an issue of guilt or some form of effort and human works. Each time Satan begins his court case against a believer, God the Father, as the Supreme Court Judge says, "The case is dismissed." You see, it is truly a family matter between you and your perfect Father, the only judge of righteousness.

Another definitive scripture is Rom 6:10 which says, "For the death that He died, He died to sin, once and for all." Jesus Christ conquered sin and resolved the sin issue once and for all. The cross is His ultimate victory in the Angelic Conflict, silencing forever the blasphemous appeal of Satan. In eternity past, it was inevitable that once Satan realized that God had sentenced him, he would cry out for an appeal. While he tried to justify his right to an appeal trial, he was also busy maligning God's character. Satan did this to build up his own false courage from his evil thinking and self-centered arrogance. The blasphemous appeal of Satan was based on some legal principle, possibly one which is heard in today's day and age: "How can a loving God put His own creatures into the lake of fire forever?" I will state this now and let it resonate as you go forward in the book. We do not get an answer to every question mankind has from the Bible. (However our Lord's victory on the cross and His Word give us all we need to know in this life.) God is gracious and allows us to look through a large window into spiritual knowledge. He gives us plenty of guidance in life within the realm of the Bible; however, some questions are left for eternity. In Deu 29:29 the Bible tells us that there are secret things of God that belong to Him, and the things He reveals belong to us. For example, it is revealed that "it is not God's will that any should perish" (2Pe 3:9); " . . . for we know that Jesus Christ died, not for our sins only, but for the sins of the whole world" (1Jo 2:2). The only reason anyone ever goes to the lake of fire is that they continue to insist on using their free will to follow in the path of Satan.

The actual blasphemous appeal of Satan is unknown to us. There are many believers today who do not even believe in a literal hell or lake of fire. There is teaching that it is a figure of speech or metaphor. For example, certain cults sponsor this type of thinking such as the Jehovah's witnesses who do not believe in the lake of fire. The smart believer will not give them the time of day!

> "If anyone comes to you and does not bring this teaching, do not receive him into your house, and do not give him a greeting;" (2Jo 1:10)

They have the same question that is posted above: why would a loving God do this? God did not see fit to record for us the actual appeal of Satan but we can venture a pretty close guess. We can see the fact that an appeal trial was filed from the lapse of time between the sentence of the fallen angels (Mat 25:41) in eternity past and the execution of that sentence at the termination of human history (Rev 20:10).

> "Then He will also say to those on His left, depart from Me, accursed ones, into the eternal lake of fire which has been prepared for the devil and his angels;" (Mat 25:41)

> "And the devil who deceived them was thrown into the lake of fire and brimstone, where the beast and the false prophet are also; and they will be tormented day and night forever and ever." (Rev 20:10)

The very fact that the sentence has not been carried out and that Rev 20:10 reveals that the sentence will be carried out at the end of human history motivates our conclusion. We see that human history is the time of the appeal trial. This appeal takes place between the passing of the sentence in eternity past and the execution of that sentence at the end of the Millennium. So, it is our time now to be a vital part of the intensified stage of the conflict. Eze 38 through 39 tells of a future invasion of Israel by a vast coalition of nations that surround it. As we read the headlines in the newspapers of today and witness the conflict in the Middle East, it is not hard to imagine that this invasion, prophesied over 2,600 years ago, could be fulfilled in our lifetime. Eze 36-37 predicts a gathering of the Jews to the nation of Israel, which will be followed by this massive invasion. For 19 centuries the Jewish people were scattered throughout the world. Until May 14, 1948 there was no nation of Israel to invade. With the nation of Israel now a reality, the stage seems set for the war that will usher in the Tribulation and the rise of the Antichrist. As you read Eze 38 and 39, it is not just the creation of the nation of Israel that makes this prophecy seem likely to be fulfilled in the near future. The nations that God tells us will form this coalition against Israel seem more likely now than perhaps ever before to form just such an alliance. To understand the prophecies of Ezekiel about this future invasion, it is important to understand who the players will be. There are many theories as to who will join in this future invasion of Israel.

> "And the word of the Lord came to me saying, 'Son of man, set your face toward Gog of the land of Magog, the prince of Rosh, Meshech, and Tubal, and prophesy against him, and say, 'Thus says the Lord God, Behold, I am against you, O Gog, prince of Rosh, Meshech, and Tubal. And I will turn you about, and put hooks into your jaws, and I will bring you out, and all your army, horses and horsemen, all of them splendidly attired, a great company {with} buckler and shield, all of them wielding swords; Persia, Ethiopia, and Put with them, all of them {with} shield and helmet; Gomer with all its troops; Beth-togarmah {from} the remote parts of the north with all its troops— many peoples with you.'" (Eze 38:1-6)

However, even though we will not be around for this revolution, remember that no matter what type of spiritual warfare exists now, do not assume that you have no power in this battle. It is the power we gain from Bible doctrine and the filling of the Holy Spirit that launches us forward into combat, prepared to take the witness stand like Job if need be. All things are possible through Christ (Mar 9:23), it all comes down to that simple word that people find so difficult to apply: FAITH.

Faith may seem like a simple word, but faith in our Lord Jesus Christ is the power to win in the Angelic Conflict, and to overcome any obstacle in our lives, even the worst attacks from the kingdom of darkness.

> "Truly I say to you, whoever says to this mountain, 'Be taken up and cast into the sea,' and does not doubt in his heart, but believes that what he says is going to happen, it will be granted him. Therefore I say to you, all things for which you pray and ask, believe that you have received them, and they will be granted you." (Mar 11:23-24)

Our faith can have an impact in this Angelic Conflict that we cannot even imagine! As we have seen, human history is not only coterminous with the appeal trial of Satan and his fallen angels, but human history is the actual courtroom for the trial, and mankind was created to be part of that trial. The structure of this angelic trial can be viewed in the same light as the American jurisprudence system, which provides analogies for the appeal trial of Satan and his fallen comrades.

Let us begin to note the order of events in the angelic trial. A trial is known to have three phases:

1. The formal presentation of the case. This is when the prosecution presents its case, followed by the defense presenting its case (God is the prosecution in this case).
2. The rebuttal phase: the rebuttal arguments of the prosecution followed by the rebuttal arguments of the defense (Satan).
3. The closing arguments then are allowed after all evidence and arguments have been fully presented.

Satan's formal presentation in the appeal trial corresponds to the Old Testament and ancient human history. The trial phase truly began with the fall of man in the garden and continues until the beginning of the dispensation of the Hypostatic Union. When mankind was created it was done in order to duplicate the conditions of the prehistoric Angelic Conflict. This provides both evidence and precedence for Satan's appeal trial during human history. The fall of man in the Garden of Eden duplicated the fall of Satan in the garden of God, both environments were created in perfection by the hand of God. The trial phase in the court of appeals is essentially Old Testament history that can be viewed back in Genesis 3 where it all began. God created man as a rational creature but a lower creature than the angelic creatures that were already in existence. This was a form of lower-scale duplication of the same conditions that existed in the prehistoric Angelic Conflict. Man was given the opportunity to choose for or against God with one command from God, only one thing was forbidden.

> "The LORD God commanded the man, saying, 'From any tree of the garden you may eat freely; but from the tree of the knowledge of good and evil you shall not eat, for in the day that you eat from it you will surely die.'" (Gen 2:16-17)

In the Hebrew, *muth muth* is the doubling of the verb which refers to "Dying spiritually, you will die physically." Now we all know the rest of this piece of human history, but it is important to note the subtle approach of Satan in chapter three of Genesis. The crafty serpent asked the question.

> "Now the serpent was more crafty than any beast of the field which the Lord God had made. And he said to the woman, 'Indeed, has God said, 'You shall not eat from any tree of the garden?'" (Gen 3:1)

Notice the slick approach toward the woman and the twist on God's words. The Lord was clear that any tree was available except one, Satan makes it seem as if none are available. Satan tried to make the woman conscious of the forbidden as though God had held something back from her. Temptation is one of Satan's trump cards in the game of life, always showing you something appealing that is just out of reach or something better than what you have.

> "When the woman saw that the tree was good for food, and that it was a delight to the eyes, and that the tree was desirable to make one wise, she took from its fruit and ate; and she gave also to her husband with her, and he ate. Then the eyes of both of them were opened, and they knew that they were naked; and they sewed fig leaves together and made themselves loin coverings." (Gen 3:6-7)

With the fall of Adam, Satan climbed back on top of the throne to planet Earth, becoming the world ruler from this point forward. From this position Satan begins his appeal trial. Unbelievers, and the average Christian as well, have little or no knowledge of what is going on over the course of human history as related to the spiritual realm. The last thing they would suspect is that their own unintentional involvement in this conflict is crucial. Satan is capable of blinding the masses, this is highlighted time and again in the scriptures.

> "And even if our gospel is veiled, it is veiled to those who are perishing, in whose case the god of this world has blinded the minds of the unbelieving, that they might not see the light of the gospel of the glory of Christ, who is the image of God." (2Co 4:3-4)

So, the first Adam failed and fell, and then the second Adam came on the scene to be the strategic resolver of the Angelic Conflict, as well as to share that resolution with winner believers throughout the ages. Therefore, now in the dispensation of the Hypostatic Union and in the dispensation of the Church Age, the prosecution presents its answer to Satan's case: the rebuttal phase of the trial, from the birth of Jesus Christ until the Rapture of the Church. The third and final phase of the courtroom battle contains the closing arguments, which will take place from the Second Advent of Christ to the end of the Millennium.

Planet Earth is the courtroom and had been the courtroom prior to mankind's being placed in it. According to Eze 28, Satan led all the angels on earth to worship God. Later, the human race was created upon a stage or courtroom called planet Earth. Earth had been active with angelic creatures and a conflict long before the human race was designed by God. We are part of the evidence, arguments, and precedents in this angelic trial. Basically, God entered His evidence by creating man just as the angels were created, innocent (perfect) with the potential to love and to worship God through right decisions. However, angels also had the potential to become imperfect through negative decisions, just as mankind had that potential. The similarities between the human race and angelic race are very apparent and intentional on God's part. Mankind is created lower than the angels for a period of time, that period covers the appeal trial. So, we have both angels and man with free will and beginning in a perfect environment. The fall of Satan is followed by the fall of Adam, not by accident or sheer luck, nothing is by accident with a perfect God. It is all a divine plan, the divine timing and the divine similarities all for a reason and purpose. Both creatures developed an attitude of rebellion. Satan swept away a third (possibly more) of his fellow creatures as noted in Rev 12:4, and Adam's fall resulted in the fall of mankind, as we see in Rom 5:12. The scripture refers to one man (Adam) allowing sin to enter the world, so death spread to all because all have sinned.

You can rest assured that God provided a path to salvation for fallen angels just as He did for fallen man. Accepting salvation would have been as simple as a positive thought toward the plan of God, no works or merits needed, simply believe or agree with God. The similarities are unmistakable, and viewed through the scriptures it becomes so very apparent what is going on in the spiritual realm. The Word of God reveals some type of reconciliation for the fallen angels in Col 1:20, Phi 2:10, and Heb 2:2. This is why we have elect angels (believers) and fallen angels (unbelievers). The human race is seen as believers and unbelievers, all offered a choice from their free will, with the same decision the angels had, to be for or against God (see Joh 3:36). Exercising free will is offered to both creatures, and we see the angelic division and the two categories in Rev 12:7-8, 1Ti 5:21, and Mat 25:41 as well as Mar 8:38. The fact that human history is analogous to a courtroom or judicial system is lost on the unbeliever, and even escapes the believer who is negative, but in the end they will view the Truth for what it is, the divine plan of God in action in this appeal trial.

The rebuttal phase of the trial on the prosecution side is coterminous with the Christocentric dispensations (the Hypostatic Union and the

Church Age). Christocentric dispensations refer to two periods of time (dispensations) in human history where Christ lives inside of humanity. It is during those two periods of time that God presents His case, revealing His justice and righteousness as well as His love.

> "By common confession, great is the mystery of godliness: He who was revealed in the flesh, Was vindicated in the Spirit, Seen by angels, Proclaimed among the nations, Believed on in the world, Taken up in glory." (1Ti 3:16)

Our Lord and the invisible heroes in the Church Age are the main witnesses for the prosecution. When we see God's justice within this court case we can look at the fairness He displays in dealing with the issue of fallen mankind and the judgment of sin. God's righteousness is revealed by the fact that He was willing to forsake His own Son for the judgment of fallen man's sins. God's love is revealed by the offer of salvation put forth for ALL creatures by a simple act of faith upon His Son. *It is faith alone in Christ alone.* So, in any fair trial we need witnesses and real evidence, cold hard facts to come to a conclusion and to get an outcome that serves up the proper justice. The laws of evidence demand investigation of each accusation, and legitimate evidence is based upon two or more witnesses independently agreeing and their stories corroborating the same outcome or fact. Some of the questions laid upon this courtroom have been: Is God just? Is God fair to all creatures? How can a loving God have a lake of fire for His creatures? This is where witnesses like the Lord Jesus Christ and positive believers enter into the testimony portion of the case. In ancient times as well as with the Jewish law of the Old Testament, without witnesses you could not even proceed with a murder trial. It was a process that took two or more witnesses that had collaborating accounts for a trial to be conducted accurately. They were interrogated independently to see if their testimony was compatible.

> "A single witness shall not rise up against a man on account of any iniquity or any sin which he has committed; on the evidence of two or three witnesses a matter shall be confirmed." (Deu 19:15)

> "If anyone kills a person, the murderer shall be put to death at the evidence of witnesses, but no person shall be put to death on the testimony of one witness." (Num 35:30)

This is why the Lord, in Mathew chapter 26, was put through a type of kangaroo court in the dead of the night (another issue not allowed during this time period), so the legalistic leaders of the church and government could attempt to get lying witnesses!

> "Now the chief priests and the whole Council kept trying to obtain false testimony against Jesus, so that they might put Him to death. They did not find any, even though many false witnesses came forward. But later on two came forward," (Mat 26:59-60)

So, the two key witnesses in the appeal trial of the Angelic Conflict are the humanity of Christ, when God lived within man in the dispensation of the Hypostatic Union, and the Church Age believer, in the only other dispensation where God lives in man. This is why the early church was told in Act 1:8, "You shall receive the power when the Holy Spirit comes upon you. You shall be My witnesses both in Jerusalem and in all of Judea and Samaria and to even the remotest part of the earth." The power made available to believers in the Church Age is phenomenal. We have been given more power to witness for the integrity and love of God than even Job had in the Old Testament. In this conflict, Jesus Christ is the strategic victor, the number one witness. In Rev 1:4-5 it refers to "the One (Jesus Christ) who is (now and constantly) and who was (eternity past) and is to come (Second Advent), and then Christ is referred to as "the faithful witness, the firstborn of the dead, and the ruler of the kings of the earth." Any individual who is a witness for God in the Angelic Conflict will be remembered forever, and we see again the witness reference coming up in Rev 2.

> "I know where you dwell, where Satan's throne is; and you hold fast My name, and did not deny My faith even in the days of Antipas, My witness, My faithful one, who was killed among you, where Satan dwells." (Rev 2:13)

The terms witness or witnesses, as well as many military terms and analogies, are used in the Bible constantly, which should be proof enough for mankind to realize the conflict and battle that has been taking place all around us since the beginning of time. Even in the Tribulation period God will have two witnesses.

> "And I will grant authority to my two witnesses, and they will prophesy for twelve hundred and sixty days, clothed in sackcloth." (Rev 11:3)

So Jesus Christ is the first witness, and believers who follow Him and glorify God in this conflict are the second category of witnesses. There is a third group of witnesses, called Christian marriage, which we will study in detail in the next chapter.

Also acting as witnesses, in Revelation there is a reference to open books, two sets of books that can be interpreted as witnesses regarding the human race.

> "And I saw the dead, the great and the small, standing before the throne, and the books were opened; and another book was opened, which is the book of life; and the dead were judged from the things which were written in the books, according to their deeds." (Rev 20:12)

Two sets of books, the first being a record of every good deed performed by the human race. If a deed or good work is done in the flesh it is simply wood, hay, and straw to be burned up. The second book includes the names and list of the entire human race throughout history. This pertains to the unlimited atonement, but there are names blotted out because they are the ones who rejected Christ as Savior. This final judgment is covered in Rev 20:13-15, where it states that the sea and Hades give up the dead and all are judged according to their deeds. This is called a second death, if anyone's name is not found in the book they too will be thrown down to the lake of fire just like Satan.

Our Lord Jesus Christ in His humanity, in hypostatic union, is considered the chief witness in the conflict. Jesus Christ in His deity could be classified as a strategic witness as well, because it is His strategy that formulated the plan and then executed it.

Then we can classify winner believers or mature believers as tactical witnesses. By tactical we mean that we have to do the same job as a witness but in a lesser form, because no one can be an exact copy of Christ. Again we see a military term which is related to combat. This tactical stance is like a military action. The definition for tactical is "relating to combat tactics involving actions or means of less magnitude or at a shorter distance from the base of operations than those of strategy." The strategy was accomplished by Christ on the cross, followed by the death, burial, resurrection and then the ascension. The believer accomplishes the tactical victory in this conflict by advancing to a level of spiritual maturity and becoming an invisible hero within the warfare, as witnessed by angels and eventually mankind when all is revealed. This is why the Church Age is of such great importance in the Angelic Conflict. After Jesus Christ in the dispensation of the Hypostatic Union as the chief witness, the Church Age presents the primary evidence, the witness that can shut the case closed.

Believers with knowledge of what is truly going on in the world have a personal sense of destiny and can relax during stressful periods in history. They know what is happening in the invisible realm, while the visible realm fumbles through this life. Never in human history has a believer's life been more important than right now, the intensified stage of the Angelic Conflict. After Jesus Christ won the victory at the Cross, Satan and his kingdom have increased their attack on witnesses for the prosecution, which gives all of us an incredible opportunity to glorify Jesus Christ in this conflict, by reflecting His love and His character no matter how intense the opposition. How we execute the plan that God has for our life is the critical factor right now. One positive individual can have more impact than a whole army of unbelievers who could care less about God. This is a time of equal privilege and equal opportunity. There are no excuses such as race or gender issues, nothing that a person can fall back on to say that they could have done better in the Pre-designed Plan of God if only they had not been held back by some difficulty or unfair situation. It is not your environment that matters, God has provided everything for each one of us to become invisible heroes and to glorify Him, no matter where we come from. It did not matter where Saul of Tarsus came from, our Lord can use anyone to reflect His glory in the Angelic Conflict! It is a level playing field for all people when it comes to this Angelic Conflict. The prosecution (God) presents the Lord Jesus Christ and then follows the testimony of winner believers.

CHAPTER 8

The Third Witness

The Angelic Conflict has three Church Age witnesses. One is the Lord Jesus Christ (Rev 1:5, Jesus Christ, the faithful witness). The second is the believer who fulfills the plan of God for his or her life.

> "I have fought the good fight, I have finished the course, I have kept the faith (a reference to the invisible hero of the Church Age);" (2Ti 4:7)

A third witness is not necessarily needed in a trial. However, there is a third witness in the Angelic Conflict i.e. the witness of Christian marriage. This principle definitely needs some concentration and requires an understanding of the importance of comparing scripture with scripture. The Bible states that only two witnesses are needed concerning a legal dispute or proof for evidence.

> "On the evidence of two witnesses or three witnesses, he who is to die shall be put to death; he shall not be put to death on the evidence of one witness." (Deu 17:6)

> "A single witness shall not rise up against a man on account of any iniquity or any sin which he has committed; on the evidence

of two or three witnesses a matter shall be confirmed." (Deu 19:15)

Just as the Lord Jesus Christ and the winner believer are tested and interrogated separately, so too will Christian marriage be tested and interrogated separately. The individual witness or invisible hero is of great importance as the second witness, but a good Christian marriage carries a strong message to Satan and the fallen angels as well. To concentrate on this chapter do not focus on your own marriage, or lack thereof, but understand that we are all viewed in the individual realm first in terms of becoming a witness in the Angelic Conflict. This chapter and the doctrine of the third witness can apply to a broken marriage or a rock solid marriage, a divorced individual or someone years away from the wedding altar. Bible doctrine is there for current reference, past examination, and most importantly future use! So it pertains to all of us who want to grow in spiritual knowledge and become invisible heroes in the plan of God. For those of you who are married and do not see any spiritual light at the end of the tunnel, that does not mean that this doctrine may not apply to your future situation.

For those who are no longer married and especially those who are single there are important applications for what may be coming your way very soon. In light of this subject we need to keep in mind at all times:

> "In fact, that spiritual peace and prosperity from the source of the God, which surpasses or rises above and beyond all comprehension, shall garrison your hearts (your thinking) also your motivation (minds) in Christ Jesus." (Phi 4:7)

"This spiritual peace and prosperity from God, which is beyond all human understanding, shall guard your hearts and give you victory in every area of your life. God the Holy Spirit has illustrated this principle with one of the most sensitive areas of relationship in life and that is marriage. I am not talking about worldly marriage but Christian marriage and the mystery behind it. The information about it given in the age of mystery doctrine (the Church Age) is some of the greatest intelligence for the defeat of the powerful creature known as Satan and his genius plot concerning human history. Satan and his fallen angels know all about this subject and they have done such a magnificent job of deception in this area that the average believer disregards and rejects Biblical information concerning this subject. This is partly because they have failed in marriage and partly because it has not been taught properly from the Biblical perspective. A wise man is strong, and a man of knowledge increases power (Pro 24:5), so information is power! When information is the metabolized mind or thinking of Jesus Christ and is the special spiritual intelligence required for our victory, then we will have made available to us everything we need to understand and to combat the situation.

This type of information may have been labeled classified or off limits to creatures of both races (angelic and human) but is no longer concealed as the mystery doctrines were, because there has been an unveiling process that took place at the finished work of our Lord Jesus Christ upon the Cross. It only remains a mystery or secret because of willful ignorance. I say that because, if a believer desires Truth and is motivated to seek it out, God will teach or lead the individual (Joh 7:17, Jer 29:13, Heb 11:6) to a place or person who will feed them. Just like the unbeliever who has a genuine desire to know Christ will find salvation in their pathway sooner or later. God does not play hide and seek with positive people who have true motivation and desire for His words and His wisdom.

> "Now to Him who is able to establish you according to my gospel and the preaching of Jesus Christ, according to the revelation of the mystery which has been kept secret for long ages past, but now is manifested, and by the Scriptures of the prophets, according to the commandment of the eternal God, has been made known to all the nations, leading to obedience of faith;" (Rom 16:25-26)

Notice the "revelation of the mystery" was kept a secret but is now available throughout the Scriptures. And just who is the one to teach or decipher the Scriptures so as to be accurate and on target with the information? The average believer cannot pick up a Bible and gain the wisdom that was given from the original language and then be able to fully comprehend it all and move forward to apply it in their life without confusion. There is a purpose and reason that God gave some as apostles, and some as prophets, and some as evangelists, and some as pastors and teachers (Eph 4:11), and they are not to be thought lightly of or dismissed by members of the church. These are serious positions of authority that are worthy of respect and compensation. They are life-long gifts or studies, efforts that occupy a man's time more so than a full time job in the worldly realm.

> "Let a man regard us in the manner, as servants of Christ, and stewards of the mysteries of God." (1Co 4:1)

Any teacher of the Word of God is charged with a very serious assignment and is responsible to be a shepherd who teaches his flock. They have to communicate classified information and the only way to get it across is through the exegesis of the New Testament epistles (exegesis means the grammatical and syntactical analysis of the passage from the original languages). This is what develops in the life of every believer who becomes an invisible hero. A good example of this is seen in the book of Philippians, and when it is truly studied you can see the big picture. We can see a connection between the maximum glorification of God, for which believers are created, the resolution of a pre-historic Angelic Conflict, a related notion, and then born again believers who receive God's highest and best. Ephesians 1 refers to hidden assets, or the release of the assets. But the average Christian cannot gather all that information or connect the dots so to speak and view the big picture of what God is showing them without a pastor-teacher.

There is in the most elevated section of heaven, in the very preeminent district, a place in which the Lord Jesus Christ Himself is dwelling. In that same place He is guarding for us something that is on deposit (Eph 1:3, 1Pe 1:3-4): we are talking about phenomenal wealth for the soul and for the believer throughout time and in the eternal state.

> "Blessed be the God and Father of our Lord Jesus Christ, who has blessed us with every spiritual blessing in the heavenly places in Christ," (Eph 1:3)

This wealth is conveyed to the believer as part of a manifestation of the glory of God and to the glory of His grace at the moment when the believer contributes to resolving the prehistoric Angelic Conflict by living the spiritual life and glorifying God to the maximum through the different forms of testing. It is the positive believer who endures the tests and trials of time here on earth who can reach maturity and push through into evidence testing and receive the greater blessing in the eternal state and fantastic blessings in time. Receiving the highest and best from God (Mar 10:29-30) is reserved for the invisible hero.

> "Jesus said, 'Truly I say to you, there is no one who has left house or brothers or sisters or mother or father or children or farms, for My sake and for the gospel's sake, but that he shall receive a hundred times as much now in the present age, houses and brothers and sisters and mothers and children and farms, along with persecutions; and in the age to come, eternal life.'" (Mar 10:29-30)

Blessings are poured out upon that person in time and cannot be contained. This has an overflowing effect that will shower out onto family and friends, the community, and even the nation. King David recognized this type of blessing when it occurred within his own life when he said in Psa 23:5, "My cup overflows," speaking about his cup overflowing from God's grace. David had blessing overflow to his family and to his military ventures, even overflowing to his loyal followers. David had a positive impact on his nation and generation (Act 13:36) because of his love for God.

> "And after He had removed him, He raised up David to be their king, concerning whom He also testified and said, 'I have found David the son of Jesse, a man after My heart, who will do all My will.'" (Act 13:22)

> "For David, after he had served the purpose of God in his own generation, fell asleep, and was laid among his fathers, and underwent decay;" (Act 13:36)

Thousands of years later David still has a profound effect on believers when we simply study a book like Psalms. The Church Age believer's impact will not be made known until the end of the Angelic Conflict. We do have some hints as to the situation of positive believers in time when we study the book of Revelation. In chapters two and three there is the mention of rewards and blessings imputed to winner believers, but it is difficult to comprehend it all in this current stage of the conflict. What can be evaluated is the importance of eternal fame in heaven compared to the fleeting fame many obtain here in the cosmic system.

> "For what will it profit a man if he gains the whole world and forfeits his soul? Or what will a man give in exchange for his soul?" (Mat 16:26)

In your own spiritual walk and personal sense of destiny, you have the capacity right now to have phenomenal opportunity and potential through your marriage to impact this conflict in a magnificent way. The spiritual life is unique and was pioneered by the Lord Jesus Christ and was passed on and revealed in detail for every believer in the Church Age to imitate. No one lived this unique spiritual life before the humanity of Jesus Christ, and then it was passed on with two added extras which are both extremely important:

1. Problem-solving device number one, rebound (1Jo 1:9).
2. Problem-solving device number ten, occupation with the Lord Jesus Christ.

This is not the imitation of hypocrisy or plagiarism, nor has this anything to do with academic dishonesty. It is perceiving and learning the proper doctrine needed to follow and fulfill the spiritual life for the Church Age believer. This was first pioneered by the Lord Jesus Christ and then penned and taught to us, especially by the apostle Paul, the apostle to the Gentiles, as stated in Rom 11:13. "But I am speaking to you who are Gentiles. Inasmuch then as I am an apostle of Gentiles, I magnify my ministry." Therefore, consider the following passages:

> "Therefore I exhort you, be imitators of me." (1Co 4:16)

> "Be imitators of me, just as I also am of Christ." (1Co 11:1)

> "Therefore be imitators of God, as beloved children;" (Eph 5:1)

> "You also became imitators of us and of the Lord, having received the word in much tribulation with the joy of the Holy Spirit," (1Th 1:6)

> "Remember those who led you, who spoke the word of God to you; and considering the result of their conduct, imitate their faith." (Heb 13:7)

> "Beloved, do not imitate what is evil, but what is good." (3Jo 1:11)

> "Brethren, join in following my example, and observe those who walk according to the pattern you have in us." (Phi 3:17)

"You have been created to participate in this battle and to bring glory to God in doing so."

> "Worthy are You, our Lord and our God, to receive glory and honor and power; for You created all things, and because of Your will they existed, and were created." (Rev 4:11)

Isa 43:7-21 states that everyone who is called by the name of Jesus Christ was created for the glory of God.

> "Everyone who is called by My name, And whom I have created for My glory, Whom I have formed, even whom I have made." (Isa 43:7)

> "The people whom I formed for Myself, Will declare My praise." (Isa 43:21)

So, a very vital question to answer after salvation is "What Now?"

> "My Father is glorified by this, that you bear much fruit, and so prove to be My disciples." (Joh 15:8)

> "This is good and acceptable in the sight of God our Savior, who desires all men to be saved and to come to the knowledge of the truth." (1Ti 2:3-4)

It cannot be laid out any more clearly and precisely than in these verses and several others throughout the Bible. This takes the right attitude and motivation and should be evaluated by you and no one else, except your mate for the purpose of fellowship, concerning the Lord Jesus Christ and your marriage. Such questions need to be answered if you desire to be a winner believer in the divine institution of marriage. Are you operating in the parameters within the plan of God? Is His Word the number one priority in your life? Is there a real relationship between you and your savior Jesus Christ? This is the gauge or guide issue within your own soul that you need to answer for yourself!

The formal trial, or Satan's presentation of his appeal, was presented between the creation of the first Adam and the incarnation of the second Adam (or the last Adam), the Lord Jesus Christ. Have you become aware of the Angelic Conflict and the trial you are a part of as well as its implications for the human race? Between Genesis 2:7 and the creation of the first Adam, and Mat 1:25, the birth of the Lord Jesus Christ, who is called the last Adam in 1Co 15:45, is the presentation of the formal trial we call the Angelic Conflict. The first Adam failed and sinned which is known as THE FALL. The last Adam would come on the scene and become the strategic victor of the Angelic Conflict, as well as sharing that victory over Satan and the kingdom of darkness and death, with all believers. We call this THE VICTORY, as well as sharing His victory with winner believers who have executed the Pre-designed Plan of God and fulfilled their very own personal sense of destiny, sometimes called "fighting the good fight, and finishing the course" (2Ti 4:7). This victory for all believers is also found in:

> "But when this perishable will have put on the imperishable, and this mortal will have put on immortality, then will come about the saying that is written, 'Death is swallowed up in victory. O death, where is your victory? O death, where is your sting?'" (1Co 15:54-55)

> "But thanks be to God, who gives us the victory through our Lord Jesus Christ." (1Co 15:57)

> "For whatever is born of God overcomes the world; and this is the victory that has overcome the world—our faith. And who is the one who overcomes the world, but he who believes that Jesus is the Son of God?" (1Jo 5:4-5)

FOR WINNER BELIEVERS

There are at least five categories of crowns for victorious believers in the Word of God (crowns and other phrases used in the Bible give our finite minds a glimpse of the unbelievable blessings and rewards God has for us). These crowns or rewards are described for us in human terms, as we are given some insight into what they are like in the Word of God. For example, consider the following passages in the light of our Great Victorious God:

> "But just as it is written, 'Things which eye has not seen and ear has not heard, And which have not entered the heart of man, All that God has prepared for those who love Him.'" (1Co 2:9)

> "For this reason, I bow my knees before the Father, from whom every family in heaven and on earth derives its name, that He would grant you, according to the riches of His glory, to be strengthened with power through His Spirit in the inner man; so that Christ may dwell in your hearts through faith; and that you, being rooted and grounded in love, may be able to comprehend with all the saints what is the breadth and length and height and depth, and to know the love of Christ which surpasses knowledge, that you may be filled up to all the fullness of God. Now to Him who is able to do exceeding abundantly beyond all that we ask or think, according to the power that works within us, to Him be the glory in the church and in Christ Jesus to all generations forever and ever. Amen." (Eph 3:14-21)

> "Oh, the depth of the riches both of the wisdom and knowledge of God! How unsearchable are His judgments and unfathomable His ways! For who has known the mind of the Lord, or who became His counselor? Or who has first given to Him that it might be paid back to him again? For from Him and through Him and to Him are all things. To Him be the glory forever. Amen." (Rom 11:33-36)

Truly our God and Lord and Savior Jesus Christ is beyond words to describe, His blessings stagger our imagination and His love is incomprehensible.

> "Who is a God like You, who pardons iniquity and passes over the rebellious act of the remnant of His possession? He does not retain His anger forever, because He delights in unchanging love." (Mic 7:18)

> "I am the Lord, and there is no other; Besides Me there is no God. I will gird you, though you have not known Me; That men may know from the rising to the setting of the sun That there is no one besides Me. I am the Lord, and there is no other." (Isa 45:5-6)

> "Remember this, and be assured; Recall it to mind, you transgressors. Remember the former things long past, For I am God, and there is no other; {I am} God, and there is no one like Me, Declaring the end from the beginning And from ancient times things which have not been done, Saying, 'My purpose will be established, And I will accomplish all My good pleasure,' Calling a bird of prey from the east, The man of My purpose from a far country. Truly I have spoken; truly I will bring it to pass. I have planned {it, surely} I will do it." (Isa 46:8-11)

All these passages reveal in one way or another the glory of God. I could give you hundreds of verses and passages which describe that our God is an awesome God!

Remember that when Moses deeply desired to see the glory of God, His glory was revealed in His unbelievable mercy and grace, His infinite desire is to give to us, no matter what it would cost Him to save us.

> "Then Moses said, 'I pray You, show me Your glory!' And He said, 'I Myself will make all My goodness pass before you, and will proclaim the name of the LORD before you; and I will be gracious to whom I will be gracious, and will show compassion on whom I will show compassion.'" (Exo 33:18-19)

In Isa 30:18, the Hebrew idiom reveals that our Lord is "tapping His foot" because He cannot wait to give graciously to His people, even though this was written to people who had failed over and over!

> "Therefore the LORD longs to be gracious to you, And therefore He waits on high to have compassion on you. For the LORD is a God of justice; How blessed are all those who long for Him." (Isa 30:18)

Our Lord did not just say, "It is more blessed to give than to receive," but He Himself lives in that every moment! We can always live in confidence because that is His heartbeat toward us!

Our gracious Lord desires to give us eternal rewards beyond our imagination! Consider with me some of the Victor's crowns which are available to all believers who have executed the Pre-designed Plan of God and fulfilled their very own personal sense of destiny. Some believers will have the crown of righteousness for loving His appearing or being totally occupied with the Lord Jesus Christ as they "walk in the good works which God prepared beforehand" with the result of producing divine good.

> "For we are His workmanship, created in Christ Jesus for good works, which God prepared beforehand so that we should walk in them." (Eph 2:10)

> "In the future there is laid up for me the crown of righteousness, which the Lord, the righteous Judge, will award to me on that

day; and not only to me, but also to all who have loved His appearing." (2Ti 4:8)

Some believers will have the crown of life for enduring trials, heartaches, and disasters, as they glorify the Lord in the Angelic Conflict.

"Blessed is a man who perseveres under trial; for once he has been approved, he will receive the crown of life which the Lord has promised to those who love Him." (Jam 1:12)

"Do not fear what you are about to suffer. Behold, the devil is about to cast some of you into prison, that you may be tested, and you will have tribulation ten days. Be faithful until death, and I will give you the crown of life." (Rev 2:10)

Some will have the incorruptible crown for mastering their old sin nature, also known as the "old self," in Eph 4:22, and the "flesh," in Rom 13:14, and the "perishable seed," in 1Pe 1:23. It is also called "sin" in the singular in Rom 7:8-9,11,13,14,17,20,23,25, just to name a few.

Our Lord longs to give incredible blessings and rewards to anyone who lives for Him in this Angelic Conflict! These include not only our eternal rewards or "crowns" but also special and unexpected blessings in time. Regarding these unexpected blessings, a little laughter is permitted here if you have what every believer needs, a sense of humor. Do you know that under the "first mention principle" the first time that laughter is mentioned was when a man of faith laughed mentally at some of the promises of God, namely his libido being energized and stimulated at age 99, almost 100 (by the way without Viagra)! They in fact did have holistic medicines. They believed that lettuce, fennel, ginger, radishes, coriander, and (believe it or not) pomegranates were libido boosters. They were also fond of pearls dissolved in wine. However, none of these things could aid at all in this situation! Abraham, who was called the father of our faith in Rom 4:16, enjoyed, as a part of the promises of God that he laughed at, his wife's womb being opened and ready not just for recreation, but for copulation, and the promises of God to Abraham were fulfilled. I am sure that they enjoyed the increase of their recreation in the sexual realm because of their marriage being held in honor as in Heb

13:4. By the way, a little advice is to be noted here (no extra charge), the Bible teaches that it is virtue that inspires and fulfills the marriage bed, not experience. For the greatest sexual organ found in both the man and the woman is the mind and heart, not the genitalia.

I am grateful to some of the translators of our new translations who, in academic honesty, will tell you that their focus was not really the literal accuracy of every word but simply to shed further light on the interpretation of the passage. Some of the passages may be difficult to understand because of the change of language from the original language. Some of the words have also changed their meaning from time to time throughout history. I say all of that because in the Contemporary English version we read the following translation of Pro 5:1-23:

> "My son, if you listen closely to my wisdom and good sense, you will have sound judgment, and you will always know the right thing to say. The words of an immoral woman may be as sweet as honey and as smooth as olive oil. But all that you really get from being with her is bitter poison and pain. If you follow her, she will lead you down to the world of the dead. She has missed the path that leads to life and doesn't even know it. My son, listen to me and do everything I say. Stay away from a bad woman! Don't even go near the door of her house. You will lose your self-respect and end up in debt to some cruel person for the rest of your life. Strangers will get your money and everything else you have worked for. When it's all over, your body will waste away, as you groan and shout, 'I hated advice and correction! I paid no attention to my teachers, and now I am disgraced in front of everyone.' You should be faithful to your wife, just as you take water from your own well. And don't be like a stream from which just any woman may take a drink. Save yourself for your wife and don't have sex with other women. Be happy with the wife you married when you were young. She is beautiful and graceful, just like a deer; you should be attracted to her and stay deeply in love. Don't go crazy over a woman who is unfaithful to her own husband! The Lord sees everything, and he watches

us closely. Sinners are trapped and caught by their own evil deeds. They get lost and die because of their foolishness and lack of self-control." (Pro 5:1-23)

That passage states the advice from David to his son Solomon and it is a little clearer in that newer translation. The point is that some words lose their impact when they are translated from one language to another. For example, the word gay originally meant happy. Now, of course, it has to do with a sexually perverted lifestyle or an abomination to the Lord, as in Lev 18:22. However, what does the Bible say about marriage and the sexual relationship between the husband and his wife?

"Marriage is to be held in honor among all, and the marriage bed is to be undefiled; for fornicators and adulterers God will judge." (Heb 13:4)

Remember, there is no place for condemnation or guilt here because of problem-solving device number 1, which is rebound (1Jo 1:9). Remember that your past does not matter, it matters if you forge ahead and continue to press on! (Phi 3:13-14) Anyone, regardless of their past, has a tremendous opportunity to grow into an invisible hero and to receive special blessings in this life, and incredible eternal rewards!

These eternal rewards are even beyond our ability to imagine. Some believers will have the crown of rejoicing for being soul winners, 1Th 2:19. Some will have the crown of glory for being willing to feed the flock of God, 1Pe 5:4. Therefore, there is the warning regarding crowns in Rev 3:11, "I am coming quickly; hold fast what you have, so that no one will take your crown." The same warning is given in 2Jo 1:8, "Watch yourselves, that you do not lose what we have accomplished, but that you may receive a full reward."

So, tremendous eternal rewards and blessings, as well as remarkable and unexpected blessings in time, are given to anyone who becomes a witness for God in this historical trial. The rebuttal phase of the Angelic Conflict involves three kinds of witnesses: Jesus Christ (the Chief Witness), the believer who glorifies God as an invisible hero, and Christian marriage.

Christian marriage is truly unique and has a purpose in the divine order and plan of God. The standards and values are above the norm and are outlined very well in Eph 5:22-33.

> "Wives, be subject to your own husbands, as to the Lord. For the husband is the head of the wife, as Christ also is the head of the church, He Himself being the Savior of the body. But as the church is subject to Christ, so also the wives ought to be to their husbands in everything. Husbands, love your wives, just as Christ also loved the church and gave Himself up for her, so that He might sanctify her, having cleansed her by the washing of water with the word, that He might present to Himself the church in all her glory, having no spot or wrinkle or any such thing; but that she should be holy and blameless. So husbands ought also to love their own wives as their own bodies. He who loves his own wife loves himself; for no one ever hated his own flesh, but nourishes and cherishes it, just as Christ also does the church, because we are members of His body. For this reason a man shall leave his father and mother, and shall be joined to his wife; and the two shall become one flesh. This mystery is great; but I am speaking with reference to Christ and the church. Nevertheless, each individual among you also is to love his own wife even as himself, and the wife must see to it that she respects her husband." (Eph 5:22-33)

These standards are higher than any standards that have ever been communicated to mankind, through the Mosaic law or otherwise. There is no way to reach these standards and values except by fulfilling the spiritual life that God has designed. After Paul describes the guidelines for marriage, he says; "This mystery is great, but I am speaking with reference to Christ and the church" (Eph 5:32).

The institution of marriage has existed in one form or another since the Garden of Eden, so the mystery is not simply just that. It cannot be what the average preacher or commentator says when they refer to the church as the bride and the Lord as the bridegroom, or the analogy in the Old Testament where Israel is said to be the bride and the Lord her husband. Neither of these has any mystery or even vagueness to them, they are clear-cut analogies.

The mystery goes back to the Garden of Eden and all that Adam lost when he fell and all that the second Adam (Jesus Christ) restored and how all this relates to the Angelic Conflict. Not only did the Lord restore everything Adam lost, but He enlarged it and enriched it. We can understand and experience a measure of these principles in the spiritual realm right now; however, we will abide in them and experience them in totality in the eternal state.

So, the mystery Paul speaks of in Ephesians points back to the Garden of Eden. The absolute righteousness that the first Adam lost is now duplicated and imputed in the spiritual realm to the believer in the Church Age who receives a double righteousness under the principle of a double portion for the heir. However, this righteousness now comes directly from being in union with the Lord Jesus Christ and is accompanied by a brand new nature which can never be improved upon or lost. We are told in 1Pe 1:23, "for you have been born again not of seed which is perishable but imperishable, that is, through the living and abiding word of God." This seed is also in view in passages like 1Jo 3:9, "No one who is born of God practices sin, because His seed abides in him; and he cannot sin, because he is born of God." Therefore, any person who has believed in Christ, by faith alone, will remain in that state of perfection forever (Rev 22:11).

Therefore, what the first Adam lost in the Garden of Eden, the second or the last Adam restored, and much more. The perfection of the original environment found in the Garden of Eden is now revealed and duplicated in the spiritual realm in the Pre-designed Plan of God for the Church Age today. However, even this environment will be consummated someday as we enter into the ultimate environment of perfection in the eternal state (Rev 21:1-4). And so, the first Adam lost his perfect righteousness in the original fall of man, but it was restored and perfected by our Lord's victory upon the cross. Also, the perfect environment found in the garden of Eden was also lost by the first Adam, but brought back, improved upon, and restored by the Lord Jesus Christ manifested by the Pre-designed Plan of God in the Church Age. This restoration will reach its ultimate status of perfection in the perfect environment found in the eternal state forever.

> "The Lord is not slow about His promise, as some count slowness, but is patient toward you, not wishing for any to

perish but for all to come to repentance. But the day of the Lord will come like a thief, in which the heavens will pass away with a roar and the elements will be destroyed with intense heat, and the earth and its works will be burned up. Since all these things are to be destroyed in this way, what sort of people ought you to be in holy conduct and godliness, looking for and hastening the coming of the day of God, on account of which the heavens will be destroyed by burning, and the elements will melt with intense heat! But according to His promise we are looking for new heavens and a new earth, in which righteousness dwells." (2Pe 3:9-13)

However, there was one more thing that the first Adam lost. Because of the Angelic Conflict, the last Adam—the Lord Jesus Christ—gives some believers the opportunity to recover and to glorify Him with a certain principle. By doing so in the Angelic Conflict we put another nail in the coffin of Satan, and this all refers to the mystery we are highlighting in Eph 5:32, "This mystery is great; but I am speaking with reference to Christ and the church."

The first Adam and the woman also lost in the Garden of Eden the original design of marriage, conceived by God for the purpose of virtue, love, and intimacy. However, this can now be experienced in the spiritual realm for believers in the Church Age and gives us a glimpse of the eternal marriage between Christ and His bride for all of eternity (Rev 21:9). But this takes submitting to the Word of God as it was written and not finding loopholes and angles that would exclude the husband or wife from operating in doctrinal principles. A fine example is the following verse in Eph 5:22 where it states, "Wives, be subject to your own husbands, as to the Lord." One of the main areas that the woman struggles with concerning the man is that of respect. In the Greek it reads like this: "Hai gunaikes tois idios andrasin hupotassesthe hos to kurio" which says in effect, "The wives to your own husbands submit as to the Lord."

Now, you ladies must be thinking that the adjective "idios" which seems very similar to our English word idiot, is fitting for your husband. However, take a look at the word gunaikes which is similar to goonie and apply that to yourselves! The noun gunaikes could then be used in the humorous statement: "You goons obey your idiot husband." That statement alone speaks volumes about the worldly relationship of marriage. Most marriages today mirror words like idiot or goon to describe the husband or wife. This is one main source of erosion that breaks down the foundation of marriage, disrespect and the name calling that follows it. It becomes easy to disrespect someone once you see all their flaws and failures when they have seemingly let you down. Familiarity is the real enemy within long-term relationships, be it friends or family but especially in marriage. The woman is said to need respect for the man in the realm of marriage because it is an area of weakness for women.

This is not because man is any greater than woman in the eyes of God, but it is a divine order that God has chosen. In fact, many women are mentally stronger or more intelligent than the man they married. In some cases, God has allowed the man to be the authority because the woman would become too controlling or her emotions would make her a weak leader, but no matter what the reason, it is clear that the man is the head in the relationship of marriage.

> "But as the church is subject to Christ, so also the wives ought to be to their husbands in everything." (Eph 5:24)

This is the absolute and dogmatic truth as it states everything and does not even hint to partial submission or a 50/50 agreement, but that the man is the authority in the marriage. The Bible teaches to honor and respect authority in all realms, but it can be difficult for many women to follow in their daily lives. There is a hint of the depth of the riches both of the wisdom and knowledge of God in this particular area of marriage as it relates to the Angelic Conflict. Perhaps this is one of the reasons why the Scripture relates the woman's area of submission in marriage as an integral part of the Angelic Conflict, and something the angels notice. In 1Co 11:9, we read, "for indeed man was not created for the woman's sake, but woman for the man's sake."

> "Therefore the woman ought to have a symbol of authority on her head, because of the **angels.** However, in the Lord, neither

is woman independent of man, nor is man independent of woman."(1Co 11:10-11)

Now, there is also another area that can destroy the spiritual significance of marriage in both the man and the woman, the area of hypersensitivity and bitterness. However, it is the man that seems to be weaker in this area, just as ladies may struggle with the area of respect. This is why Col 3:19 says, "Husbands, love your wives, and do not be bitter against them." Most husbands will say, "How can I love her when she is constantly nagging or complaining and being critical?" The answer is found in doctrine, and it all points to impersonal unconditional love, the same love Christ has for all mankind.

> "Husbands, love your wives, just as Christ also loved the church and gave Himself up for her." (Eph 5:25)

This is not a passive, distant love because it is impersonal, it is powerful enough to protect the object of the love and to tolerate its failures, but has enough emotional control not to take everything personally or take it to heart. Jesus Christ gave Himself up for the Church, so that is in no way a passive or a distant love, but a powerful one that overcomes all our failures.

> "So husbands ought also to love their own wives as their own bodies. He who loves his own wife loves himself (spiritual self-esteem) for no one ever hated his own flesh, but nourishes and cherishes it, just as Christ also does the church." (Eph 5:28-29)

So ladies, you better find a man that respects and loves Jesus Christ and himself enough to operate with this type of integrity. The man better have some confidence and spiritual self-esteem to be a good leader in his authority position in the marriage. This is not the confidence that the world promotes but the confidence that develops from a relationship with God that eventually matures a person spiritually. The fact is, if both parties have reached at least the stage of spiritual self-esteem, any relationship can flourish, be it friendship, business, and most certainly marriage. When Christ is the glue that holds a relationship together it is the strongest bond! When a marriage fulfills the spiritual life corporately, the marriage becomes a corporate or collective witness for the prosecution of Satan! That marriage receives the very highest and best from God beyond any human expectation, as well as the recognition of that marriage throughout the eternal state, fame in the place that will last forever. This is described as a fortune that cannot decay or be broken (Mat 6:19), a reward that endures forever (Joh 6:27).

If we live in the power of the Word of God, even in marriage, our lives will have an impact that will last forever, just as our eternal rewards will. So the kingdom of darkness will strongly oppose anyone who lives as a witness for God during human history, especially since the time of the strategic victor, Jesus Christ. We can surely say that the Lord Jesus Christ is the star witness in the angelic trial. The period from 4 BC to 30 AD is when Jesus Christ was pioneering the spiritual life, passing all the spiritual tests and trials put in front of Him, including evidence testing as in Mat 4:1-10. After that temptation, our star witness went to the Cross without sin or blemish (2Co 5:21, 1Pe 2:22-24), offering Himself without spot to God by means of the Holy Spirit in Heb 9:14.

In Rev 3:14, Jesus introduces Himself to the church at Laodicea, a church that was failing and faltering, and He calls Himself the originator of the creation from God, the one who is preeminent over the creation including both angels and mankind, the faithful and the true witness. He is called "ho martus," the Witness, and then the Greek says "the faithful and the true one" which means He was the star witness. In fact, Jesus Christ closes the entire book of Revelation with this announcement: "I Jesus, have sent My angel to testify to you these things for the churches. I am the root and the offspring of David, the bright morning star" (Rev 22:16). This Star, the offspring of David, this Witness, The Lord Jesus Christ, is forever the star witness for the prosecution of Satan in human history. In fact, that is what the invisible heroes of the Church Age receive in Rev 2:28, the Order of the Morning Star. There should be no wondering why Satan has targeted Jesus to destroy Him. Even before His birth Satan began a campaign to stop the coming of Jesus Christ. Looking back into Genesis 6 we can see the introduction of the Nephilim, who were nothing more than an experiment to pervert the bloodline of mankind. Nephilim are beings who appear in the Hebrew Bible, specifically mentioned in the Book of Genesis and the Book of Numbers, they are also mentioned in other Biblical texts and in some non-canonical Jewish writings. The Nephilim refer to the mixed offspring of heavenly beings (fallen angels) who came to earth and had sexual intercourse with women.

> "Now it came about, when men began to multiply on the face of the land, and daughters were born to them, that the sons of God saw that the daughters of men were beautiful; and they took wives for themselves, whomever they chose." (Gen 6:1-2)

Genesis 6:4 implies that the Nephilim have inhabited the earth in at least two different time periods—in antediluvian times and afterwards. If the Nephilim were supernatural beings themselves, or at least the progeny of supernatural beings, it is possible that the giants of Canaan spoken of in Num 13:33 were the direct descendants of the antediluvian Nephilim, or were fathered by the same supernatural parents. Had it not been for Noah and his household the kingdom of darkness would have infected every human being on earth over the period of a few generations.

So Satan's kingdom was intent and focused on destroying Jesus, from trying to destroy His lineage and the Jewish people in the Old Testament so He could not be born true humanity, to destroying all the children 2 years and under in Bethlehem (Mat 2:16), to tempting and trying to distract Jesus throughout His whole life on earth right up to His spiritual death on the Cross. Satan not only tempted and attacked Jesus in His evidence testing in the wilderness (Mat 4, Luk 4), but throughout His whole life.

When Satan failed miserably in his attacks on Jesus Christ as the star witness, and Jesus defeated his case totally on the Cross, he increased his attacks on the individual believer, now in the Church Age. When we discuss the second witness in this appeal trial, it is centered on the individual believer and his or her role in the conflict. This individual believer has to live in the role of invisible hero to truly make an impact in the heavenly courtroom. This dispensation of the Church Age has and can yield a great many witnesses. Look at the apostles who were tortured and put to death for their faith. In the Old Testament, we can see great men and women of God standing in the conflict and becoming mature and powerful witnesses for God to use. In Heb 11:2 all the way to Heb 12:1, we see a great cloud of witnesses from the Old Testament.

And before our Lord ascended into heaven He said, "But you shall receive power when the Holy Spirit has come upon you; and you shall be My witnesses both in Jerusalem and in all Judea and Samaria, and even to the remotest part of the earth." This is a reference to Church Age believers bearing witness in the conflict. The corporate witness is the third witness which we now know is Christian marriage. So, the second witness (individual believer) and the third witness (either one mature believer in the marriage or two) have existed since the beginning but have now come to center stage because the star witness has finished upon the stand. We can say that, as of October 30 AD until the Rapture, Church Age witnesses have the floor.

The Christian marriage then becomes very important, and it emerges in a very different realm from worldly marriage. Marriage is a sensitive subject to begin with, but it must be dealt with from divine viewpoint and must remove the issue of hypersensitivity. The Christian couple must learn to be objective, not subjective, to succeed in the conflict. First and foremost, a Christian couple should be made up of a man and a woman, hopefully under the right man and right woman principle. And this falls under the principle of God designing a certain woman for a certain man. Notice it is singular, not one woman for several different men or vice-versa, or living in human viewpoint such as: "Let's keep trying different ones until we find the one we think is God-sent."

In Gen 2:18 we read, Then the Lord God said, "It is not good for the man to be alone; I will make him a helper suitable for him." And as you read on in Genesis, you see that God created every beast of the field, "but for Adam there was not found a suitable helper" (Gen 2:19-20). God made it clear that a pet or animal can never have the intimacy of a man and woman or husband and wife, nor should they. So God is going to bring forth a helper or an ezer. This is the Hebrew noun which means a responder and fulfiller. God then performs the first surgery upon the earth as He removes a rib, and from this rib He would bring forth a great source of pleasure and pain for the man! As the humorous saying goes,

"God made Adam and He rested; then God made the woman and since then no one has rested."

> "The LORD God fashioned into a woman the rib which He had taken from the man, and brought her to the man." (Gen 2:22)

God designed or built the woman for the man. The reference here is to be fashioned or built, not created. Adam was unaware of what he even needed at this time, but his radar was certainly up now! But what Adam *wasn't* doing was seeking and chasing after anything. In Gen 2:22 the Lord brought the woman to the man. There was no game of hide and seek, or Adam club—hopping looking for the one with the shortest skirt and the highest heels. God made it happen, bringing the woman into the man's path. Men, please do not misinterpret the intention of God here, and that would be to sit at home waiting for an angel to drop off the right woman into your living room. It is the intention of God to show His timing and His method of bringing the right people or situation together. Stop working the odds and looking for the angles in an attempt to obtain the things you think you need in life, be faithful to God and He brings it forth to you. In fact, as you pursue your relationship with the Lord, blessings will follow you as in Psa 23:6, so just follow God and let them catch up!

And Adam said, "This is now bone of my bones, and flesh of my flesh; She shall be called Ishshah (woman), because she was taken out of Ish (man)." (Gen 2:23)

The next verse makes an interesting statement that has been the root of more than one marital problem over the years. In verse 24 it states; "For this cause a man shall leave his father and mother." Now the truth of the situation is that Adam and Eve did not have a mother or father in the human sense of the word. But yet it states that when marriage enters the picture the parents are to get out of the picture! This passage, as many Biblical passages do, is setting a precedent. Under the first mention principle, when you establish precedent, it is to show that this is a firmly established principle from the beginning of time to the end of human history. What this passage is laying down is a privacy policy that marriages and those connected to married couples should respect. Keep your nose out of the bedroom and the personal affairs of other people. We all know some in-laws, relatives, and close friends who cannot seem to do that one thing that God is telling them to do in this verse.

Interference in a marriage is a dangerous and rocky road to go down as it can start off with innocent advice and end with broken relationships and broken hearts. No one knows all the facts or realizes what truly goes on behind closed doors, so the best thing for people to do in the case of marriage is to work on your own relationships, not someone else's. The last part of verse 24 says: "and they shall become one flesh." This is a pattern of intimacy that God is putting forth, a special closeness for husband and wife to experience, excluding other people from that tight bond. These were patterns and rules set into place to keep marriage sacred and safe from outside forces. Just as there is one edification complex for one soul (one developed system of thinking), and every believer has their own unique relationship with the Lord, there is one man for one woman in God's unique design.

> "For this cause (analogy between the universal church in Christ in the previous verse) a man shall leave his father and mother, and shall cleave to his wife; and the two shall become one flesh. This mystery is great (in context, the oneness of the soul of the believer with the Lord Jesus Christ, through the Word of God, developing the mind of Christ); but I am speaking with reference to Christ and the church." (Eph 5:31-32)

Our relationship or intimacy with Christ on earth depends upon our soul structure, for God has designed a system of perfection of thought patterns developing in your soul relating to our relationship with the Lord Jesus Christ. In God's system, the woman is commanded to respect the husband. It does not say that she is commanded to personally love the husband, that should be a natural occurrence with the right woman. The man is commanded to love the woman. She should not be struggling with loving her husband if she married the right man, but the man can struggle with this issue and it appears that God is forewarning the men who get married to be aware of it.

"Nevertheless, each individual among you also is to love his own wife even as himself, and the wife must see to it that she respects her husband." (Eph 5:33)

The word used here for respect is the present middle subjunctive of the verb phobeo, meaning not only respect, but an awe, and to treat in high regard with reverential obedience. Respect is the key to this relationship between the woman and her right man. Love can fluctuate for a woman, and she may at times feel angry enough to hate her right man because he will be able to evoke very strong emotions from his right woman. Anyone under authority will at times reject the authority or resent it, but when they truly recognize the authority they will always submit to it.

Ladies, if you find a man attractive or even feel love for him, that is not as important as the respect you have for him, that should be your gauge. Whether feelings of anger, love, or hate come from the woman toward the man, it is respect that should remain in operation for the relationship to move forward. If the woman cannot respect the man that she is going to marry, she should not enter into the divine institution of marriage until she does so. If a man does not have unconditional love for his wife, he is not ready for marriage as well. In the spiritual realm, if a woman struggles with respecting authority she is not ready for marriage. As man and woman grow spiritually, both will develop in their souls what God designed for marriage. What will develop within the man is an initiating, aggressive type of love which is very important. The relationship between husband and wife who develop the mind of Christ is one of the greatest gifts God can give. There are three prominent grace gifts from Christ to man delineated in Scripture:

    a. The right woman: God built her, Gen 2:22.
    b. Salvation: God did it, Joh 19:30.
    c. Bible Doctrine: God thought it, 1Co 2:16.

A vital principle: This list is not the order of importance, because in the order of importance it is salvation that should come first. The second priority would be to find your right pastor-teacher and study hard to gain the mind of Christ. Then, thirdly, would come the time for finding the right person to spend your life with, after you have grown spiritually and

God has put the right person in front of you. In all of human history, the right woman is the oldest human gift given to man from our Lord. However, the fall of man did change their relationship somewhat, which is a part of our study concerning the mystery. So whether it is a gift of right pastor-teacher or right woman these gifts are designed to fit you perfectly. In Deu 32:4 it says, "His work is perfect, for all His ways are just."

> "Every good thing given and every perfect gift is from above," (Jam 1:17)

God created you so He knows what is good for you. We think we know what is good for us, yet God knows us even better than we know ourselves. In Mat 10:29-31 we read, "Are not two sparrows sold for a cent? And yet not one of them will fall to the ground apart from your Father. But the very hairs of your head are all numbered. So do not fear; you are more valuable than many sparrows." Any gift from God takes positive volition to receive, as you will not even recognize what God is trying to give you if you do not stay in His plan.

The gifts of God are always perfect and always abundantly beyond all that we can ask or think (Eph 3:20), including our opportunity as witnesses in the rebuttal phase of Satan's appeal trial in history. When a marriage fulfills the spiritual life corporately, that marriage becomes a corporate or collective witness for the prosecution of Satan. Then the marriage is glorifying God and can receive the blessing of the highest and best from God. Under Election, God wills His highest and best and provides the believer with the capacity to receive that highest and best. How often do you think husbands and wives in our day and age think about glorifying God? Most marriages are more concerned about what they can *get* from their relationship than what they can *give*.

The ones that do stay positive and glorify God will endure attacks from the kingdom of darkness, who will definitely try to get at one or both of the positive believers in the marriage. However, God will carry them through it and bless them on the other side of the adversity, much like He did with Job. So in Eph 5:22 all the way into Eph 5:32, the apostle Paul teaches on some of the finer points of marriage, and he then finishes with the reference to the mystery of the bride of Christ and the Church Age.

> "For this cause a man shall leave his father and mother, and shall cleave to his wife; and the two shall become one flesh. This mystery is great; but I am speaking with reference to Christ and the church." (Eph 5:31-32)

The word for mystery is the Greek noun musterion. At the time that the Bible was written, there were numerous mystery cults which flourished throughout the ancient world, and although the secrets of these groups were closely guarded, everyone knew that these secretive organizations existed. Everyone knew that there were certain rituals and formulas and rites under which these cults would operate, called musterions or mysteries. Therefore, the apostle Paul used this word to describe the Church Age, which was entirely unknown prior to our Lord's announcement of the Church Age (Joh 16; Luk 24:49). The Church Age, of which we are all part, and its doctrine, were never mentioned in Old Testament prophecy, but instead were fully developed in the New Testament epistles. Paul states in Rom 16:25-26, Col 1:25-26, and Eph 3:3-6 that this mystery is now revealed.

> "Now to Him who is able to establish you according to my gospel and the preaching of Jesus Christ, according to the revelation of the mystery which has been kept secret for long ages past, but now is manifested, and by the Scriptures of the prophets, according to the commandment of the eternal God, has been made known to all the nations, leading to obedience of faith;" (Rom 16:25-26)

> "Of this church I was made a minister according to the stewardship from God bestowed on me for your benefit, so that I might fully carry out the preaching of the Word of God, that is, the mystery which has been hidden from the past ages and generations, but has now been manifested to His saints, to whom God willed to make known what is the riches of the glory of this mystery among the Gentiles, which is Christ in you, the hope of glory." (Col 1:25-27)

It is this body of doctrine known as mystery doctrine which sets the Church Age apart from other dispensations. The mystery doctrine of the Church unveils the characteristics unique to the Christian way of life. And, it is important to note that the mystery pertains to the Church alone. Now, how important is mystery doctrine? Well, mystery doctrine actually tells the believer what he must do now that he is a Christian. Where there is ignorance concerning mystery doctrine there is ignorance concerning how to live the Christian life. Most believers today are living in some false system of spirituality that they have substituted for mystery doctrine, such as emotionalism, legalism, etc. Mystery doctrine reveals the divine assets that God has given to each Church Age believer and His directions for using those assets. God has magnificently provided everything for us and has thoroughly instructed us so that as Ephesians 4:1 says, we can "Walk in a manner worthy of our calling." In 2Co 5:17, "Therefore, if anyone is in Christ, he is a new [spiritual] creation," which refers to a secret not known in the past. This is a secret way of life not given in the Old Testament and this same word is used in the following verses:

In Rom 16:25-26—a mystery that was kept secret for long ages past but is now manifested.
In 1Co 2:7—the mystery points to God's wisdom.
In 1Co 4:1—Paul states that the apostles (teachers) are stewards of the mysteries of God.
In Eph 3:9—Paul says that he is to shine the light on this mystery.
In Col 1:26—this mystery which was hidden is now manifested by believers.

This is not highlighting a singular piece of knowledge but a series of several different doctrinal principles that can now be uncovered. The exciting part of this is that Christian marriage has the ability to operate in this mystery and to be involved as a witness for the Lord. After the first man on earth failed and damaged his perfect environment and perfect marriage, the second Man came on the scene to restore all that he lost, even greater than it was at first! As 1Co15:47 reveals, "The first man is of the earth, earthy; the second man is the Lord from heaven," or 2Co 5:17 "Therefore if anyone is in Christ, he is a new creature; the old things passed away; behold, new things have come." Gal 2:20 reveals our new life: "I have been crucified with Christ; and it is no longer I who live, but

Christ lives in me; and the life which I now live in the flesh I live by faith in the Son of God, who loved me and gave Himself up for me."

We have all been given tremendous opportunities as the nature of God reveals to us. But, just what will you choose to do with the time and opportunities that God gives to you? Adam had perfect environment and perfect righteousness that God had given him, as well as the gift of intimacy with the right woman, and he lost all three! The Lord replaced all that Adam had lost for himself and mankind with His perfect justice and righteousness resulting in a perfection that goes way beyond man's imagination. A Christian marriage can experience that perfection in time if they put Christ at the center of their relationship. Their focus on Christ results in becoming witnesses in something which dates back to before the beginning of human history, the Angelic Conflict!

Remember that under the Jewish laws of evidence, it was stressed that there had to be more than one witness.

> "But if he does not listen {to you,} take one or two more with you, so that by the mouth of two or three witnesses every fact may be confirmed." (Mat 18:16)

Paul made the very same statement in 2Co 13:1, "This is the third time I am coming to you. Every fact is to be confirmed by the testimony of two or three witnesses."

The laws were set so that each witness was to be interrogated separately and in the end all the testimony had to be exact. The Lord was interrogated alone concerning the issue of being the Son of God and possessing perfect righteousness (Mat 4:1-11; Luk 4:1-13). The Lord was tempted to use His divine power or to perform human good, but the devil could never succeed in getting Jesus Christ to fail in those areas. Jesus Christ never gave in to sin or human good, never strayed from the plan of God for His life, and always relied upon divine solutions. This made Him the perfect witness and the star of the trial, one of the many meanings behind Rev 22:16, "I, Jesus, have sent My angel to testify to you these things for the churches. I am the root and the descendant of David, the bright morning star."

> But He answered and said, "It is written, 'Man shall not live on bread alone, but on every word that proceeds out of the mouth of God.'" (Mat 4:4)

> "For we do not have a high priest who cannot sympathize with our weaknesses, but One who has been tempted in all things as we are, yet without sin." (Heb 4:15)

In this intense conflict, Jesus Christ was a faithful witness and He stood His ground when the tests and deceptions came His way. So, if your desire is to go forward to become an invisible hero, as an invisible hero, you will face similar tests and challenges, and the witness stand will become a hot seat for you as well. Will you stand in the GAP and take the heat, or will you run? You may be tempted to leave the place God has assigned for you. Maybe you will not follow through on the commitment that you made to God or perhaps your attitude will change toward the Word of God. These are all areas that Satan and the kingdom of darkness will tempt you in and try to drag you away, if you give them just a little space in your soul to do so.

> "And do not give the devil an opportunity." (Eph 4:27)

There is a private cross examination that the kingdom of darkness is allowed to do with every believer. Those believers who are classified as the positive ones get double attention and more attacks because they become the important witnesses.

> "Because to you it has been graciously given with reference concerning Christ, not only to believe in Him, but also to suffer on behalf of Him." (Phi 1:29)

> "Indeed, all who desire to live godly in Christ Jesus will be persecuted." (2Ti 3:12)

So, the kingdom of darkness will attack any growing believer, and especially those who are married and growing spiritually together. However, with divine power, Christian marriage can glorify God in powerful ways. First of all, when both parties operate in the supernatural power of living the spiritual life within the marriage, this not only restores the original design, but a divine union which Satan attempted to destroy forever. This takes two invisible heroes living in the Word of God as the *top priority* in the relationship, not money, status, approval, emotion, or anything else, not even each other, and that is the difference between worldly and Christian marriage.

This is why it is so important to grow up spiritually and concentrate on your own walk with God, to get the focus off your friends or mate and get it on yourself. To get the focus off your friends or mate and get it on yourself, of course, does not mean to become selfish or to live for yourself, but that you cannot push or shove another person toward spiritual maturity, nor are you responsible for anyone else in the spiritual realm. You must operate under such principles as: "Work out your salvation with fear and trembling;" (Phi 2:12)

> "Who are you to judge the servant of another? To his own master he stands or falls; and stand he will, for the Lord is able to make him stand." (Rom 14:4)

> "But you, why do you judge your brother? Or you again, why do you regard your brother with contempt? For we shall all stand before the judgment seat of God." (Rom 14:10)

> "So then each one of us shall give account of himself to God." (Rom 14:12)

> "But each one must examine his own work, and then he will have reason for boasting in regard to himself alone, and not in regard to another. For each one will bear his own load." (Gal 6:4-5)

The only thing you can do is to be an inspiration for others to follow, but that also takes a positive attitude toward God from all parties involved.

> "Let your light shine before men in such a way that they may see your good works, and glorify your Father who is in heaven." (Mat 5:16)

Ladies, if your husband is not on board with the plan of God, you can set the example by respecting him while still going forward in the plan of God for your own life. Men may even be won over by the behavior of their wives, even without a word! (1Pe 3:1) Men, if your wife has a negative attitude toward Truth, you just love her and keep moving forward in the plan of God, by operating in your role within the marriage (not complaining but doing what God has mandated you to do) as in 1Co 7:3, "The husband must fulfill his duty to his wife, and likewise also the wife to her husband."

Eph 5:25 "Husbands, love your wives, just as Christ also loved the church and gave Himself up for her;"

Eph 5:28 "So husbands ought also to love their own wives as their own bodies. He who loves his own wife loves himself;"

Col 3:19 "Husbands, love your wives and do not be embittered against them."

1Pe 3:7 "You husbands in the same way, live with your wives in an understanding way, as with someone weaker, since she is a woman; and show her honor as a fellow heir of the grace of life, so that your prayers will not be hindered."

Husbands can still bring glory to God even though their wife may be negative toward the Gospel or negative toward doctrine, by always praying and believing that one day they may eventually see the light and get with the plan of God. If not, if you become the witness God has designed you to be, that is all that counts in the end. Forget past mistakes or worldly counsel and get on board with the plan of God, and that will strengthen your marriage. God designed the union of the man and the woman physically, sexually, soulishly, and even spiritually, yet people do not go to His Word for advice in the area of marriage. As far as dwelling on past mistakes or failures is concerned, that is a sure way to keep a relationship down. Whether you are the innocent party or the guilty party, you have to learn to forgive as Christ forgave and move forward, always remembering how infinitely God has forgiven you! (Luk 7:47)

> "For if you forgive others for their transgressions, your heavenly Father will also forgive you. But if you do not forgive others, then your Father will not forgive your transgressions." (Mat 6:14-15)
>
> "Be kind to one another, tender-hearted, forgiving each other, just as God in Christ also has forgiven you." (Eph 4:32)
>
> "Bearing with one another, and forgiving each other, whoever has a complaint against anyone; just as the Lord forgave you, so also should you." (Col 3:13)
>
> "For as in Adam all die, so also in Christ all will be made alive." (1Co 15:22)

Realize what God has done for you, what the Cross offers you, and how you are washed clean when you go to the Lord. Nothing is more freeing than forgiveness and new opportunities or a fresh new slate, after you have really made a mess out of things in your life! Guilt, shame, and condemnation do nothing to energize the human spirit, it is all bondage and slavery. The principles from the Bible concerning marriage cannot be forced upon someone nor can they be manipulated to happen from the flesh. It is the fruit of the Spirit (Gal 5:22-23) that produces reverence and unconditional love in a marriage, not the efforts of our flesh.

These doctrinal principles happen naturally when a believer is positive toward Truth and spends more time filled with the Holy Spirit than living in the old sin nature. This is why the emphasis is on individual growth and becoming what we are all designed to be in the Angelic Conflict. This type of attitude will help any individual, who is a second witness as an invisible hero, to become a third witness. The ultimate goal is the restoration of the marital relationship as it was originally designed by God before the fall. It takes both the husband and wife working in conjunction to form a spiritual bond that the kingdom of darkness cannot penetrate. When the Christian marriage can rise to a level that it faces attacks and does not fold under cosmic pressure, it is a marriage that can be a powerful witness and stand right on the front line of the angelic battlefield without hesitation. Even the angels observe a woman or man operating in doctrine while engaged in a marriage. What a powerful statement in favor of our Lord!

> "For man does not originate from woman, but woman from man; for indeed man was not created for the woman's sake, but woman for the man's sake. Therefore the woman ought to have a symbol of authority on her head, because of the angels." (1Co 11:8-10)

To become victorious in view of angels may seem overwhelming, but we can receive all the guidance we need from God through the filling of the Holy Spirit and Bible doctrine circulating in our souls. The Word of God gives us those magnificent options called the problem-solving devices (footnote) and all the divine power we need to execute the Pre-designed Plan of God.

For the marriage of two believers to excel and glorify God, it demands the highest form of virtue that has ever existed. Fulfilling this requires the two problem-solving devices known as personal love for God the Father and impersonal love for all mankind. When a woman starts to react to her husband, the solution to her problem is not whose fault it is, but to respond to the Lord Jesus Christ with her personal love for God, and in turn respond to her husband with an impersonal unconditional love. For the man it is a role of leadership, that same role Christ has over the church, as a protector and the one who will sacrifice. We have seen the mandate for a husband is to love the wife. This is a true, honorable, and virtuous love that can express itself through actions like sacrifice and going the extra mile for the wife, believing the best and loving her even when she is wrong in a situation. Even the problem of our nation becoming weaker is at the root a problem with the institution of marriage. We have raised up generation after generation of children without the proper role models or guidelines of the Word of God ingrained in their lives. The breakdown of respect for authority is at the core of a nation that begins to crumble. However, remember that even in the environment of perfection, the human beings involved in the first marriage failed. So, do not be tough on your own marriage or your own mate. Remember that no matter what, leave the past in the dust and press on to the things which lie ahead! (Phi 3:13-14)

A divine institution is established as a guide for all mankind to follow, but a Christian institution is for the believer only. Even an unbeliever can have a level of happiness or success when they follow the parameters God has put into place under divine institutions. However, the divine institution of marriage is something God ordained since the beginning of human history, but the Christian marriage is part of the resolution of Satan's trial and has a unique testimony to give. When Adam and the woman fell in the garden, you can see God make modifications within the institution of marriage right on the spot after the fall. For example, sex in the Garden of Eden was for recreation only, for refreshment for a husband and wife. After the fall and subsequent spiritual death, a second purpose was added: procreation and perpetuation of the human race. Keep in mind that God knew in eternity past that mankind would need a solution for the angelic trial to have its time and witnesses for the courtroom battle ahead. Once again we see God multi-tasking and dealing with several solutions that all fix a certain problem or future event as only He can do. One swipe of God's finger and a thousand solutions play out to many different problems all connecting and converging with perfect timing and divine endings in a manner that escapes the mental capacity of the human mind.

Marriage has always held a special place in human history and in the eyes of God, but in the Church Age, marriage has become dramatized, as a very special witness for the prosecution, with all angelic eyes upon us. 1Co 4:9 says, "For, I think, God has exhibited us apostles last of all, as men condemned to death; because we have become a spectacle to the world, both to angels and to men."

> "Therefore the woman ought to have a symbol of authority on her head, because of the angels". (1Co 11:10)

> "I solemnly charge you in the presence of God and of Christ Jesus and of His chosen angels, to maintain these principles without bias, doing nothing in a spirit of partiality." (1Ti 5:21)

In the Old Testament, angels used to teach mankind, as with Abraham, Lot, Jacob, Moses, David, etc., but in this dispensation of the Church Age, mankind now teaches the angels, as in Eph 3:10 which says, "so that the manifold wisdom of God might now be made known through the church to the rulers and the authorities in the heavenly places."

Angels did not know about the intimacy of Christian marriage, so they would have to learn that from observing. Angels do not experience the types of relationships and difficulties we have here on earth, so they have to learn from watching human history unfold. In Mat 22:23-30 we once again have the legalistic crowd, the Sadducees, questioning our Lord concerning resurrection and intimate relationships in eternity. During the questions Jesus Christ clearly states that marriage is an earthly vow and angels are not involved in this union.

> "But Jesus answered and said to them, 'You are mistaken, not understanding the Scriptures nor the power of God. For in the resurrection they neither marry nor are given in marriage, but are like angels in heaven.'" (Mat 22:29-30)

Angelic observation and opposition are both at a maximum level in this stage of the conflict; therefore, your marriage and your ability to become a witness all ride on your level of spiritual growth. So, when God allows the kingdom of darkness to thrust you upon the witness stand concerning Christian marriage, will you be ready? This world was designed as a theater or a courtroom for human drama to unfold for all eyes to see, as in 1Co 4:9 "we have become a spectacle to the world, both to angels and to men." The word spectacle is theatron, a theater in the ancient world. The angels observe all the drama in human history and the Angelic Conflict. Angels (1Co 11:10) particularly observe the woman's reflection of her relationship with the Lord as she shows respect to her husband.

To glorify our Lord in view of the angels is an incredible challenge, since it is marriage that causes the most grief and confusion for many people. Marriage is demanding and filled with double-trouble as we are told in 1Co 7:28, "But if you marry, you have not sinned; and if a virgin marries, she has not sinned. Yet such will have trouble in this life, and I am trying to spare you."

In marriage, there are two distinct personalities, two sets of wants and needs, two old sin natures and two sick heads (Isa 1:5) under one roof. If the marriage does not have Christ at the center it is sure to be even more difficult and confusing. True fellowship and friendship is a fantastic thing when it is grounded in Bible doctrine.

> "As for the agreement of which you and I have spoken, behold, the Lord is between you and me forever." (1Sa 20:23)

It is very rare to have true fellowship, because true fellowship is based upon doctrine resident in the soul between people who think with the thoughts of God, that common bond that only the mind of Christ can bring to any relationship in life.

> "I am a companion of all those who fear Thee, And of those who keep Thy precepts." (Psa 119:63)

The kind of people we all need as companions or friends are those who respect God and keep His doctrines. Remember that you become like those you are close to! As the wisdom of David and Solomon tells us:

> "My eyes shall be upon the faithful of the land that they may dwell with me; He who walks in a blameless way is the one who will minister to me. He who practices deceit shall not dwell within my house; He who speaks falsehood shall not maintain his position before me." (Psa 101:6-7)

> "He who walks with wise men will be wise, But the companion of fools will suffer harm." (Pro 13:20)

This passage has a wonderful lesson in friendship woven into it. David had developed a strong bond with Jonathan and he felt closer to him than to any other companion he had.

> "I am distressed for you, my brother Jonathan; you have been very pleasant to me. Your love to me was more wonderful than the love of women." (2Sa 1:26)

This was because of the integrity and trust that David and Jonathan had and the special bond that developed from sharing a relationship with God.

God designed such relationships and intimacy with others from the beginning; however, even in a state of perfection, the man and the woman both failed. This opened the door for marriage to become a divine institution for anyone, not just believers. The unfortunate situation in our day and age is that Satan could take a marriage between unbelievers and compare it to a Christian marriage, and often there would be little or no difference. There are certain standards and doctrinal principles that need to be functioning for the Christian marriage to exceed and surpass the common cosmic marriage, even if the cosmic marriage is based upon the virtue that two unbelievers can attain through following the laws of divine establishment. If such standards are met in a generation, you can count on that generation's being influenced by both unbelievers' obeying and following the laws of establishment and a pivot of mature believers, whose execution of the Predesigned Plan of God brings blessings to fall upon that nation. When those standards disappear you can count on divine discipline to follow. I think you are getting the idea and grasping the magnitude of Christian marriage.

The principles needed in any organization are freedom, authority and values. An organization can be the U.S. Army, the big bank down the street, the small bakery on the corner, or your marriage. The intimacy of a divine relationship like marriage does not exclude it from having the structure of any other organization. In fact, your marriage is designed to prosper when it has structure and the plan of God is at the center. Those three areas again are:

1. The husband's love for himself manifested by his spiritual-self esteem, and his impersonal unconditional love for his wife.

    "Husbands, [impersonally unconditionally] love your wives, just as Christ also loved the church and gave Himself up for her;" (Eph 5:25)

    "So husbands ought also to love [impersonally unconditionally] their own wives as their own bodies. He who loves his own wife loves himself;" (Eph 5:28)

    "Husbands, [impersonally unconditionally] love your wives and do not be embittered against them." (Col 3:19)

2. The wife's unconditional respect for her husband, based on her relationship with Jesus Christ.

   "Wives, {be subject} to your own husbands, as to the Lord." (Eph 5:22)

   "But as the church is subject to Christ, so also the wives {ought to be} to their husbands in everything." (Eph 5:24)

   "Wives, be subject to your husbands, as is fitting in the Lord." (Col 3:18)

   "In the same way, you wives, be submissive to your own husbands so that even if any of them are disobedient to the word, they may be won without a word by the behavior of their wives," (1Pe 3:1)

3. Forgiveness. This one is the one that seems to be ignored the most. Before you start to harbor any bitterness in your marriage toward your mate, it is wise to remember the words of our Lord in the Gospels. For example, Mat 18:23-35 is a powerful picture of our Lord's forgiveness toward us and how we are to reflect that to others.

   "For if you forgive others for their transgressions, your heavenly Father will also forgive you. But if you do not forgive others, then your Father WILL NOT forgive your transgressions." (Mat 6:14-15)

   Many individuals have been so hurt in their marriage and have put limits upon their forgiveness toward their mate, and yet they forget . . .

   "Then Peter came and said to Him, 'Lord, how often shall my brother sin against me and I forgive him? Up to seven times?' Jesus said to him, 'I do not say to you, up to seven times, but up to seventy times seven.'" (Mat 18:21-22)

The number seventy times seven refers to no limits on forgiveness. However, forgiveness does not necessarily mean reconciliation and having to stay in the marriage. There may be too many wounds and scars which are almost impossible to heal. The real issue is operating in grace orientation, impersonal love, and occupation with the Lord Jesus Christ which glorifies God in the Angelic Conflict. Remember, both the elect and fallen angels are watching, learning grace and seeing the very love and forgiveness of God being manifested in the marriage. Both the filling of the Spirit and the Word of God are being magnified as God is being glorified in the courtroom trial of the Angelic Conflict.

> "God is spirit, and those who worship Him must worship in spirit and truth." (Joh 4:24)

The believer in the Christian marriage as a member of the Church Age operates with the fantastic invisible assets made available only to believers in the Church Age. These include the Baptism of the Spirit, the Indwelling of the Trinity, Mystery Doctrine of the Church Age, and Divine Omnipotence. All of these give believers the power to accomplish commands like Eph 4:32, "Be kind to one another, tender-hearted, forgiving each other, just as God in Christ also has forgiven you." And then Eph 5:1, "Therefore be imitators of God, as beloved children." Notice that being kind to one another, tender-hearted, forgiving each other, makes us imitators of God and beloved children who "walk in love, just as Christ also loved you and gave Himself up for us, an offering and a sacrifice to God as a fragrant aroma," (Eph 5:2).

> "So, as those who have been chosen of God, holy and beloved, put on a heart of compassion, kindness, humility, gentleness and patience; bearing with one another, and forgiving each other, whoever has a complaint against anyone; just as the Lord forgave you, so also should you." (Col 3:12-13)

Notice that having a heart of compassion and forgiveness reflects the character and soul of Jesus Christ, who graciously gave Himself up for us (even the angels watch this closely!). If more Christian marriages operated under divine power and spiritual growth, those believers would glorify God in the realm of the Angelic Conflict. For any organization to succeed it has to recognize a final or ultimate authority as well as offer freedom for growth and creativity. But freedom without authority is anarchy, just like authority without freedom is tyranny. Many so-called leaders do not understand authority or simply abuse it to hold power over others. To avoid anarchy, freedom must have values, and authority must have virtue to avoid tyranny. The authority in marriage belongs to the husband, but this authority must be exercised in virtue love with integrity. This is when personal love for God provides motivation as well as leadership within the marriage. The freedom aspect belongs to both husband and wife, but is highlighted here to allow the man to realize that the wife is not a slave or servant given to him by the divine power of God. No one in marriage should be forced or manipulated by the other out of their personal rights. The husband should never become a tyrant who strips his wife of freedom, which we all truly value. Friendship, love, or intimacy cannot survive under the pressure of a dictator. A woman will lose her love for a man that violates certain principles like freedom or forgiveness.

Therefore, Eph 5:25 says, "Husbands, love your wives, just as Christ also loved the church and gave Himself as a substitute for her."

God does not assign a leadership role without responsibility. The husband really needs to understand love and forgiveness and not allow temper tantrums and bitterness to get into his soul. The woman is to respect and honor the authority of the husband (Eph 5:33). A wife must adjust her life to revolve around her husband and not expect him to adjust and revolve around her. A good soldier or employee anticipates what their authority will need to succeed and then prepares or operates accordingly. The third law, forgiveness, can help with the first two laws mentioned. Often it will be this third law of forgiveness that will save the marriage.

Gentlemen, you cannot expect a woman to respond to your soul when it is filled with anger, bitterness, jealousy, or any of the mental attitude garbage of this world. The soul is where the real spiritual connection takes place. This is where the right man and right woman will recognize each other. The problem is that we destroy or chip away at this ability to recognize the right one if we allow the world's viewpoint and patterns to infiltrate our souls. Premarital sex is the big culprit in destroying this recognition mechanism and causes grief and confusion even after finding the right one. The world system will set you up for unrealistic expectations and allow your soul to harden, becoming vile and vindictive as well as implacable. Any man will have a hard time loving a worldly woman with a tainted soul. And a woman must have freedom in a relationship to respond to the man. This all points back to Satan's cosmic system failing miserably to replace the perfection God offers us. The highest form of love between human beings is found in the woman as a responder and the cosmic system slowly takes that away from her.

In marriage, virtue and values always meet in one place, coalescence of bodies and coalescence of souls. Most people have unrealistic expectations of others and especially what marriage should live up to in their lives. The freedom that Bible doctrine offers, if you grow in it, will take pressure off the marriage. The wife will not lose respect for the husband and the husband will not fall out of love for the wife, because the focus is on the Lord and not the flesh of the mate! When expectations are removed and forgiveness flows freely in a relationship both parties begin to relax and enjoy the relationship more. Look, in less than a hundred years (Mat 22:30), you are not going to be married to that person anymore. So, for some, the agony and suffering will be over forever and for others the love boat will dock permanently. For those of you who love to be in love and are forever tangled up in infatuation, it will be over and men, that means no more flowers or chocolate because Valentine's day will cease to exist. For the people that live for today or are so wrapped up in human relationships and worldly lusts, the shock of it all coming to an abrupt end when Christ returns might be overwhelming. Sadly enough many believers are really just living as worldly individuals wrapped up in the details and emotions attached to the devil's world. They are the ones who will be surprised when the Angelic Conflict comes to its final dramatic conclusion.

So your motivation is vital: what do you seek day in and day out? Is it the promises of the world that you seek, the opportunity for riches and pleasure that motivates you? So, at this point, you have realized that the Christian marriage is unique and of great importance in the overall view of human history and you know why! You now see the Christian marriage as the third witness in the Angelic Conflict, why we have been created! This helps remove any hypersensitivity between husband

and wife because you are working for a greater cause, your focus is on glorifying God, not on what you can get from the relationship. When your own happiness and desires become secondary in the marriage, only then can the marriage escalate to a spiritual level that is beyond human comprehension. You will then find true happiness that can only come from your relationship with God.

The happiness that many people seek from marriage actually first comes from a personal relationship with God, and is not to be sought out with another person. No one should be expected to be someone else's happiness! If you are not content by yourself in difficult times, you certainly will not be content with another person in those same difficult times.

> "Not that I speak from want, for I have learned to be content in whatever circumstances I am. I know how to get along with humble means, and I also know how to live in prosperity; in any and every circumstance I have learned the secret of being filled and going hungry, both of having abundance and suffering need." (Phi 4:11-12)

It is amazing how the world seeks marriage counsel from so-called experts, but the Bible used a man that quite possibly was a bachelor or from many accounts, was single for most of his life, as the marriage expert. Paul's conclusion was that he could do all things through Christ who strengthened his soul. Let us look at a few other counseling statements from the Biblical marriage expert Dr. Paul.

> "Are you bound to a wife? Do not seek to be released. Are you released from a wife? Do not seek a wife. But if you marry, you have not sinned; and if a virgin marries, she has not sinned. Yet such will have trouble in this life, and I am trying to spare you." (1Co 7:27-28)

Can that be any clearer for those that feel a need to be married soon or a need to jump from one relationship to the next? It states that there will be trouble. Two old sin natures that are under one roof does not equal peace and harmony. For most people marriage becomes a distraction or their main priority so that everything else falls by the wayside.

> "But this I say, brethren, the time has been shortened, so that from now on those who have wives should be as though they had none." (1Co 7:29)

This is not Paul telling men to neglect their wives but that our focus should be on Jesus Christ. This is a reminder of how easily we become distracted from the plan of God and pulled away from our calling. Your marriage will not be important one hundred years from now, and it should not be the center of your life, our lives should revolve around Jesus Christ alone.

Col 3:1-3: "Therefore if you have been raised up with Christ, keep seeking the things above, where Christ is, seated at the right hand of God. Set your mind on the things above, not on the things that are on earth. For you have died and your life is hidden with Christ in God."

We tend to put the emphasis on the temporary items of this world. The things we see in front of us seem so important but have little value in the eternal state.

> "But have nothing to do with worldly fables fit only for old women. On the other hand, discipline yourself for the purpose of godliness;" (1Ti 4:7)

> "... for bodily discipline is only of little profit, but godliness is profitable for all things, since it holds promise for the present life and also for the life to come." (1Ti 4:8)

Enjoy one another now in time, forget the insignificant flaws and failures, and just focus on your part in the angelic trial. Ladies, in eternity it will not matter that he leaves the toilet seat up after he is done in the bathroom. Men, it will not matter that she takes an hour to get ready every time you leave the house together. Learn to live for Christ and watch your relationship take on a new light, as you live in light of eternity. Paul describes how useless the folly and efforts of this world are in 1 Corinthians 7:30, and he makes the point that living for anything other than Christ is futile.

> "And those who use the world (worldly viewpoint), as though they did not make full use of it; for the form of this world is

passing away. But I want you to be free from concern (anxiety, worry). One who is unmarried is concerned about the things of the Lord, how he may please the Lord; but one who is married is concerned about the things of the world, how he may please his wife, and his interests are divided." (1Co 7:31-33)

A poet once wrote, "Only one life, 'twill soon be past, only what's done for Christ will last!" In our lives, truly only what is done *by* Christ will last. The fruit of the Spirit, Gal 5:22-23, developed in us by the power and the Word of God, is what glorifies our Lord and lasts forever.

Then Paul states how the human mind is easily divided or drawn away from the relationship with Christ when we are not single.

> "This I say for your own benefit; not to put a restraint upon you, but to promote what is appropriate and to secure undistracted devotion to the Lord." (1Co 7:35)

The Greek word for undistracted is the adjective aperispastos meaning to be free from domestic problems, free from household duties and chores of family or home. It also points to a fatigue that comes from worry or anxiety. Now, the word for devotion is the Greek adjective euprosedos, meaning to sit with relaxation and confidence (as Mary did in Luk 10:38-42), also meaning to be steady and attentive or diligent. This really is saying "having your undivided attention." It is interesting how a celebrity can go on trial and millions of eyes are glued to the TV set, yet God is offering all of us an opportunity to be involved in the greatest trial in human history and the majority simply reject the offer. So many believers and unbelievers are too busy and occupied with family, business, and what society has to offer to even recognize their role in the Angelic Conflict, and that is truly pathetic.

The Lord has a way of dealing with the excuse crowd, the "yeah but" group. In Luk 14:21 He told the servant to go out and get the poor, the blind, and crippled and He will use them! That is why 1Co 1:27 carries so much weight, because Jesus Christ will use the weak to confound the strong, the fools to shame the wise ones of the world.

> "But God has chosen the foolish things of the world to shame the wise, and God has chosen the weak things of the world to shame the things which are strong," (1Co 1:27)

The Lord does not need the powerful worldly men or women, in fact they usually have no humility and lack the proper motivation to be used in the plan of God. All of this is an example of why you need to be mature in the Word of God before you are married, because it will be a distraction or it can lead you astray from your calling within your church. Marriage can be a great blessing or a painful curse, and it all depends upon the two people involved and where they stand in their relationship with God. This subject should inspire you to focus in on your place as the second witness in the conflict, becoming the invisible hero God initially designed all of us to be. You may even be in a horrible marriage and become a great witness because of it! If you marry a negative person, it is no excuse for you to become negative and lose your rewards in time and eternity. You have the power to fulfill God's plan for your life in a good marriage or a bad marriage. No one should hold your fate and your happiness within their hand, no one should become a slave to someone's mood or a bad environment. Being married to an unbeliever or negative believer is an opportunity for spiritual growth, not grounds for divorce.

> "But to the rest I say, not the Lord (the Lord did not cover this in His earthly ministry), that if any brother has a wife who is an unbeliever, and she consents to live with him, he must not divorce her. And a woman who has an unbelieving husband, and he consents to live with her, she must not send her husband away." (1Co 7:12-13)

The world system has designed the throw-away relationship, not God. Divorce is the last resort in a very difficult marriage that has no other avenue to go down. In fact, in the Bible, there are only a few principles that approve of divorce at all. When you face the issue of a spouse telling you to choose him or her over the Word of God you can refer to Act 5:29, "We must obey God rather than men."

Ladies, it is not disrespectful to study Bible doctrine on your own time, it is part of the plan of God to grow up spiritually and to obey God rather than man. When an unbelieving spouse sees how you treat him because of the Word of God he may just have a change of heart.

> "In the same way, you wives, be submissive to your own husbands so that even if any of them are disobedient to the word, they may be won without a word by the behavior of their wives, as they observe your chaste and respectful behavior." (1Pe 3:1-2)

What wife would not want a loving husband who will go that extra mile for her, and what husband would not want a wife who respects him and treats him as the king of the household? And ladies the next few verses cover the fact that you should make an attempt at looking good for your husband and having that gentle and kind spirit because it is just such things that are considered precious in the sight of the Lord.

> "Your adornment must not be merely external—braiding the hair, and wearing gold jewelry, or putting on dresses; but let it be the hidden person of the heart, with the imperishable quality of a gentle and quiet spirit, which is precious in the sight of God." (1Pe 3:3-4)

Your spiritual growth can even bless your family as this next verse points out.

> "For the unbelieving husband is sanctified through his wife, and the unbelieving wife is sanctified through her believing husband; for otherwise your children are unclean, but now they are holy (sanctified or blessed by association). Yet if the unbelieving one leaves, let him leave; the brother or the sister is not under bondage in such cases, but God has called us to peace. For how do you know, O wife, whether you will save your husband? Or how do you know, O husband, whether you will save your wife?" (1Co 7:14)

So once again it is the spiritual growth of the individual that is the key, that is really all we can account for in the end. No one is responsible for your spiritual life but you! Only eternity will reveal the impact you had as a spiritual believer glorifying God in even the most challenging relationships in life!

Chapter 9

The Strategic Victory of the Angelic Conflict

The strategic victory of the Angelic Conflict in human history can simply be summed up in two words: The Cross. As we begin this chapter, there needs to be clarity and definition of our Lord's work upon the Cross and His saving ministry. This needs to be clearly understood when defining the Lord's humanity as being judged for our sins on the Cross. It is my intention in this book to make certain you know why He did the work as well. All have sinned and fallen short of the glory of God. The term "all" here refers to those who are born into sin (human race) or have chosen to sin (angelic race), as was made clear in previous chapters.

So with all creatures unable to avoid sin, we had a dilemma that only a divine solution could resolve. The Cross not only solved all problems in this area, but It was also the strategic victory that God implemented in eternity past.

> "And when you were dead in your transgressions and the un-circumcision of your flesh (your human nature is unacceptable to God), He (God the Father) made you alive together with Him (Jesus Christ), having forgiven us all our transgressions, having

canceled out the certificate of debt consisting of decrees against us, which was hostile to us; and He has taken it out of the way, having nailed it to the cross." (Col 2:13-14)

The verbal construction "having cancelled" is the aorist active participle from ezaleipho meaning to blot out, to cancel, to erase, to eradicate, or to obliterate. The term was actually used as a gambling statement, used when a debt or an IOU was cancelled. It has the meaning of a pressure situation or an overwhelming burden being dealt with, so the IOU gets paid for you. The fact that this type of IOU was taken care of, completed, and cancelled out should be a great relief to the one in debt. It was removed permanently, never to be brought up again. Notice in verse 14, the sentence reads, "He has taken it out of the way," which is referring to sins (it) or a debt that was surely owed.

In fact, this verse implies a certificate of debt consisting of decrees against us. Before it was removed or cancelled, God had to blot out or cancel this debt by paying it or washing it away with some power. The aorist tense speaks of that point in time when the entire IOU was paid or wiped clean. So this phenomenal pressure and deep debt is removed for the entire human race. This means all human beings from the beginning of time right up to the moment of the last judgment had this real IOU or debt, that hung around their necks, removed with one act. This divine, supernatural act of grace is revealed by His work on the Cross. The Cross cancelled out everything on the human debt list. As noted in verse 13, when we were dead in our transgressions, He (God) made us alive together with Christ. We not only have been graciously forgiven but He also made you alive together with Him.

Satan hates the work that Christ preformed upon the Cross, and he spent all his time in the Old Testament trying to cause that event to never come to pass. Satan was furious when the cancellation of sins within human history from the past and present as well as future was completed and wiped off the table in the courtroom. What many believers do not realize is that their first point of contact with God is with His justice, not His love. The Cross is where the justice of God was the first divine attribute that had to be completely satisfied with the sinless perfect offering of the humanity of our Lord Jesus Christ.

"For we do not have a high priest who cannot sympathize with our weaknesses, but One who has been tempted in all things as {we are, yet} without sin." (Heb 4:15)

"Who (Jesus Christ) committed no sin, nor was any deceit found in His mouth; (1Pe 2:22)

"For Christ also died for sins once for all, the just for the unjust, in order that He might bring us to God, having been put to death in the flesh, but made alive in the spirit;" (1Pe 3:18)

"He made Him who knew no sin to be sin on our behalf, so that we might become the righteousness of God in Him." (2Co 5:21)

"For it was fitting that we should have such a high priest, holy, innocent, undefiled, separated from sinners and exalted above the heavens;" (Heb 7:26)

These passages and many others teach that God was completely satisfied with His judgment of His Son upon the Cross, which completely covered any issue with sin. The only sin that was left was the sin of unbelief in His Son. Our Lord completely solved every last detail and planned it all out in eternity past. When you study the essence of God you have to be mindful of the divine order and the perfect steps that God the Father takes to operate even in the smallest realm of life. When you look at the essence of God, His divine nature and His mode of working are beyond what we as limited, flawed creatures can comprehend. We can never put God in a box and must always settle on the conclusion that He is infinite and more complex then we will ever understand, even in eternity we will fall far short of ever really grasping His depths and ways.

"Oh, the depth of the riches both of the wisdom and knowledge of God! How unsearchable are His judgments and unfathomable His ways!" (Rom 11:33)

What we can conclude is the certainty that His essence is revealed in time. The Cross was payment in full and complete satisfaction to God the Father. God is perfect righteousness, so He cannot have fellowship with anything but righteousness. The work on the Cross is the point of contact for all flawed creatures to become righteous through Jesus Christ, gaining perfect righteousness for fellowship with God the Father. This is why we have some interesting principles of doctrine along with some interesting questions that we will deal with later on in this book.

Here is a little taste of coming attractions or questions and thoughts some of you may have.

One key word in the Bible is HOLY, the translation of the Greek adjective dikaios, used to express the uniqueness of the Lord Jesus Christ. The word is used eight times in the Scriptures for the Lord Jesus Christ. Two of the key verses are found in Rev 15:4 and 16:5.

> "Who will not fear, O Lord, and glorify Your name? For You alone are holy; For ALL THE NATIONS WILL COME AND WORSHIP BEFORE YOU, FOR YOUR RIGHTEOUS ACTS HAVE BEEN REVEALED." (Revelation 15:4)

> "And I heard the angel of the waters saying, "Righteous are You, who are and who were, O Holy One, because You judged these things; (Rev 16:5)

Only the Lord Jesus Christ remains experientially holy, yet in four verses this word is used as an adjective for angelic beings. If Jesus Christ is called the only Holy One (Rev 15:4) which can only refer to the fact that He alone is the Only One who remains experientially holy, and the elect angels are called holy, how can this be unless they were made holy after they were found unholy? There is a syllogism in this i.e. the fact that Jesus Christ is the only Holy One. Since others, men, angels, things are called holy, His unique holiness must be in that it is perpetual, not merely present. Angels are called holy and thus must have been made holy from a status of not being holy, just like the Christian. In Rev 7:10-12 resurrected believers praise the Lord for salvation and the angels join in by twice saying "amen" in which they concur, agree, express that they believe it! Believe what? Salvation. They say "amen" concerning salvation because they personally understand it. In the Tribulation, while angels bring divine judgment upon the earth, no angel is allowed to execute this judgment apart from Jesus Christ because He alone is worthy (see Rev 5:2-5). In Psa 89:5-8, "No one is perfect but Jesus Christ."

Not only is God just and holy, but God is also Omnipotent (all powerful). He has the power to do whatever He wants to do for us, but before He can use that power for us, His justice has to be satisfied. God is also Sovereign, but before God can operate from His sovereign will on our behalf, propitiation must take place. He is Omniscience (all knowing), using this power to recognize any problem or difficulty before it ever occurs. God has all solutions but the solutions are useless unless God's justice is first propitiated. God is Immutability (unchangeable). He cannot change; therefore, He could never have fellowship with sinners unless the justice of God had already bridged that great gap between flawed creature and perfect Creator. He is love, but His love cannot step into action until the justice side of the situation is satisfied. God is Veracity (Truth), but His Truth cannot be given to us until the justice is completed. God is Omnipresence (everywhere), and though this never changes in the lives of creatures positive or negative, He cannot come in to comfort us unless His justice approves. God is Eternal Life, but He can never give that to anyone until justice is met. So by this simple breakdown of the essence of God, we can see that sins are not the issue. The Cross wiped sins off the face of any legal document that Satan brings to the divine courtroom, in justification God has legally declared every believer perfectly righteous. He is free to give us His perfect righteousness because He is totally satisfied with the work of His Son paying for all sins on the Cross. (In time, whenever any believer confesses sins he is restored to fellowship with God, so even in our experience in time, we do not have to let our sins separate us from walking in fellowship with our Lord.) Our certificate of debt has been forever cancelled! This leaves only one sin as an issue for definite entry into the lake of fire, the sin of unbelief.

> "He who believes in Him is not judged; he who does not believe has been judged already, because he has not believed in the name of the only begotten Son of God." (Joh 3:18)

Now the certificate of debt consisting of decrees against us and which was hostile to us is made up of certain principles such as the fact that we owe God perfect righteousness and a perfect life and there is no way to pay off that debt. This is totally impossible to pay because this IOU of fallen man is nothing that any creature can work off. We were born hopeless and helpless as sinners and we are saved by grace, not earned or deserved, just freely given and available upon the simple agreement that Christ is the God-man who is our Savior. No good deed, no system, no concept or guilty feeling wipes the slate of unbelief clean. This barrier is too high and too wide for us to overcome in our flesh. God has broken that wall down and left an entrance into the divine side of eternity if we are willing to join Him there.

God was able to do all this without compromising His divine nature and character, at the same time as He also left open an arena for Satan to state his case and to have his shot at the title. If you do not understand the grace of God in all that took place on the Cross, you will be a sucker for pseudo—systems of spirituality and false concepts of fellowship with God. In fact, many so-called normal folks get pretty crazy when they begin to buy into works programs and false concepts of Christianity. The fact is that most believers who do not begin to metabolize real Truth and solid doctrinal food after salvation are simply babes in the cosmic system and will be sucked up into some type of false teaching sooner or later. We were designed to live on Bible doctrine. Those that do not sadly end up starving to death spiritually, they eventually go from being nice, normal Christians with right motivation to being loonies and weirdoes, and no one wants to have a conversation with them. Sometimes they end up on the extreme end of the spectrum involved in activist groups that become violent or very confrontational people. The Bible states in Mat 4:4 that man should not live on bread alone but from the words that proceed from the mouth of God.

> "I have not departed from the command of His lips; I have treasured the words of His mouth (doctrine) more than my necessary food." (Job 23:12)

It is only the grace of God that can turn spiritually dead, deeply indebted creatures into noble, royal priests in time (not just in eternity) for all the angels to witness. The debt that was so hostile and negative for us was nailed to the Cross and taken out of the way (Col 2:14), this is the evident cancellation of our sins and a fatal stab into the side of Satan. This cancellation was like a heavyweight body blow, delivered with precision, speed, and accuracy upon a frail opponent. I can just see Satan and the whole kingdom of darkness seething with rage, wondering what are they going to do now as they felt that strike in their gut, and it rattled them and brought them to their knees. As fierce and devastating as the Cross is in the Angelic Conflict, the fact is that most believers do not even recognize the work upon the Cross. This is a credit to Satan's tireless efforts to blind the human race from Truth. The world has several religious programs that fill believers up with guilt, leaving them feeling condemned, or ashamed, and many arrogant believers follow right along with the façade, buying into that program. These are people who know nothing of grace or of the work upon the Cross.

Heb 8:12 tells us, "For I will be merciful to their iniquities, And I will remember their sins no more." Hebrews 10:17 says God will forget the lawless deeds and sins. Mic 7:18-19 tells us that God is said to not only pass over our rebellious acts, but to pardon our sins and cast them out to sea! Where do believers, and worse yet some Christian spiritual leaders, get the guilt and shame-game from? Guilt and shame have a tendency to develop two types of thought patterns within most people because they bring a person to a weak point, where they feel so low about self that they have to make a change (in their own strength), or they simply dwell in it and fall into depression. Most people will end up driving themselves away from God and His plan and they will use one of two thought patterns. The first is the "I'm not good enough, never will be, so screw this religion crap!" The second is the "little engine who could" thought pattern. Here people chug upward out of guilt and shame by using programs, human power, and any other fleshly technique they can find in the world. All the while saying, "I know I can, I think I can, I know I can," but none of it touches the grace of God or taps into the power of the Holy Spirit. It is a human works program and will always lead to the arrogant statement of "Look what I did!" In reality all they did was to clean themselves up for the devil's world. No glory to God, and this points directly back to the five "I wills" of Satan.

Sin-conscious people cannot have a solid relationship with God, their fellowship is hindered by guilt and shame because anything that is not of faith is sin. Satan has designed the world system around blinding people from the Truth of salvation and the Truth of grace. When Satan cannot blind someone, he will do everything in his power to help them forget, or cloud the Truth, to keep them confused. God has stated since the beginning of human history that sins are not the issue. We can see that from Old Testament verses such as Isa 38:17 and Psa 103:12, where God is said to have cast sins behind His back and removed them as far as the east is from the west. In fact any study of Abraham, Jacob, and David (to name just a few) shows God's grace toward sinners, blotting out huge errors and flaws in which these men willingly operated during their spiritual walk.

> "He has not dealt with us according to our sins, nor rewarded us according to our iniquities." (Psa 103:10)

In Psa 85:2 God is said to cover our sins as well as to forgive what we have done against Him. Similar verses you can study in the New Testament apply even more to the Church Age. In Rom 11:27 it is said that God takes away sins. Even Paul quoted David from Psa 32 where it reads; "Blessed are those whose lawless deeds have been forgiven, whose sins have been covered."

The problem for most believers is that they buy into the lies of the kingdom of darkness. This shows the magnificent blinding effect that Satan has brought to bear in this world concerning the work of Jesus Christ upon the Cross. You may read this and think, "What have I done to deserve all my sins being forgiven?" The answer is nothing!

> "Your sins are forgiven for His name's sake." (1Jo 2:12)

No wonder why Satan hates the Cross. It could not be made any easier, nor could there be a swifter technique to deal with sins than by this act of gracious forgiveness by God, offered to fallen man by a simple acknowledgment. When we think of love and grace we cannot ask for God's character and nature to be any more deeply rooted in these virtues than what He shows us at the Cross. As we delve deeper into Colossians and get into Col 2:15 we can see the victory of the Angelic Conflict at hand.

"When (at the Cross) He (God the Father) had disarmed the rulers and authorities (fallen angels), He made a public display of them (all angels), having triumphed over them through Him." (Col 2:15)

God has disarmed the rulers and authorities or the angelic forces of evil which are all under Satan's rule. The Cross truly broke the back of Satan, and God did this while cancelling out sin and reconciling fallen man to His Royal Family. God defines multi-tasking as He deals with problems, solutions, and future issues with one act that will all intertwine at a later date to fit His perfect plan. You venture a guess as to why the Cross broke the back of Satan if he was already sentenced, and you need look no further than the conflict we are currently encountering. Satan appealed his first judgment in eternity past, the Cross was the place of his second judgment.

When the verse says a public display it comes from the Greek word deigmatizo, meaning to display captives. The triumphant display of captives ("triumphed over them") is a military march or parade that occurred in ancient times when a victorious army came home with the spoils of war and the prisoners were brought into the kingdom. Hence the importance of understanding isagogics, which is a method of interpretation of the Bible. Isagogics is basically having knowledge of the time and historical setting in which a verse was written. The term triumphal procession is the Greek word thriambeuo, a verb used to represent this special exhibition that took place when the Roman army marched in from a victory. It is to be a time of celebration, a victory dance in the form of displaying enemy prisoners and all that the victor has taken from the battle. This is used for a reference to Operation Footstool which began the triumphal procession in heaven and will include a triumphal procession on the earth with the Second Advent of Jesus Christ.

So we can see the importance of this procession in ancient times, but the point here is that it also relates to the Lord Jesus Christ, His resurrection after three days and His ascension to heaven. Christ was on the earth for 40 days before ascending up to the right hand of the Father and He would have been very similar to a returning general, a war hero returning from conquering a battlefield full of enemies, bringing them home in chains. The victory parade would have Satan and his fallen angels trudging out first, most likely escorted by elect angels because angelic convocations include all angels. So there would have been a moment on earth when things were pretty quiet because all the demons were in the procession as the Lord Jesus Christ took His seat upon the throne. The fallen angels would have been allowed back to their activities and a full reign in earth's atmosphere once again until the Second Advent. It is then that Operation Footstool kicks into gear, at which point the thousand year incarceration will begin for the fallen angels. The Lord has had one victory parade already with the kingdom of darkness shackled and beaten, the second will be the final judgment.

As highlighted in Eph 4:8-10, when He ascended on high, He led a host of captives and gave gifts to men. It covers the fact that Christ descended to earth as well as went upward to the heavens with the captives. This is the Lord's triumphant procession through billions of light years of space into the second heaven, or stellar universe, which ended with the Father's command of "Sit down at My right hand." And you will hear and see the Father not only say sit at My right hand but, "Sit down at My right hand until I make Your enemies Your footstool."

Chapter 10

The Importance Of The Hypostatic Union

To begin this chapter we must clarify what the Hypostatic Union is, and what the term truly encompasses, so that there is no confusion as this book progresses. To put it in plain terms it is the two natures of Jesus Christ: the true humanity and the true deity in one body or being, forever! Jesus Christ is the unique God-man, not a mixture of two, but the full concept, power, and ability of God and man in one person. This is not an easy thing to wrap your head around, and it may never fully make sense to the human mind. We are limited creatures in understanding things in the spiritual realm. No matter how far we grow we can never fully reach the level of intellect that can digest every aspect of God. But when you see or hear this term Hypostatic Union the first thought that should come to mind is the Lord Jesus Christ in His unique and divine body.

Jesus Christ is not one-half God and one-half man. He is 100% God and 100% human and will always have a divine nature and a human nature. Christ is so unique that it can sometimes be truly indescribable to the common man. It takes a doctrinal believer with positive volition to grasp this concept and to be able to move forward to study His work on earth, in heaven, and especially upon the Cross. He did not always exist eternally as the God-man but as God.

> "The Jews said to Him (Jesus Christ), 'Now we know that You have a demon. Abraham died, and the prophets (also)'; and You say, 'If anyone keeps My word, he shall never taste death.' Surely You are not greater than our father Abraham, who died? The prophets died too; whom do You make Yourself out (to be)?" (Joh 8:52-53)

Sometimes the Lord would speak from His humanity and other times He would speak from His deity, as here in Joh 8:52-58. In His deity Christ tells the Jewish leaders that He truly knows God because He is God.

The Jews therefore said to Him, "You are not yet fifty years old, and have You seen Abraham?" Jesus said to them, "Truly, truly, I say to you, before Abraham was born, I Am." (Joh 8:57-58)

Jesus Christ is stating that He existed before Abraham ever was on the earth. This type of statement sent the legalistic leaders of that age into fits, because He was pulling doctrine out from the Old Testament referring to the moment when God spoke out to Abraham and Moses. His words were the exact terms that God used to the Old Testament saints, and this was coming from a young man who appeared to be only alive for thirty years. In Joh 10:30 the Lord said from His deity, "I and the Father are one." Then there were times when Jesus spoke from humanity such as the following verse:

> "After this, Jesus (notice He's called Jesus, emphasis on His humanity), knowing that all things had already been accomplished, in order that the Scripture might be fulfilled, said, 'I am thirsty.'" (Joh 19:28)

God does not get thirsty, but in His humanity Jesus Christ does. Though the Hypostatic Union may be difficult to understand in our day and age, imagine the confusion and frustration it must have caused in that time, when the church leaders were not to be questioned! The leaders of church and politics of that day and age were the ultimate in authority, and they were believed to be the closest people to God and His words. This is why their arrogance grew because they were elevated and even elevated themselves to be god-like. But as we are noting in this chapter there is only one being who is both man and true God, and that is Jesus Christ.

We can see the anger it caused when they took up a violent stance against our Lord as in Joh 10:31. The Jews took up stones again to stone Him. Jesus Christ said in His humanity in Joh 14:28, "You heard that I said to you, 'I go away, and I will come to you.' If you loved Me, you would have rejoiced, because I go to the Father; for the Father is greater than I." So, it is vital that you understand the Hypostatic Union because the Scriptures can be twisted to make Jesus Christ appear as only a man, and that is not the case. There were times when He spoke from both His deity and His humanity.

> "What then if you should behold the Son of Man (humanity) ascending where He (deity) was before?" (Joh 6:62)

There are some false teachings that point to Christ as a prophet and not as God. The scripture above (Joh 14:28) speaks of the Son's human nature, not His divine nature. This has to be made clear because to believe that Jesus Christ came to us simply in human form to die for the sins of all mankind is not the full doctrine, and leaves the deity of Christ completely removed from the gift of our salvation. Perhaps you would question why God becomes a man, or why the Son within the divine Trinity becomes a human being. The answer is that Jesus Christ had to become perfect humanity to be our savior, to be the high priest and mediator between God and man. Jesus Christ had to fulfill the Davidic covenant, displaying the truth that a Son (in the line) of David would rule forever.

Jesus Christ as God could have nothing to do with sin. God can only reject or judge sin, it is that simple, only humanity could bear our sins. Jesus Christ stepped forward from the Trinity to receive the imputation of humanity to take the judgment for sins, and He did so with no hesitation. In 1Pe 2:24 it is said that He bore our sins upon the Cross. We see Jesus Christ as this mediator between mankind and God in scriptures such as Job 9:32-33 and

1Ti 2:5-6. To be this type of divine mediator He would have to be both equal to God the Father and also equal to the entire human race!

> "For there is one God, and one mediator also between God and men, the man Christ Jesus." (1Ti 2:5)

Jesus Christ had to become true humanity to be a priest. A priest must be a man in order to represent man before God. Jesus Christ is known as the high priest after the pattern of Melchizedek noted in Heb 7:1-8 and 7:14, as well as Heb 10:5-14. For our Lord to be a king He had to become human, and He had to fulfill the covenant of David, which would show that his humanity was derived from the line of David.

> "Concerning His Son, who was born of a descendant of David according to the flesh." (Rom 1:3)

When studying the Hypostatic Union within Scripture there are many passages that make this point clearly and concisely.

> "In the beginning was the Word, and the Word was with God, and the Word was God." (Joh 1:1)

> "And the Word became flesh, and dwelt among us, and we beheld His glory, glory as of the only begotten from the Father, full of grace and truth." (Joh 1:14)

Passages from Joh 1:1-14, Rom 1:2-5, 1Ti 3:16, Heb 2:14 and Phi 2:5-11 all document the Hypostatic Union in one realm or another.

During the dispensation of the Hypostatic Union the devil made every effort to tempt, torment, and even assassinate in order to stop our Lord and to cancel the work upon the Cross before it would get accomplished. As usual, when the devil and his crew came against the plan of God, they failed. The work that took place on that Cross was the destruction of any military foundation that Satan had laid up to that point. It is most likely at that time of the finished work upon the Cross that Satan and his fallen mob began to truly become desperate and to feel the sting of defeat creeping up on them.

The Angelic Conflict

The temptations that Satan laid out for the humanity of Christ prior to the Cross are proof positive that the kingdom of darkness was on full active duty trying to destroy the grace and salvation power that the Cross would accomplish. We can see three unique temptations from Satan to attempt to distract the humanity of Christ to try to get Him to stumble and fall, as noted in the books of Luke and Matthew. God cannot be tempted, but man can.

In Luk 4:1 we read: "And Jesus, full of the Holy Spirit, returned from the Jordan and was led up by the Spirit in the wilderness." In verse 2 it goes on to say that "He (Jesus) was in the wilderness for forty days and the temptation from the devil was great." This was a temptation to be independent from God the Father. The word used for Jesus is Iesous, meaning Savior, and is never used for the description of Deity but only for the humanity of Christ. The Greek verb for the phrase "was led up" is in the passive voice from the verb "ago" which means the humanity of Christ received the action of that verb as part of a test. He was being led into evidence testing.

When a believer reaches a certain level of maturity, he or she is allowed upon the witness stand in the Angelic Conflict. It is there that Satan and his demons are allowed to push, prod, and test a mature believer. They do so to get a result in their favor, much like a badgering, aggressive lawyer who tries to squeeze a statement from a witness. But with God in the divine seat of judgment we are tested to our limits but not beyond, and it is surprising the limits a mature believer can endure. Satan is allowed much grace in this conflict and will use everything in his dirty book of tricks!

Satan can use disaster, division within relationships, confusion, misunderstandings, as well as being allowed to stoke the fire of someone's old sin nature to get them to fail and leave the plan of God. Very few items are off the list when it comes to witness testing in the conflict. Satan may test your health, or your wealth, as he did with Job, bring in family problems and divisions within your circle of friends, or almost anything to stress your soul and shake your faith. But God knows your strengths and the inner power that you have gained from your relationship with Him. That is why the statement, "Adversity is inevitable, but stress is optional" holds so true in this conflict. It is your mental capacity that is tested most of the time. It is your volition that will fail you, not so much Satan's pressure.

Your turn on the witness stand may come and go quickly, or may be sustained for a longer period, and the trip to that stand is not always a one-time event. Life in the cosmic system is loaded with tiny tests and experiments to see how far you have grown, or if the kingdom of darkness can distract you. God does test His disciples and Satan is allowed to have time to go after you. This is a conflict and also a heated court battle, never lose sight of that fact! We are all responsible for our own growth and free will decisions. So when the time of difficult testing comes it is only the person in the mirror who is to blame for any failure. Failure will happen to flawed human creatures so you can gain knowledge from a mistake, when you rebound, recover, and grow up in the spiritual realm. The human race was created for this conflict and to glorify God in time you must learn to adjust to this invisible warfare, because it is why you are here.

We can witness the growth and spiritual stages our Lord went through when He was on planet Earth. In Luk 2:40 we see Jesus Christ as a child who began to grow strong physically and spiritually, gaining wisdom. The grace of God was upon Him because He pushed forward and gained knowledge about the plan of God for His life.

> "And Jesus kept increasing in wisdom (momentum from the doctrine) and stature, and in favor with God (personal love for the Father) and men (impersonal love for mankind)." (Luke 2:52)

We see spiritual autonomy or a spiritual independence when we see the fact that Jesus kept increasing or growing in the spiritual realm. We can see His maturity or the finished product in Joh 1:14 where it states "the Word became flesh and dwelt among us, and we beheld His glory full of grace and doctrine." Matthew was positive that Jesus was ready to step into the divine position of authority to lead the way when our Lord was baptized. This was the beginning of His ministry among the human race, noted in Mat 3:16-17. The heavens opened up when Jesus came up from the water and the Spirit of God descended down upon Him.

> "Behold a voice out of the heavens, saying, 'This is My beloved Son, in whom I am well-pleased.'" (Mat 3:17)

So we can see that Jesus was ready for the cross-examination (Luk 4). He was well prepared for Satan's barrage of temptations and confusing word games. In Luk 4:2 the word *tempted* is referring to what Satan was doing to Jesus. It comes from the Greek word *peirazo* meaning to make proof of, test, examine, or scrutinize. This was used to describe the enticement employed to test the humanity of Christ, to test the character and virtue He had regarding His dependence upon the Father. If there was no conflict or court case occurring then why was Jesus Christ put in such a position to be tempted? It was God the Holy Spirit leading Jesus into this situation which displays two key points we have been noting: i) first, there is cross examination occurring involving the kingdom of darkness and ii) second, Jesus was mature enough to deal with it. A pastor or a spiritual leader that denies the existence of a conflict or spiritual trial has no clue about the Bible or why we are here on this earth.

> "Make sure no advantage be taken of us by Satan; for we are not ignorant of his schemes." (2Co 2:11)

During this historic trial of the Angelic Conflict it is not God tempting us, but the Holy Spirit who leads us to the test. It is the devil who does the cross examination, not God.

> "Let no one say when he is tempted, 'I am being tempted by God', for God cannot be tempted by evil, and He Himself does not tempt anyone.'" (Jam 1:13)

We can see the defense attorney Satan in action during this appeal trial trying to confuse and discredit the chief witness in Luk 4:3 as he tells Jesus, "If You are the Son of God, tell this stone to become bread." Satan knows that the humanity of Christ is very hungry at this point. Jesus Christ could have acted independently from God's plan and put a five course meal in front of both of them with merely a thought. We have already studied how to manipulate and discredit a witness, and we can see the defense attorney working his angles. Satan is once again using

Truth mixed with lies to tempt someone as was the case in the Garden. Satan knows the power of God and realizes what He is capable of and how easily the Lord could make anything appear in an instant, all the while knowing the weakness in the human body and need for food.

Satan opens with a verbal examination, saying, "Ei huios ei tou Theou" which in translation means, "If You are the Son of God, and You are," meaning that Satan certainly recognized Whom he was tempting. The verb "to be" is actually translated "you are" and it is a present active indicative of the Greek word eimi, stating his recognition of who he was dealing with. Again you can see the Truth of doctrine or the weaving of a fact of theology into the sentence, and then he slides in with the temptation or deceptive part. This is why Satan's trump card can be religion because man-made religions and legalistic teachings always have a hint of Truth mixed in with the falsehoods. The moment of testing arrives when the false statement and temptation are put forth and the Lord must choose self-reliance or waiting on God's timing.

> "For we do not have a high priest who cannot sympathize with our weakness, but One who has been tempted in all things, yet without sin." (Heb 4:15)

It is the same for the Church Age believer: do we do it our own way, or do we wait on God and do it His way? Do we become frustrated and snoop around the cosmic system for a quick fix, or do we go to God for all of the solutions? These two questions are the essence of daily life in this angelic court battle. The small battles and tests that later become larger and more potent within the court room is what the conflict truly encompasses. This is why we have access to the history of the Old Testament saints and the one true role model for the Church Age, our Lord and Savior Jesus Christ. It was written for our benefit, for our education, and for the principle of warning us of the schemes of the devil. Never misconstrue the Bible as just another book on ancient history, because it was divinely established and preserved for this conflict and our spiritual growth.

The world teaches us to be cut-throat and to go out and capture all we can while we are here, but how often do we learn to be patient and wait on the timing of God? Human nature has difficulty waiting in line at the grocery store, much less waiting for God to come through when the pressure is really turned on. Ask anyone who has waited for something special and ask if it was worth it, and you will hear testimony after testimony that it was worth the wait!

Jesus could have used His power (deity) to satisfy any need at any time, and it would not have been an act of immorality or evil, yet it would have put him outside the plan of God so that would have been a sin. You may question why an all-powerful God turning a stone into a piece of bread is a sin, yet in this case it would have been. It would have been not only a sin that screamed of independence from the Father, but a sin that would have destroyed human history as we know it. This same sin Satan displayed in perfect environment, independence from the Father. Satan would have loved to be in front of the Supreme Court of Heaven saying, "Look at your Son! He is just like me; He is independent from Your plan."

This is known as the doctrine of kenosis which says that during the dispensation of the Hypostatic Union, our Lord Jesus Christ voluntarily restricted the independent use of His divine attributes in compliance with the Father's plan. Jesus lived among men as an equal, living in limitations, and by doing so He established in His humanity a spiritual life which is an example for the Church Age believer. Certain functions of His deity continued, such as holding the universe together as He operated as a man here on earth. We can see Satan attack His kenosis in this chapter, and that is why it is a unique situation of temptations that He faced. Jesus Christ gave up divine powers and as a man had to operate within the power of the Holy Spirit, and use Biblical problem-solving devices and the power of the Word of God to see Him through. Jesus Christ had to concentrate on the plan that the Father had laid out for Him using His humanity. Jesus Christ metabolized Bible doctrine and circulated doctrines through his soul, then incorporated it into daily life and applied Biblical principles to move His ministry forward. Jesus Christ used problem-solving devices like faith in His Father, power from the Holy Spirit, unconditional love for others, love for the Father, a personal sense of destiny, grace orientation, doctrinal orientation, and sharing the happiness of God. These are all problem-solving devices that we believers have available to us on a daily basis as well. We actually have two more than the ones our Lord used: rebound and occupation with the Lord Jesus Christ. The Lord did not depend on deity to solve His problems, and He is the example to follow.

Jesus Christ stuck to the plan and trusted that God the Father had it all under control. He studied the Word of God daily and then applied it to His life. This is all that we need to do to become aware of the schemes of the devil and to stand in the gap during this conflict. When and if God decides to remove us from the pressure situation it is His volition, and all a part of His plan. Whatever God does not remove you from, He intends for you to bear it. Jesus Christ refused to function independently of the Father's plan and at no time did He rely upon His own omnipotence during the incarnation.

We can recognize that the sin of independence is usually not an overt one like sins of the tongue or adultery. However, it carries the same weight or even more so than overt sins, because it is a mental separation from God. This is why at times you need to evaluate the distractions in your life like work, marriage, friendships, social life, or career goals. None of these are considered sin, but they can take you away from the plan of God. Anything that pulls you away from God and puts the plan of God at the bottom of life's priority list could be the tool Satan is using to get you to become independent from the Creator. Once you become independent from God you are living in the same sin as Satan. What we see here is the humanity of Christ passing the test without calling upon His Father or His own deity to remove Him from the situation. Jesus Christ stuck to the plan and remained in the faith, knowing that the Father is in control of the situation.

We let the little things distract us, yet Jesus Christ had Satan himself attacking His humanity at a point of weakness. In 2Ti 2:4 it says not to get entangled in the affairs of everyday life. In Luk 8:14 it states that worry and riches and the pleasures of this life will choke us and we will not bring forth fruit. We can never face the temptations that Christ did because for most believers Satan will never attack them directly. Jesus Christ was unique and had the ability to snap His fingers and have stones turned into food, we do not have that power. You can spend your bread to get stoned, but you will never be able to tell a stone to become bread! The fact that we are not deity, and that Satan can only be in one place at one time can reassure us of the fact that we will get little direct attention from Satan himself. Satan is not going to chase after John Doe the positive believer directly, but he does have an army of demons that can antagonize, test, and gather information on that positive believer.

> "And Jesus answered him, 'It is written, 'Man shall not live on bread alone.'" (Luk 4:4)

Jesus used the most potent weapon that mankind has: Truth! That is what would get Him through the test. In fact Jesus Christ used nothing but doctrine to establish His stand against the devil.

> "It is written, 'You shall worship the Lord your God and serve Him only.'" (Luk 4:8)

> "It is written, 'You shall not put the Lord your God to the test.'" (Luk 4:12)

A miracle is not the answer that removes us from a test or difficulty. In fact, a miracle is not as powerful as faith and operating from a positive position using doctrinal thoughts to bring forth positive actions. When God performs a miracle it requires only His sovereignty. When a positive believer can apply Bible doctrine to a situation it is the highest function that any human being can obtain in this conflict, much greater than God rescuing a believer. How do you think it must appear to the fallen angels when a weaker species can stand against such great attacks by using God's power? Satan is made to look inferior in that situation and all the angels witness it. Instead of relying on human power we rely on God's power, and that shows all who witness the event that God is fair and just, by not interfering yet still giving us the tools and knowledge to guide us through the challenge against a stronger opponent.

The mind of Christ is the Bible, so says Joh 1:1 and 1Co 2:16, so it is there for us to learn and to use to go forward in this battle. Satan hates that a believer can solve his or her own problems with the power of Bible doctrine and the filling of the Holy Spirit. Satan looks like a coach that has a losing team playing against weaker opponents. It is the equivalent of a local high school football team beating up on the Super Bowl champs. This knowledge and power that the Bible can give to a believer is something that has the kingdom of darkness in a state of frustration every time it is applied. It is God's power being used by weaker creatures against the stronger angelic creatures that not only hate God, but should have an advantage in this conflict.

The unique temptations that are noted in Luk 4:1-13 and also in Mat 4:1-11 were designed by Satan to get the humanity of Jesus to operate in the deity of the Lord Jesus Christ to halt the plan of God. This would have given Satan his opportunity in the courtroom to shout out, "Guilty! Unfair, You have been unjust and unfair as I pointed out from the beginning of time!" Notice that the Lord did not use prayer or miracles to escape the scrutiny of Satan, Jesus used the Word of God and applied it precisely. Most people seek out God for their rescue and do so wishing on a miracle or dropping to their knees in prayer asking God to remove the situation. We see our role model Jesus Christ operating in an intelligent, cool headed-manner using only the words of the Father as His defense. Jesus met the challenge head on with Truth from the only source of Truth, the Bible! There were no angles or false solutions needed when dealing directly with Satan himself, only divine power from the Father. To pray for strength in time of suffering is blasphemous since under the Pre-designed Plan of God, strength is provided in another way, through the power of the Spirit (Act 1:8) and the power of the Word of God (Heb 4:12). We can also see that God knew His Son had reached a level of spiritual maturity to be able to sit face to face with Satan and be tempted, tested, and put on display in the courtroom. You see, a miracle is the easy way out, the simple solution, and it only takes God's will and omnipotence to perform. Paul prayed for the removal of a thorn in the flesh, as we can see in 2Co 12, and this was a false solution as Paul would learn. It is the grace of God that is sufficient to get us through the difficult times as he was reminded.

For God to give maximum blessing to a believer or even to reconcile a broken relationship is much more difficult than God turning a stone into bread. This is because in the case of blessing and reconciliation it takes the creature's free will to line up with God's will for that to take place. A miracle proves nothing in the Angelic Conflict. It only shows God coming to the rescue of mankind, and gives Satan more ammunition to promote negative propaganda toward the Father. We are not designed to be helpless in the battle, we are equipped for spiritual warfare and we are to stand firm in our faith proving the kingdom of darkness to be wrong. It has been allotted for every believer to have his or her battle and stand against the powers of this world.

> "For to you it has been granted for Christ's sake, not only to believe in Him, but also to suffer for His sake." (Phi 1:29)

We are commanded to suffer hardship in the spiritual battle as good soldiers for Christ in 2Ti 2:3. If Satan can wear you down and get that beaten, defeated nature to arise within your soul, you will eventually detach from God's plan and begin to attach yourself to the ways of the world. This is the sin of independence we have noted since chapter one. Our Lord was hungry enough to be tempted to create food from a stone, but He did not separate Himself from the plan of God. He did not act independently, but instead used the power of the Word of God instilled into His human soul. Jesus reached back to a scripture in Deuteronomy 8:3, where it states that "Man cannot live on bread alone but by every word that proceeds out of the mouth of God." This shows that doctrine was the priority and circulating deep within His soul, because the pressure was on and Jesus Christ applied what he had learned.

The Word of God is alive and powerful as noted in Heb 4:12. The power we need to avoid cosmic independent thinking is the WORD! If Satan was so intent on having Christ become independent what makes you think that this is not his plan for believers in the Church Age? This arrogant, independent line of thinking is connected to legalistic people, self-righteous believers, those on the path of crusader arrogance and those living in moral degeneracy. They have a form of godliness but have denied its true power as in 2Ti 3:5. Spiritual victory within the plan of God truly relies upon the Word of God that penetrates ever more deeply within your soul. It is a far greater weapon than any schemes that the kingdom of darkness has developed or any cosmic viewpoints. We are dealing with an army of divinely built creatures of the highest caliber, and we need weapons that will withstand the mental and physical assault that these angelic creatures can use to bombard us. If you had to play a life or death chess match against a genius adversary, would it not be smart to have the training and knowledge given to you before the match? Not just training and knowledge ahead of time, but the training and knowledge from the current chess champion of the universe. Bear in mind that the kingdom of darkness is not only far superior to human beings in almost every aspect, but its agents are invisible and manipulating the majority of people (believers and unbelievers) to fail in this battle. We as believers have the power, but most reject it through negative volition toward the Word of God.

> "You are from God, little children, and have overcome them; because greater is He who is in you than he who is in the world." (1Jo 4:4)

Satan even offered the Lord a chance to by-pass the pain and humiliation of the Cross when he showed Jesus the world that God had allowed him to rule over.

> "And he led Him up and showed Him all the kingdoms of the world in a moment in time. And the devil said to Him, 'I will give You all this domain and its glory; for it has been handed over to me, and I give it to whomever I wish.'" (Luk 4:5-6)

What Satan was attempting was not only to halt the plan of God for the humanity of Christ, but also to cancel the Second Advent and to offer Jesus Christ a chance at being a king right then and there. The Father's plan was for Jesus Christ to receive all the kingdoms of the world after the work on the Cross was complete and after sins and the Angelic Conflict had been resolved. The offer Satan put forth is legitimate, as he has supreme power on planet Earth at this time in human history. Satan has the ability to bless human beings in time when it is connected to worldly desires. But Jesus has so much doctrine that He was well aware that there is no Crown without the Cross!

Satan is willing to promote without the effort or plan of God coming to fruition. This type of promotion is false and typical for the kingdom of darkness, offering a person the reward for no effort or endurance in the plan, believer or unbeliever, deity or humanity. Satan has no shame in his promotional scams. As we move forward to the next verse we see a familiar pattern as Satan uses a third class condition unlike the first class condition we have seen in Luk 4:3 (if you are the Son of God, and You are . . .).

> "Therefore if You worship before me (maybe you will, maybe you will not), it shall be Yours." (Luk 4:7)

The pattern is deception and confusion with the words of Truth and God's plans for our life. Satan does have power in the worldly realm and most believers can be fooled by this fact. When Satan states, "For it has been handed over to me (by Adam), and I give it to whomever I wish," he is relating a true fact. But the pattern of Truth, peppered with lies and deception, is obvious to a trained believer, who will not be twisted and spun sideways like the majority who are blinded by Satan.

Jesus makes it clear that He knows the plan of God for all creatures in verse 8, by stating, "It is written, You shall worship the Lord Your God and serve Him only." This statement is strong and refers more to an obligation or contract to be fulfilled, or a decree of law, than a mere comment that Jesus uttered to His adversary in an attempt to resist temptation. Jesus Christ was letting it be known that God was the author of the plan, the designer of the world, and that Satan offers a false promotion. This was a warning to all of us as well that there is nothing under the sun that Satan can offer that can replace the plan of God.

What we see in these tests are attacks on Christ in His humanity, attacks on God's plan and His Word and attacks on the power of the Trinity. The first temptation tested the Lord's relationship to the ministry of the Holy Spirit (3rd person of the Trinity). The second temptation tested the Lord's relationship to the plan of God the Father for His life (1st person of the Trinity). Now the third test comes in the form of testing the Lord's relationship to the Word of God (Christ, 2nd person of the Trinity).

"And he (Satan) led Him (Jesus) to Jerusalem and had Him stand on the pinnacle of the temple, and said to Him, "If You are the Son of God, throw Yourself down from here." (Luk 4:9)

This word used for *pinnacle* is the Greek noun *pteurgion*, meaning the highest point on a temple. This was Herod's porch which was a 450 foot drop! Satan told Him to jump off, to toss Himself down upon rocks, a 450 foot plunge. Satan, having a great knowledge of doctrine himself, was well prepared for the Deu 8:3 verse that stated that Jesus would only live by the Word of God. Satan followed right on with verses 10 and 11 of Luke 4, saying that he knew the angels of God would rescue Him before a stone would ever touch His feet. It is actually a verse from the book of Psalms that Satan used.

> "No evil will befall you, nor will any plague come near your tent. For He will give His angels charge concerning you, to guard you in all your ways. They will bear you up in their hands, lest you strike your foot against a stone." (Psa 91:10-12)

What the devil wants the humanity of Christ to hear is: "If you live by the Word of God then there is no danger in leaping off a 450 foot porch, so prove it!" What Satan is doing is using correct doctrine with a false application, a distortion of Scripture which is not uncommon in the devil's world. Moses was the likely one to have written this Psalm, and Moses was the one who had written Deu 8 as well. Satan is wise beyond any human comprehension and this is one great example of the mental game he can play with anyone during human history. Keep in mind that he is testing the God-man, Jesus Christ, and not stuttering in his evil game. Makes you wonder how easily he can toy with the human mind that has little or no doctrine to shield it. This temptation is related to false doctrine therefore dealing with the relationship of Bible doctrine. As there is resistance to the devil's word game and deceptive motives we see the entrance of Bible doctrine into the mix as Satan accurately quotes Scripture, but removes it from the original context. Satan goes right into doctrine when he cannot find another opening in the defense, and this is what he does time and again throughout human history. Satan uses a Biblical passage and twists it out of context, but never loses the Truth aspect of the verse, so it seems legitimate. This verse is not written as a dare to Jesus Christ to tempt death because He will be protected, but Satan has managed to dress it up in that fashion without any major changes to the written words. This again points to Satan's one true desire since the beginning, and that is independence from the Father.

Independence is something he has always thought about, acted upon, and promoted since his fall. This temptation could have been the crowning achievement of Satan, and he would have truly been exalted by his followers if the humanity of Christ had fallen apart during the forty days in the desert. Instead the humanity of Christ used Bible doctrine as a defense weapon and turned the temptations back. The lesson of the temptations is truly the subtle twist and play on words that Satan uses against our Lord. It is the example we need to remember when dealing with false teachings, worldly concepts, and human viewpoint in our daily lives.

Most con-men use some facts and truth to move their scam past intelligent people and get to their goal. As we sit back now and look at this scripture, (Psa 91) we can examine it and plainly see that it is absurd to think that Jesus Christ was supposed to tempt fate in relation to any scripture. However, the way Satan led Jesus up to it was very clever and slowly deceptive. Satan used the slow deceptive tactic, mixed with subtle lies, and waited for his opponent to be worn out, hungry, tired, and near confusion. This brings us to an issue that we face in the Church Age, namely that the average Christian has no discernment about what the Word of God says and what deceptions the kingdom of darkness uses in religion today. The nonsense that is taught on a regular basis is not related to Bible doctrine, yet is widely accepted in Christian communities around the world. There is more nonsense and deceit within many churches in this world than there is in greedy corporations and businesses.

God does not condone nonsense and unreasonable action, yet this is the foundation of several popular religions in our world. Jesus Christ sticks to the real issue and Truth when confronted with deception and nonsense. Jesus used the scripture of Deu 6:16 when He stated emphatically, "You shall not put the Lord your God to the test." When the Lord said this He was saying, "your God" meaning that He (Jesus Christ) was God and He is the one who created Satan. In that statement it was the equivalent of saying to Satan, "Do you realize that you are testing God?" Satan knew He was God by the statement that was made in the first test, when basically Satan was saying, "You are God so turn this stone into bread." Jesus Christ used the proper scripture in the right context and put Satan in his place. Satan was attempting to be slick with the word games, but Jesus Christ in His humanity was able see right through it by sticking with the plan of God and applying the Scriptures accurately to the problem.

> "And when the devil had finished every temptation, he departed from Him until an opportune time." (Luk 4:13)

This verse is the conclusion of one test, but it also shows that the kingdom of darkness always makes a return trip and is relentless in the area of attacking Truth and positive believers. Satan had to quit because he was stumped and frustrated at this point. Arrogance usually has two directions when it becomes frustrated, either it lashes out and seeks to destroy, or it will flee the scene and fester on the sidelines until another opening presents itself. Arrogance will not last under the spotlight of Truth and integrity, it wilts and becomes emotional. Jesus Christ never said that Satan must stop the test because He is God. Jesus never became physical in His humanity or went on the attack, never showed signs of frustration. Instead, He was steadfast and true.

> "Submit therefore to God. Resist the devil and he will flee from you." (Jam 4:7)

Jesus Christ did not rebuke or attempt to bind the devil. He stood in the Truth of Bible doctrine and let the white, hot light of His Father's words sear the Prince of darkness.

There is a victory celebration that follows as noted in Mat 4:11 which states that when the devil left Jesus, the angels of God came upon the scene to minister to Him. The Greek word for *minister* is *diakoneo* which refers to a form of service, or to wait upon someone offering food and drink. You can bet this was the finest meal and victory celebration that anyone could have had.

In closing the issue of the Hypostatic Union it should be said that Jesus Christ was indeed a man, and also God, in a divine combination that was made apparent during His ministry here on earth. Jesus the man suffered, struggled, and overcame all obstacles to complete the Father's plan for

His life. He therefore left the footprints for all mankind to follow when faced with adversity and challenges from the devil's world. The miracles and healings that the God-ward side of Jesus Christ performed were to establish His church here upon earth and to leave no doubt that Jesus was the divine savior and God that He claimed to be.

Never did the deity of Christ come to the rescue of the humanity of Christ during any physical or mental suffering that occurred during His walk toward the Cross or upon it. God could have healed all mankind and allowed miracles and wonders to occur every day while Christ was working out the plan of the Father. But it would have left the kingdom of darkness screaming within the divine court room, bringing charges of unfair treatment and basically causing a mistrial. The importance of the Hypostatic Union goes beyond the suffering upon the Cross, it reaches far back to eternity past and deep into eternity future, affecting the Angelic Conflict in multidimensional ways that we may never fully grasp.

Chapter 11

The Pseudo-Victory of Satan in The Original Fall of Man.

Due to the fact that God is perfect and His divine nature cannot have contact with sin, we can assume that God does not simply ignore it. In fact we can further assume that God cannot ignore or disregard sin, nor can He turn a blind eye to some sins while dealing with others. All sin is sin, and when it comes to the righteousness of God whosoever keeps one part of the perfect Law of God, but stumbles and offends in one single instance, has become guilty of breaking all of it.

When the rebellion began in the mind of Satan, God, who has all power and all knowledge, knew what His creatures thought and desired. So God could have struck down the rebellious angel, yet God chose another path. When you truly look at the choices God had it came down to only two: destroy the creatures He had created, or resolve the issue of rebellion once and for all. God, being fair and just, would not create creatures that are void of free will. What purpose would an army of obedient robots serve to a God who can have anything, do anything, and create anything? Had God created another breed of superior angels to destroy the first, it would have simply left the issue of rebellion for the future. Heaven would have been dotted with wars and rebellions if that were God's choice. God—

also being love and compassion—would not swiftly destroy His creation before there was an opportunity for repentance.

So we see the two choices of God when the rebellious thoughts within Satan sprang to life. Destroy Satan or allow a fair trial to refute the claim of Satan that he is like the Most High! This issue of arrogance and rebellion is something that God knew in eternity past would become a massive disaster for all created beings, because they are not deity but flawed in comparison to our Lord. The issue was so glaring that God knew that there would have to be a set of events and consequences that were so profound and permanent that it would forever resolve the issue of sin. This independence from God is the reason for the conflict, and the fact that free will is to exist within His creatures is the defining factor in human history. Though the human race was created to resolve the invisible war and to be the witnesses to come forth on the stand, most people do not live their life with this in mind. Most do not even take the time to understand why they have been created.

> "For even though they knew God, they did not honor Him as God or give thanks, but they became futile in their speculations, and their foolish heart was darkened. Professing to be wise, they became fools, and exchanged the glory of the incorruptible God for an image in the form of corruptible man and of birds and four-footed animals and crawling creatures. Therefore God gave them over in the lusts of their hearts to impurity, so that their bodies would be dishonored among them. For they exchanged the truth of God for a lie, and worshiped and served the creature rather than the Creator, who is blessed forever. Amen." (Rom 1:21-25)

As Paul finishes up his statement in verse 25 we can see that most people will accept false doctrine over Truth, trading the Word of God for the lies of the world. When Satan and the fallen angels rebelled against God, God could not permit rebellion without showing His hatred for rebellion and sin. This is because His righteousness and justice as well as His holiness had to be manifested. God's attitude toward the rebellion and independence from Him had to be proclaimed. However, God would permit Satan and the fallen angels the opportunity to present their case before all created creatures. Therefore, in eternity past, before the creation of the human race, God spoke the Word of Judgment and the entire world, the domain of Satan, was blasted into chaos. This is a fact backed by not only the Bible but also science which substantiates the beginning of time as we humans have recorded it. This is the event we briefly noted between the first and second verse of Genesis 1. It notes a lapse in time, a gap or space of undetermined years.

> "In the beginning God created heavens and earth (space or period of time). The earth became formless and void, and darkness was over the surface of the deep (waters)." (Gen 1:1-2)

According to the Greek Septuagint of the Old Testament the word *deep* is the same as the word *abyss* in the Greek New Testament. God is pleased to reveal the past, present, as well as future events to those that are serious students of His word. While most people are accustomed to some revelations from God concerning future events (like the book of Revelation), many will find it startling to think that God reveals ancient history and pre-historic events for us to get a clear picture of the Angelic Conflict. The Bible is truly full of divine layers of human history, angelic rebellion, invisible and visible warfare, it is loaded with solutions and answers to human life. The Bible is our owner's manual for this life and the world we exist in, and like a large onion you need to peel back the many layers to get to the core. And yes you may shed a few tears along the way! One example of God's displaying knowledge to us is revealed as Peter mentions something that many teachers totally overlook or misunderstand.

In 2Pe 3:5-6 we read, "For when they maintain this, it escapes their notice that by the Word of God the heavens existed long ago and the earth was formed out of water and by water, through which the world at that time was destroyed, being flooded with water" (referring to Gen 1:2).

When most people hear of a flood in the Bible they immediately associate the event to the flood that Noah's generation experienced. When Peter writes that the Word of God existed long ago, it is referring back to Gen 1:1.

Then in 2Pe 3:7, "But the present heavens and earth by His word are being reserved for fire, kept for the day of judgment and destruction of ungodly men."

The phrase "present heavens and earth" is related to Gen 1:3 (God said, "Let there be light"). This is making a distinction between two worlds and time periods. There was not a definition connecting the flood of Noah's time to this passage which Peter is teaching. The King James Version of 2Pe 3:6 says, "Whereby the world that then was, being overflowed with water, perished, But the heavens and the earth, which are now . . ."

This distinctly emphasizes the earth's destruction, and during the flood of Noah the earth was simply washed clean of human life, but not destroyed. At no time in the planet's history has it ever perished. So put aside the notion that it refers to the flood of Noah's time, because that is not what the original scripture points out. This destruction that Peter was teaching took place when Satan's rebellion on planet Earth was stopped by God! Mankind assumes that all things have always been as they are now, that there have been no great moments of divine intervention either to create, to reveal, or to punish, and that is just not true. Modern science says that all things continue as they were, the Bible says men are ignorant and willfully blinded (2Pe 3:5 escapes their notice). Sorry to inform anyone with little faith, but scientists and geologists were not around when Satan and his fallen angels first took over the planet! All things do not continue as they were, they began in perfection and were altered in judgment time and again. The world went on its disintegrating course until God intervened at Calvary. We see Job describing this event in Job chapter 9.

> "In truth I know that this is so, But how can a man be right before God? If one wished to dispute Him, He could not answer Him once in a thousand times." (Job 9:2-3)

Job was a man that God allowed to have divine insight. God used Job to represent Him upon the witness stand, so it would be wise to research his words and life for divine answers.

> "Wise in heart and mighty in strength, who defied Him without harm? It is God who removes the mountains, they know not

> how, when He overturns them in His anger; Who shakes the earth out of its place, and its pillars tremble" (Job 9:4-6)

Job is speaking Truth from his insight and knowledge of history.

> "Who commands the sun not to shine, and sets a seal upon the stars; Who alone stretches out the heavens, and tramples down the waves of the sea." (Job 9:7-8)

The book of Job, as it is the oldest book in the Scriptures, may be worth putting some stock in when it comes to looking at human history and events leading up to the birth of our Savior. When did God ever outstretch His hands and move mountains and cause the sun not to shine in any time in history dating back to before the birth of Christ? Science has never come forward and claimed that mountains were moved, the earth was shaken and shifted, and everything was made dark thousands of years ago. So this catastrophic wreckage Job is speaking about is the angelic rebellion at a time when the earth was different than what we see today. In fact the catastrophe which took place upon the earth is also mentioned in the Bible as having taken place within the heavens. In looking at the book of Jeremiah we also note that the heavens had no light to be seen during the early stages of earth's history.

> "I looked on the earth, and behold, it was formless and void; And to the heavens, they had no light. I looked on the mountains, and behold, they were quaking. And all the hills moved to and fro. I looked and behold, there was no man. And all the birds of the heavens had fled." (Jer 4:23-25)

It would be easy to misinterpret this vision as simply the beginning of creation, or a period when God was busy working on this Earth, but a closer look at these verses shows that the birds were already in existence along with mountains and perhaps even intelligent life forms. The next verse puts it into real perspective.

> "I looked, and behold, the fruitful land was a wilderness. And all its cities were pulled down before the Lord, before His fierce anger." (Jer 4:26)

Now, it is truly difficult to misinterpret this piece of the Scripture. The phrase "fruitful land" refers to a full agricultural setting that would need to have been developed and groomed by intelligent creatures. This statement speaks of a form of destruction for which God apparently is responsible. When in the Old Testament or New Testament history has God completely torn down valleys and mountains, darkened the earth and chased off all living creatures? He has not done so. The flood that took place during the time of Noah and the destruction of a city like Sodom and Gomorrah are not in view here.

From these verses it is obvious that this was a catastrophic incident of worldwide proportions, not a tiny isolated event or simply a flood. We can see the anger in God to the point where He shut everything down. When the light source from the sun is removed this causes the precipitation of all moisture on the earth and all waters of the earth to freeze. There are geologists who tell us that there are traces of glaciers across the whole surface of the earth with marks of a great ice cap in the center of Africa. A further reference to this event is seen in Psalm 18.

> "Then the earth shook and quaked; And the foundations of the mountains were trembling and were shaken, because He (God) was angry. Smoke went up out of His nostrils, And fire from His mouth devoured; Coals were kindled by it. He bowed the heavens also, and came down with thick darkness under His feet. And He rode upon a cherub and flew; And He sped upon the wings of the wind. He made darkness His hiding place, His canopy around Him, darkness of waters, thick clouds of the skies. From the brightness before Him passed His thick clouds, hailstones and coals of fire." (Psa 18:7-12)

The next verses cover a hailstorm of fire and severe lightning, and this is describing an event that reached around the globe, affecting land, sea, and all creatures in existence.

> "Then the channels of the water appeared, And the foundations of the world were laid bare at Thy rebuke, O Lord, at the blast of the breath of Thy nostrils." (Psa 18:15)

These events from Jeremiah, Job, and these verses in Psalms are all related to one such event that the human race did not witness, because they were not created until a much later date. God has a wrath toward sin and independence from His plan, this is noted as ungodly behavior many times within the Scriptures. God has been seen throughout the Scriptures pouring His wrath out upon ungodly people. The main reason behind such violent events is that mankind was created for the glory of God and was allowed such freedom and available blessings that it is pure rebellion for mankind to continue forward in ignorance and arrogance, day in and day out, generation after generation, yet the majority do! At certain points of time God has to strike down upon a people due to the negative volition that has developed and for their own benefit. 1Co 6:20 tells us: "For you have been bought with a price, therefore glorify God in your body."

We noted that the flood occurred in Gen 6:4-7 due to demonic possession and infiltration taking place during an extended period of human history. God cursed the ground that Adam walked on (Gen 3:17) when he and the woman rebelled against Him. The world was God's creation and the majority on this planet still rebel against Him. His Word reveals His wrath, the cataclysmic events of the Great Tribulation, and how the world will burn with fire at the end of time (2Pe 3:7-10). His wrath toward the rebellious angels will also be shown (Rev 20:10). Highlighting this principle of wrath we can see that God's judgment is fierce and unyielding when it is released. It is not difficult to surmise that the sin of independence plays the major role in almost all of these examples. The judgment in the end times will be fitting for Satan and his fallen angels because it reveals the power of God and the impotence of Satan once and for all time. God had created the universe, the heavens and earth, by His Word, and the devil laid claim to it as if he were the creator. Not only claiming to be like God, but also taking an army of rebellious angels with him in doing so. This was nothing short of a declaration of war against the Creator.

God used a word to begin the universe, and in a word He brought it crumbling down into chaos and judgment, giving Satan his first taste of dust in his mouth. A mouthful of dust is the perfect description of the defeat and frustration that must have been felt by all the fallen angels when the Lord shook the world to its very core. From the first proclamation of "I will be like the most high!" Satan was doomed for defeat and damnation. Anyone following in Satan's footsteps is in for the same "dust in the mouth" feeling.

This brings us to the pseudo-victory of Satan in the original fall of man, getting weaker creatures to stray from God, remaining ignorant about Truth and living in a state of independence! There was a time when Satan led the angels in the worship of God, and then he rebelled in his soul, which was followed by rebellious action. Then we witnessed Satan lead a rebellion of angels against God, followed by getting newly created man to also rebel, at a much later date. It is all a pseudo-victory, because God, having created all things, knew that this would occur, and He allowed a plan to be put into place far in advance to crush the rebellion after it had run its fair and balanced course. God did take immediate action upon the first sign of rebellion, but did not fully end the conflict due to His perfect righteousness and patience. God tossed the fallen angels from the heavens down to planet Earth which may have existed for millions of years.

Sometime afterward, He packed planet Earth with ice, thus imprisoning the rebellious creatures. After a holding period (perhaps millions of years), God began the act of setting up the courtroom and allowing the conflict to take on a course to prove that He is righteous and just. Mankind was then created after all was prepared and the battle lines had been set upon planet Earth.

It is interesting to think about Satan in a state of frozen incarceration, yelling into the darkness, "Let there be light!" time and time again, and of course nothing ever happened. The frustration must have escalated day after day, and year after year. The rude awakening to such a powerful creature as Satan must have been most devastating. Here is the world he was ruling over and in one fell swoop the Lord smashed it and rearranged the mountains and valleys. God shut the source of light and heat off as easily as pulling a plug on a lamp. He peppered the earth with fire and hail stones, and for the grand finale our Lord froze it all over like icing on a cake. Satan and his army were probably thrown about like ragdolls completely in disarray and despair. Satan had to have felt a bitter and deep sting of utter helplessness. This is more than likely the catalyst that sent his arrogance soaring to new heights because the rage and frustration must have been overwhelming within his bitter soul.

As we have learned, people will usually go in one of two directions after a major tragedy, and we know which way the devil went. Satan had to be the ultimate picture of frustration and failure in front of his troops. He was offering a spectacular delicacy to his followers and all they got to dine on was dirt! There they were, locked in a frozen sphere, their world disrupted and destroyed. All they had was the sinking realization that their power, unlike God's, was limited and that they did not hold the power of creation and destruction in their hands. Satan as a leader looked like a spoiled child who finally got his discipline. Anyone who follows Satan can expect not only to dine on the dust of destruction, but will surely feel the emptiness and frustration of a complete loss of power and life in the end. God has gone to extreme measures to reveal to His creatures that any form of satisfaction is never found outside of a personal relationship with Him through our Lord Jesus Christ and obedience to His will. There is no other source of joy than a relationship with God. Joy cannot be manufactured by any creature. This is why we have commands like Jer 49:20 and Jer 50:45 that say you must hear the plan of the Lord! What we see today is what happened many times in the ancient world, we see a hard heart just like the generation in the days of Jeremiah who were stubborn and stiff-necked. This stubborn attitude is not just seen in unbelievers, but also in believers in Christ. That is what causes the wrath of God, His own children denying Him and stepping away from His plan.

> "We are going to follow our own plans (independence), and each one will act according to the stubbornness of his evil heart." (Jer 18:12)

Some people are so set in their ways that God cannot reach them with a simple tap on the shoulder or a roadblock in their path. God has to drop a safe on their head to get them to wake up, and even then it often falls upon deaf ears. God goes as far as allowing their free will decisions and stubbornness to actually obtain what they think will make them happy. Even after getting what they want, in a short time, it brings them misery or confusion, and so they move on to the next item that they think will bring them contentment. Rebellion and stubbornness are born from the same womb. In Psa 78:8 it is noted that stubbornness is associated with people who do not prepare their right lobe (soul) with Bible doctrine. Jer 5:23 puts it like this: "But this people has a stubborn and rebellious heart; they have turned aside and departed."

A stubborn heart will eventually rebel toward authority and inevitably that stubborn heart steps backward instead of forward in the plan of God. This back-peddling is subtle and referred to as reversionism, and it occurs over a period of time, not instantaneously. When God deals with the stubborn believer He first allows the lusts and desires of their heart to drag them through misery. He does not drop the hand of discipline on them quickly. This is much like the self-induced misery that unbelievers experience within the cosmic system. Stubbornness to the degree we are learning here easily translates into the sin of independence.

> "Yet they did not obey or incline their ear, but walked in their own counsels and in the stubbornness of their evil heart, and went backward and not forward." (Jer 7:24)

Let us get back to that time of frozen discipline placed upon the kingdom of darkness. It could be a safe guess to say that it was probably an extended period of time, thousands or perhaps millions of years. God does not have the restraints of time that the human race has. To God ten thousand years is barely a weekend, much less equal to a long jail sentence. Geologists tell us that millions of years were necessary to bring about some of the phenomena which are found on the earth today. Scientists and Biblical scholars all have their own set of numbers and events in an order they believe to be factual. However, the truth is that none of that can or will ever be proven. So there is much that remains in the realm of theory, and probably will remain there until the Second Advent of Christ when some of the invisible veils and mysteries will be lifted.

What we can see is the Spirit of God moving over the surface of the dark waters of earth in Gen 1:2. What was about to happen was that the arrogant one—who bragged and boasted about being like the Possessor of heaven and earth—was about to be exposed. Satan probably thought he was getting out the message proving how powerful he still was, and that he was getting another crack at having his own little heaven right here on earth. All this was being observed by a legion of worshipping angels that were at his beck and call. To some degree he was correct.

By this point of the incarceration there had to be a group of defeated angels who were ready to cut ties with Satan, but probably still had a healthy fear of his powers. There was also probably another group that had grown just as heated and bitter as Satan after such a long period under cold wraps. Maybe there was a group that was apathetic and could be swayed either way. No matter what the dynamic was at this point of the lockdown, they all knew something was brewing as Gen 1:3 came into view when God said, "Let there be light." And there was light. The whole God-head was working in unity to set a very dramatic stage for what was about to be the appeal trial of the universe. Satan had to be steaming when he saw that a word from the mouth of God brought everything to light! Satan knew something important and universe-altering was about to take place, and he had no control over any of it. This earth that he had assumed would be his heaven, his realm of authority, was shaken from his grasp with ease, frozen and stalled in time as if it never existed.

The shining light through the desolate waste, glaring into that frozen capsule, must have been a shocking experience for all the fallen angels after such a long time in darkness. Satan had to realize at this point that God still considered the earth His and under His sovereignty, and that there was a process about to begin that would certainly involve him.

So the divine command went forth and the light pushed back the curtains of darkness: the stage, planet Earth, was barren (formless and void). There were no characters or scenery upon the face of the surface, and this judgment had been witnessed by all angelic creatures on both sides of the conflict. There could be no doubt left about how God looks upon rebellion after the events that had transpired prior to this thawing-out process. As Gen 1:2 tells us, it was God Himself moving about the earth's surface, and for the next six days the Lord would design and create like a supernatural artist filling a blank canvas. The fallen angels who had sworn their alliance to Satan must have caught a glimpse of the utter wasteland that was once their stomping grounds when light first touched the earth. They had to feel the pangs of desperation and anguish at how easy it was for God to build, destroy, and rebuild again, yet their leader had limited powers compared to this. Finally after six days of scene-shifting, beauty and wonder were on display for all angels to see. It was then that God gathered up the dust of the earth and breathed life into the first human, a creature that was obviously much less than an angelic creature.

> "What is man that thou dost take thought of him? And the son of man, that Thou dost care for him? Yet Thou hast made him a little lower than the gods (angels), and dost crown him with glory and majesty!" (Psa 8:4-5)

Heb 2:6-7 makes a similar statement, asking why God cares so much about the human race and that for a time the human race shall be lower than angels. The earth was the scene of the crime so to speak, and God had wiped it clean and prepared it for the court case, and now we see a witness being brought upon the scene. Victorious vindication was the wheel that was being set in motion. God had no desire to destroy the earth completely, but rather to shake it up, alter what was in existence and begin again. The challenge to His authority had been attempted, but God knew it would not be the end.

God, who is all knowing and all powerful, is always aware of His design and creation so the attitude of the fallen angels even in captivity was no shock to God. The bitterness that was swelling up in the souls of most of the fallen angels and especially within Satan was no surprise. For a fair and just God, it is fitting to allow His creatures the freedom and opportunities to prove their point. So this transformation of the planet Earth was the real beginning of Satan's chance to prove his point, to protect his bitter attitude, and to gain some form of real authority over a lower creature, to show what type of leader he is compared to God. What the fallen angels had no clue about was the fact that Jesus Christ would become a man and one day would be standing in the garden of Gethsemane just before He would be sentenced to death and make a statement like this:

> "I glorified Thee on the earth, having accomplished the work which Thou hast given Me to do." (Joh 17:4)

Satan was unaware that the coming fall of man and the redemption provided by Christ would bring a mighty company of believers. God could raise them to the very throne of heaven without the remotest possibility that any one of them would ever claim any power in their own right. In Heb 2:9 it states that Christ will taste death for everyone, and His suffering will bring many into glory. Look at Heb 2:10, "For it was fitting for Him, for whom are all things, and through whom are all things, in bringing many sons to glory, to perfect the author of their salvation through sufferings."

When the sons and daughters of God are in heaven and work in the divine government of the Lord, they will be the first to acknowledge, and they will continually acknowledge, that Jesus Christ is the divine Savior and King of Kings. It is now upon the earth our time to take up our own Cross and to become soldiers for Christ in this invisible battle and to complete the resolution of the conflict. But instead, for many it is a time of selfish behavior and arrogant attitudes that dominate our race much like the father of arrogance, Satan. Paul describes it accurately in 2 Ti 3:4 as lovers of pleasure rather than lovers of God. One description of the priority that the plan of God should be in the life of a believer is covered in Matthew 10:37 when the Lord said, "He who loves father and mother more than Me is not worthy of Me; and he who loves son or daughter more than Me is not worthy of Me." The Lord puts it like this in Mat 10:38-39, "And he who does not take up his cross [God's plan for their life] and follow after Me is not worthy of Me. He who has found his life shall lose it, and he who has lost his life for My sake [following the plan of God] shall find it."

Without God moving over the waters and restoring light, the world would have remained desolate and frozen in time. This is why the scientific proof that the world is perhaps millions or billions of years old probably holds true. We have no idea how old planet Earth is, how long the pre-historic angels dwelled upon it, or how long it was packed away in a frozen prison. We have no idea of the creatures, plant life, and rock formations that existed during the time of the angelic realm before mankind came into the plan that God designed in eternity past. We can see God had a tremendous plan, and we can note the rebellion and conflict that took place before we came into existence. The rest is simply theory by flawed mankind to explain our planet's history. What can be deduced is that there is one true God, one divine creator, and not a set of circumstances or mythical gods that worked in unison to get all these wonders on planet Earth completed and working in harmony.

Believers need not concern themselves with the angelic demons that are set against them. As believers, we need not concern ourselves with the fall of mankind because, in Deu 23:5 the Bible says, "The Lord your God has turned the curse into a blessing for you because the Lord your God loves you." There was a divine strategy at work when God made mankind. Out of this creation, and the fall, there was an offering of redemption and blessing. This displays the complete revelation of the depths of the wisdom and the knowledge of God as it is noted in Rom 11:33.

This can be called the "paradox of the fortunate fall." There was no model of angelic beings used to create mankind, no power was given to humans as was the case for angels, no extra might or flight powers were ever instilled in a flesh and blood human being. Lucifer was given the most powers and strength of any of the original creatures and there is no trace of that in the human body. The speed and ability to travel light years through the heavens is not in the human DNA. The superior body and invisible veil that cloaks and protects angels is not designed for mankind. In Psa 8:2-6 it again states that for a little while man is made to be lower than angels, using the term elohims or gods when referring to angels.

> "From the mouth of infants and nursing babes You have established strength because of Your adversaries, to make the enemy and the revengeful cease." (Psa 8:2)

The key phrase is "for a little while." The divine strategy is God allowing mankind to be the less powerful within the conflict for a period of time. Out of the lowest, God shall bring the highest, out of the insignificant God shall bring forth the significant. In fact, God shall Himself condescend to be a member of this lower creation called humans. God, after dealing with man's fallen condition, will reach down to the level at which man was created and bring up new sons who shall associate with Him for all of eternity. God will use a creature lower than the angels to bring forth the victory and deal with the invisible conflict that has us entrenched at this point of our human history. Is it any wonder why the apostle Paul says in Rom 11:33, "Oh, the depth of riches both of wisdom and knowledge of God! How unsearchable are his judgments and unfathomable His ways!"

Satan had to witness the appearance of dry land and the ocean's resuming a normal flow once again. Trees and flowers sprouted as God moved over the earth, grass and mountains were rejuvenated as the sky came back into life.

Then God said, "Let the waters below the heavens be gathered into one place, and let the dry land appear"; and it was so. And God called the dry land earth, and the gathering of the waters He called seas; and God saw that it was good." (Genesis 1:9-10)

Reading further in Gen 1:11-12 we see the vegetation and fruits coming forward as God continues His work over the six days leading up to the creation of Adam. In Gen 1:14-18 we can see God creating day and night, seasons and weather patterns, expanding the stars and universe. Satan had no reason for jealousy other than the jealousy he felt about the power and ease with which God was re-creating the world. Even when God created new creatures like birds and animals it did not spark intense jealousy because these creatures had no soul and were no threat to Satan.

Then God said, "Let the waters teem with swarms of living creatures, and let birds fly above the earth in the open expanse of the heavens. And God created the great sea monsters, and every living creature that moves, with which the waters swarmed after their kind, and every winged bird after its kind; and God saw that it was good. And God blessed them, saying, 'Be fruitful and multiply, and fill the waters in the seas, and let birds multiply on the earth.'" (Gen 1:20-22)

Then intense jealousy and hatred for a creature arose in Satan and the fallen angels as they watched the Trinity bring a human being to life!

Then God said, "Let Us make man in Our image, according to Our likeness; and let them rule over the fish of the sea and over the birds of the sky and over the cattle and over all the earth, and over every creeping thing that creeps on the earth." (Gen 1:26)

God then went on to create a female of the human species and told them to be fruitful and multiply. At this point Satan's head was probably about to pop off from the pressure of jealousy. Not only did God tell them to multiply, but He blessed Adam and Eve (Gen 1:28). Satan instantly knew he had a rival, and a battle would have to ensue for supremacy on this planet! Man awoke finding himself a noble and beautiful creature with all that he could lay his eyes upon under his authority. The earth would now belong to someone else, and to make it worse for the skyrocketing arrogance within Satan, it was given over to a creature that was like a cockroach compared to a powerful angelic being! Little did the man and woman realize that they had been entered into a battle, a court case of such intensity that it would carry on for thousands of years. It was as if God was developing a weapon for His invisible warfare against the fallen angels, and that weapon was mankind. It was a weapon that at first glance appeared weak and ill—equipped to stand against such a strong rival.

> "In order that the manifold (abundant) wisdom of God might now be made known through the church to the rulers and the authorities in the heavenly places." (Eph 3:10)

God had set Satan up as the authority of this planet as we have noted in Eze 28:14, and Satan, even in a frozen jail cell, never gave up his possession of the planet. Yet he was nearby, as we can assume, witnessing the birth of a new creation that would bump him off the throne. It would not be difficult to imagine the scoffing and jeering that the demon army was involved in as they looked at the weaker species before them. It is a safe bet that they were tucked away, for the fear of being locked back up was still fresh in their minds.

At this early juncture the kingdom of darkness was not thinking of words like faith, grace, and redemption, and yet these very words, and the divine application of them, would be the real weapons causing the fall of Satan and his angels. At this point in our own history we can believe that Satan has had his fill of such words and truly hates God's grace and forgiveness, and he especially hates our Lord Jesus Christ and the finished work that happened upon the Cross. You see, grace means you do not earn or deserve anything, yet God comes through for you anyway. This concept is something that the kingdom of darkness cannot stand. Couple that grace with a weaker creature that will wait on God and has faith in His plan. This is infuriating to them! Most arrogant, self-righteous human beings get upset when grace and faith are seen in action in someone else's life. Satan promotes human merit and doing things your own way. He believes, and wants you to believe, that you can earn and deserve what you desire in life. He hates faith in God, and wants all trust and faith to be upon the creature not the Creator. Satan was created perfect and given the keys to heaven's highest and best. What more grace could God have given than that? Yet Satan rebelled. So we can see his attitude about such things as God's grace and faith in our Lord. Satan wants glory, and grace points to God getting the glory just as God's coming through for a believer with great faith gives God the glory.

> "Worthy of praise and glorification be the God and Father of our Lord Jesus Christ, who has blessed us with every spiritual blessing in the heavenly places in Christ." (Eph 1:3)

God wants His highest and best for all His creatures, but there is a protocol and a divine plan to be followed. God allows us time to grow and a free will to choose any path we desire. However, there is only one way to true blessings, and that is lining your will up with God's will while you are here on planet Earth. One of God's greatest pleasures is for Him to bless His creatures. Our Lord revealed His own desire in Act 20:35, "It is more blessed to give than to receive." This actually is a part of the plan of God for a believer's life, that they reach a level of spiritual maturity to receive great blessings here on earth, not just in eternity. God has provided everything in eternity past, it is just a matter of growing up to receive what God has already put in your escrow account.

God has a reason for all He has done for you, and this reason gives purpose to your life. God does not depend on us for glory, but He receives the glory when He can come through for us and bless us. Any system of human works is the wrong avenue to take to reach the glorification of God. He does not depend on us, rather we are to depend upon Him!

God's pleasure and glory are things that He expresses toward us, it is not something we earn. We are designed to be beneficiaries of blessing and divine provisions, not to manufacture them in our flesh.

> "Thou hast increased the nation, O Lord, Thou hast increased the nation, Thou art glorified." (Isa 26:15)

> "Then all Your people will be righteous; they will possess the land forever, the branch of My planting, the work of My hands, that I may be glorified." (Isa 60:21)

We must realize that when we rely on divine power and God's help to see us through, all the angels witness it and God again gets the glory!

> "And call upon Me in the day of trouble; I shall rescue you, and you will glorify Me." (Psa 50:15)

One book that shows the power of God coming through time and time again is the book of Exodus. Moses had to deal with a generation of people who would forget the wonders and miracles shortly after each rescue and divine work was completed! They were stiff—necked and stubborn, but God kept coming onto the scene to rescue them, even in the midst of their rebellious attitudes. We get a glimpse of what God's glory is all about in Exo 33:18-19, where He came before Moses and said, "I will show compassion on whom I will show compassion." God was letting Moses know that there are no works or gimmicks when God displays His blessing and favor, rather it is all grace. There are few things that incite the rage of Satan more than grace and faith concerning God. When a believer lives in faith and is occupied with the Lord, it is a direct contradiction to what Satan tries to promote in the cosmic system. We are showing all the angels that though we have not seen heaven, or our savior Jesus Christ, all our trust and faith will be in Him anyway! The angels have seen it all, heaven and earth, the universe and the divine presence of the Trinity, and so faith is easy for them. We mere humans are walking in blindness concerning these spiritual principles.

The human race goes to the Bible for their contact and proof of the Creator, the angels have lived it. You can see the importance of faith in this stage of the conflict, because we are strong witnesses and on display for angels to see, and they realize that a weaker creation with no physical contact with God has faith in His justice and righteousness, yet many of them did not. In fact 2Co 5:7 states that we walk by faith not by sight.

> "And without faith it is impossible to please Him, for he who comes to God must believe that He is, and that He is a rewarder of those that seek Him." (Heb 11:6)

> "So faith comes from hearing, and hearing by the word of Christ." (Rom 10:17)

The victory and glory within this invisible battle entangling us all will be settled and decided by the weakest of the creatures that God has created. Faith is important to comprehend as much as the fact that grace is given for the apparent reason that God is love and compassion, not that man did something to merit special favor.

Powerful weapons like grace and faith were not yet deployed into the conflict at the creation of Adam. So we can venture a guess that the kingdom of darkness was gloating on the sidelines as the Lord brought the first human being to life. They must have seen the weaknesses within this new creature immediately. They had divine powers of flight, the ability to travel throughout the universe, they had been created strong, beautiful, and full of powers that mankind lacked. So jealousy was not a major issue at the first glimpse of Adam. We know that arrogance hates to be ignored, or brushed aside, so there had to be the initial outrage over the fact that Adam and Eve had authority on earth. When God was putting these two flawed human beings at the helm of the planet it certainly had to spark more of the fires of pride, arrogance, and possibly even a hint of jealousy within the fallen angels. But they must have thought, "These new creatures are nothing compared to us; we will crush them like bugs!"

In the realm of challenging Satan's role as authority and his ultimate power, it could not have given the fallen angels that much to worry about. What God had done was to place an offensive force in the midst of the enemy-held territory, and any attack on that man was an attack upon God Himself. The attack would come as we witness in Gen 3:1-5, more of a backdoor approach, subtle and devious, using words and scripture that were slightly manipulated and very calculated to get the woman interested in an outside force. This was all to pique the curiosity, to tease the arrogant tendency towards independence that Satan knows is in all creatures. Satan tasted victory quite easily with this first attempt and must have impressed his demon army with his craftiness, which probably once again assured his place as the commander and chief.

The first combat attack in the Garden of Eden was a surface victory for all angelic eyes to see, but under the surface it was a seed of victory that God had planted in that garden. Satan's tactics are a forward attack on the Word of God and the goodness of God. Satan starts his attack with, "Indeed has God said," immediately playing on doubt and Truth within the Word of God, which is what he still uses in many cases today! We can see God come back with His own defensive maneuver letting Satan know that the victory is short-lived.

> "And the Lord God said to the serpent, 'Because you have done this, cursed are you more than all cattle, and more than every beast of the field; on your belly shall you go, and dust you shall eat all the days of your life. And I will put enmity between you (Satan) and the woman, and between your seed (unbelievers) and her seed (believers); He (Jesus Christ) shall bruise you on the head, and you shall bruise Him (suffering that Christ received here on earth) on the heel.'" (Gen 3:14-15)

In fact within this chapter almost all of the great doctrines which appear in the rest of the Bible can be found. The reality that Satan loves to cause division and sow the seeds of doubt is seen when he first slithers onto the scene. That is what he does today in many of his subtle attack methods. As soon as God implemented the principle of teaching Truth to new creatures, Satan crept in to steal that seed and scatter it.

> "And those beside the road are those who have heard; then the devil comes and takes away the word from their heart, so that they may not believe and be delivered." (Luk 8:12)

We see Satan doing this in our day and age, and this is a success or small victory for him each time it happens. So the temptation put in front of Eve in Genesis chapter 3 was setting the stage for this conflict to take on the real combat phase of operations. This was the first bullet fired on the battlefield between mankind and fallen angels. It is interesting to see God telling Satan to taste dust again in his defeat (Gen 3:14) just as he had tasted it earlier when God sent the mountains and valleys into shambles before He froze it over into a prison. The attacks from the kingdom of darkness always end with the "dust in the mouth" syndrome for Satan and his followers. This powerful imagery symbolizes the fallen soldier on the battlefield gasping for his last breath and having his face in the ground, tasting the dirt before he fades off into darkness.

Chapter 3 of Genesis is the introduction of human beings into the conflict, opening the courtroom doors and allowing them in to participate. We can also see one key weapon that the kingdom of darkness always uses and that is doubt. Someone with doubt toward the Word of God has little faith, perhaps no real faith to begin with. The Lord said to Peter in Mat 14:31, "O you of little faith, why do you doubt?" Faith is simply a reference to doctrine. In a verse like this He is saying that someone has not gained enough doctrine in their soul. Perhaps they did not subject themselves to enough Truth or did not apply what they learned.

> "Truly I say to you, whoever says to this mountain (major obstacle), be taken up and cast into the sea, and does not doubt in his heart, but believes that what he says is going happen, it shall be granted to him." (Mar 11:23)

In Rom 14:23 Paul states that whatever is not of faith is sin! This is made clear throughout the Bible: lack of faith as a believer is the fatal opening that allows Satan's army a shot into your soul. Doubt was the first shot Satan fired toward mankind that resulted in the fall.

> "For God knows that in the day you eat from it (tree of knowledge of good and evil) your eyes will be opened, and you will be like God, knowing good and evil." (Gen 3:5)

The woman began to doubt the goodness of the Creator. This is the present fallen condition of mankind as well, doubting the Lord, questioning His plan and in many cases His very existence. Man fell because he chose against God, and it cannot be put in a clearer and more perfect statement than that. Satan lied when he said in Gen 3:4, "You surely shall not die!" The same principle holds true in verse 5 when he told Eve, "You will be like God." What Satan was promoting was independence from the plan of God, promoting that life can be better away from His provisions. Satan was also insinuating that God had left something out, was withholding something from them, and this was planting the seed of doubt in a subtle manner. Satan went after the one area of restraint that God had placed in that garden, he attacked it with curiosity and doubt.

So here was Satan, in serpent form, flat out denying God was right and perfect. He was also using a weaker vessel, the woman, as a staging ground for his attack. As we will see shortly, mankind has that universal tendency to cover its own moral shame by a device from his or her own handiwork. Because in verse 7 in Gen 3, it says that they had their eyes opened right after they sinned, and then went to cover themselves up with leaves before running off to hide from their divine Father. Sin always separates man from God and causes us to flee from His presence.

> "And they heard the sound of the Lord God walking in the garden in the cool of the day, and the man and his wife hid themselves from the presence of the Lord God among the trees of the garden." (Gen 3:8)

In the next verse we see God searching and calling out for lost mankind. This is not to show that God has difficulty finding a lost child, but to show our Lord reaching out to us in time of trouble. God knew, in eternity past, where they would hide, but He was being the perfect gentleman and allowing time for them to make the right choice, as well as displaying His grace toward fallen mankind. In Gen 3:10 they reveal themselves and say that they were afraid because they were naked. God questions them about who told them of their naked state, and Adam goes right for the first game played by mankind, the blame game. Adam points to his wife to take the heat off himself, she points to the serpent and the game is on. Sound familiar to what happens in the world today?

These verses make for an excellent witness to the utter powerlessness of man to walk in the path of righteousness when divine grace is withheld from him. We see God deal swiftly but mercifully with the sin when He is confronted with it. God did not destroy them and the whole garden, just to re-start the conflict with a fresh couple. God was going to set the tone for the conflict and invisible battle that was about to ensue. He sent them out into the world as fallen creatures, to strive and struggle in the devil's world and to bring forth future generations to become witnesses and to glorify the Lord in this epic battle. It was never God's intention that Satan would not have access to this weaker creature, but that the weaker creature would be made stronger through a relationship with the Lord Jesus Christ. All the while the weaker creature will be dealing with the kingdom of darkness, having complete access to either God's plan or what Satan offers. The battle lines had been drawn at this point and even the kingdom of darkness had to realize that something of this nature was taking place. Before God removed them from the garden He covered their sins and was hinting to all eyes watching that mankind did have a choice and could not be washed clean or covered up by their own merits.

> "And the Lord God made garments of skin for Adam and his wife and clothed them." (Gen 3:21)

The interesting principle is that God had to sacrifice an animal to cover His two fallen creatures. It is also interesting to note that at this point the kingdom of darkness had seen how easily this new creation can fall, how truly flawed they were. Yet there also was the scene of guilt and shame being covered by God after He had made a sacrifice to take care of the sins of deceit, lying, and running from His presence. Not even the powerful angel we call Lucifer could have realized what the sacrifice was pointing to in the future, and how God the Father would deal with this feeble creation and the sin issue.

This whole scene where God clothes Adam and Eve was a powerful manifestation of the grace of God and was probably like poison in the eyes of Satan. It might be at this point that the real issue of jealousy began to sink in. All of heaven and earth was now put on notice that God was prepared to deal with the rebellion and the combat was now getting underway. God spoke and light melted away the kingdom of darkness' prison. They were snapped out of a gloomy torment with ease and thrown into a conflict. It was and is a conflict in which they would have many opportunities to strike back over the course of human history. Satan used deception as his first weapon to level mankind and to separate people from God. Though Adam and the woman were created perfect they were certainly on a lower level than an angelic creature. Satan must have had that deep burning feeling of jealousy now—pondering, does God think He can replace me with these creatures?

Satan knew he was the most powerful of all angels, the most wise and beautiful, the natural leader and original created being from the hand of God. Satan probably had thought that there was retribution coming when God froze over the earth, he might even have thought that the battle was coming to an end. Satan could never have understood or been prepared for the new soldier introduced to the battlefield. Never could Satan grasp the concept that God was going to allow the conflict to play out in this fashion. Confusion had to blanket the whole legion of fallen angels when mankind was brought up from the dust of the earth. God was not crashing down on the fallen ones with severe judgment or punitive behavior. Satan immediately went to his same old game plan, seduce and conquer the minds of these creatures just like he did in the heavenly rebellion. Set the seeds of doubt into the soul and begin the task of undermining authority that helped him sweep away the angels in the first place.

He tried to gain an alliance, seeking to offer something better or just as good as what the Father's plan was. His plan was one that had a dual purpose, remove these new creatures from the equation and separate them from the Father as a means of regaining his throne. The man and woman were intelligent and gifted in their own human abilities, otherwise the Bible would not have described them as perfect, yet Satan was overwhelming in his seduction because of his superiority over human beings. It is important to understand that everything good or bad that has come from mankind concerning personalities and human intellect originated with the first two people God created.

> "This is the book of the generations of Adam. In the day when God created man, He made him in the likeness of God. He created them male and female, and He blessed them and named them Man in the day when they were created. When Adam had lived one hundred and thirty years, he became the father of a son in his own likeness, according to his image, and named him Seth." (Gen 5:1-3)

The phrase "in His likeness" is first stated to show that God created them good, pure, and perfect, similar to His own attributes. They were also free from deep within their souls to choose their will over God's will, which resulted in what we have titled as the Old Sin Nature. We can see that the original man (Adam) and his bride had intellectual gifts that Beethoven, Michelangelo, Einstein, and Shakespeare would later possess. Contrary to what many scientists and archeologists of the modern day teach, Adam and Eve were not grunting, slurping, and groveling around on all fours like animals. If there was a form of evolution God would have revealed it. God is not the author of confusion, mankind and Satan have this area extremely well covered with no assistance from the Creator.

The violation of the plan of God began for the human race when the woman ate the fruit and gave it to her husband and he followed her lead. This was described in Gen 3:6 and it is amazing how human history has twisted and misunderstood just the concept of the fruit itself. The apple was used in early human history to describe the forbidden fruit, yet the original language never uses the word apple regarding this forbidden fruit. Some scholars have even written that grapes were the forbidden item, using this fruit to say that too many grapes of a potent kind may have caused intoxication and bad judgment. But even science will reveal that a form of decay must occur to cause the fermentation of grapes turning into wine. There was no sign of decay in a perfect garden designed by God. If you look in the Word of God, wine is designed to make the heart happy as noted in Psa 104:15 and Ecc 9:7.

> "And you may spend the money for whatever your heart desires, for oxen, or sheep, or wine, or strong drink, or whatever your heart desires; And there you shall eat in the presence of the Lord your God and rejoice, you and your household." (Deu 14:26)

Drunkenness is a sin and that is written in the Word of God plain and clear, but God does want His people to celebrate and to use whatever He has created in moderation. There are those that should stay clear from wine and strong drink because it causes them to struggle with addiction. God the Father in a perfect environment did not set man up for failure by allowing a strong fruit or drink to be within his reach so he would stumble and fall. Another tale of nonsense that has come from a study of the Garden of Eden is the Roman Catholic belief that sex was the forbidden fruit. It is one of the main reasons that they do not allow priests or nuns to get involved in marriage, as if sex in the marital realm is sinful! Sex was designed for recreation and then procreation by God. Most of this is foolish speculation, but like most things that man studies apart from the Truth of God it ends in nonsense and foolish theories. My personal belief is that the fig was the fruit, due to the fact that they used the leaves to cover up after the fall. The truth that should be told is that it is not revealed in the Bible so it is not the main concern within that passage.

Satan was able to approach the subject of the fruit because he approached the woman on the good side of her nature. This temptation would be similar to that which might come to a woman today if she were told that a certain course of action would result in advancement for her family or husband. Maybe a new house or greater financial stability would come about if only she would follow the path that this new person put in front of her. So we can say it was from good intent that she disobeyed. The road to hell is usually paved with good intentions! Satan truly had a slick approach and an easy victory in this first ground battle against the human race. But the woman knew that God had given them all that they would need and was the ultimate authority, her husband was the next in line in the chain of authority. This temptation came from neither of the authority figures. Satan successfully detached the woman from the man and more importantly from God at the point of the first bite she took.

Human nature always has that curious essence that leaves us easily distracted and dissatisfied, leading us on frantic searches for something new or more challenging. Satan learned early on that creatures have desires and lusts because he knew what had driven him to rebel. Satan's hatred for God is so deep that he would have attempted again and again to gain an advantage in this new world from which he was being excluded. A death occurred at the moment that the first human sin occurred, it is highlighted in Rom 5:12-21. This original sin was passed down from Adam to the entire human race, it is a spiritual death that is in view in this verse. What Satan had accomplished was a temporary victory, the new creatures had chosen Satan's plan over God's plan. Satan was able to supersede Adam as the ruler over planet Earth at this point, as well as instigating the rule of the old sin nature within these new beings.

> "Therefore, just as through one man (Adam) sin entered into the world, and death through sin, and so death spread to all men, because all sinned (Adam passed down the sin nature)." (Rom 5:12)

In the original language it is clear that the verse above states that all have sinned from the fact that Adam reproduced in his likeness.

> "So then as through one transgression (Adam's sin) there resulted condemnation to all men, even so through one act of righteousness (the Cross) there resulted justification of life to all men." (Rom 5:18)

The ramifications behind Satan's first assault unlocked the wheels of God's divine gears of war. What Satan believed to be a multi-faceted attack that would cripple his opponent on many fronts was used to set God's battle plan into high gear. God's plans are always more intricate, and the results more far-reaching, than any creature, angelic or human, can understand when it first is set into motion. Here Satan was on top of the world again, the leader, the victor and champion in the eyes of his troops. Yet it all traces back to God's grace and justice because the plan from the beginning was that Satan would have his opportunity as the leader, the ultimate authority, having ample time to state his case and pursue his agenda.

As we have covered earlier Satan is the god of this world (2Co 4:4) and the prince and power of the air (Eph 2:2). So once again after an easy victory Satan had seated himself in a powerful position on the earth, and we can see why he is called the god of this world. One consequence that the kingdom of darkness was not aware of at this time in human history was that Adam and Eve would vastly multiply, spread across the earth, and desire their own kind of independence. Satan may have thought that the new creatures would easily succumb to his will and his plan, but the control he would have over the human race would be fleeting and much less potent than he realized at the time of the incident within the garden.

Satan had led them away from the divine provisions and dependence on God as well as the blessings that God had showered down on them, but he certainly did not obtain a league of obedient followers. This is similar to the one who digs a pit for someone to fall into and they end up in it themselves. Ecc 10:8, "He who digs a pit may fall into it," is a fine description for the predicament Satan has gotten into. Fools plot and set traps, attempting to set others up because they are jealous or insecure. They end up in misery and confusion in the end. Evil has a nasty way of backfiring right in the perpetrator's face in the long run.

> "He has dug a pit and hollowed it out, and has fallen into the hole which he made." (Psa 7:15)

King Solomon who had great insight and wisdom stated in Pro 26:27, "He who digs a pit will fall into it, and he who rolls a stone, it will come back on him." The one who promotes self will eventually lose out. In the blind attempt to destroy others it is inevitable that operation boomerang will occur and all the destruction that is directed to others comes back upon the one who initiated it. This key area of the Word of God is where we learn to stay out of the business of reprimanding others and punishing those we think deserve it, manipulating situations in our favor and using the sneaky approach to get ahead in life.

> "And do not judge and you will not be judged; and do not condemn, and you will not be condemned; pardon, and you will be pardoned." (Luk 6:37)

At a quick glance we see the first two human beings taking the side of Satan in the initial confrontation on battlefield Earth, but things are not always what they seem. Satan used trickery and confusion and did gain a win. But his true goal was to have man step away from God and cling to his system and deny God's system or methods of survival on this planet. So the man and the woman have now gone independent, and the kingdom of darkness probably assumed they would depend on their power and system now.

Little did Satan know that self-reliance is deep within the soul of the human creatures. He did not realize that man would be much like angels in that aspect, completely having a free will and choices available to them, desires and lust deeply rooted into their nature. Man, like angels, aspires to do what Frank Sinatra sang about, to do it my way! Satan was surely fooled by this lower creation and was certainly underestimating free will and God's divine grace. The arrogance of his own independence did not come to mind when he began his attack, because arrogance, like that which consumes Satan, is blinded by its desire for success at the expense of others. In fact a good sign that a believer is stepping away from the plan of God and delving into reversionism is the arrogance of attacking and judging others. Harsh criticism and manipulative behaviors to gain what they desire all come forth from the person who is not in fellowship with God. What victory Satan had accomplished was overshadowed by the future confusion and destruction of his own plan that was set into motion at this time.

The Romans were defeated by Pyrrhus of Epirus, but the cost of the victory was so staggering that when Pyrrhus later appraised the battle, it became a standard measure for costly victories. Eventually the phrase "another such victory and Pyrrhus will be destroyed" was to come from it. Satan would slowly learn that these new creatures were not like a herd of cattle that could be prodded and easily re-directed. The kingdom of darkness would have to come to the realization that the human race and their volition could not be easily infiltrated, not even by God's supreme powers. This is the reason that the kingdom of darkness has become masters of subtle manipulation, subliminal messages, and covert actions. The lesson learned at that moment for the demon army was that man's independence from God does not mean dependence on Satan.

We have covered the two wills in the universe, God's will and Satan's. Man's will, or independence from God, does not mean man's will lining up with Satan's plan. If Satan's plan was well controlled and in full effect, and his goals were ever actually accomplished, he would be able to point to the earth and say, "See the perfection I have created? Like You (God) I have the ability to create perfect environment and to operate with love, justice, and righteousness and all is well here on earth. We do not need You!" Do you believe for a moment that Satan can hold the earth up on that kind of pedestal? The human race is made up of stubborn, arrogant, self-seeking creatures that always want to do things their own way, much like Satan in their attitudes. At no time in human history has God been able to look down on this planet and say, "Wow! Perfection, great job Satan!" So what this statement of the two wills that exist within the universe means is that you are either in the plan of God and lining up with His will, or you are like Satan and independent from the divine Creator.

There are plenty of people who do not recognize Satan's will or his ultimate desires. They are like him in the realm of arrogance and independence, but are not under his complete control. So we can say that part one of Satan's plan was a success: man fell. The second phase of the battle plan came apart at the seams because a large majority of the human race does not follow him, does not depend on his system and his will for their lives. Lewis Sperry Chafer has written some interesting insights upon this subject. For example, he wrote: "A serious question arises whether the presence of gross evil in the world is due to Satan's intention to have it so, or whether it indicates Satan's inability to execute all he has designed. The probability is great that Satan's ambition has led him to undertake more than any creature could ever administer."

At no point in human history did Satan gain full control of the human race. Adam never sold his soul to the devil, he made no side deal with the kingdom of darkness. Our spiritual death through Adam at no time affects the grace of God, in fact it illuminates it! Being born in the flesh, as spiritually dead creatures, does not hinder the power of a positive decision toward God, aided by the ministry of the Holy Spirit in common and efficacious grace. The plan was that we were to have access to His grace and redemption if we so choose. At the same time Satan has a fair and level playing field because the human race starts off in sin. Rom 5:6 shows that we were born helpless and Christ died for the ungodly.

> "For one will hardly die for a righteous man, though perhaps for the good man someone would dare even to die. But God demonstrates His own love toward us, in that while we were yet sinners, Christ died for us." (Rom 5:7-8)

Most people miss the key factor that the victory Satan grabbed in the garden was actually a profound defeat, which is the reason for human history to follow a full and unyielding course until the conflict is resolved.

Human beings choose against God daily in many cases. Free will is negative toward the plan of God, and acknowledgment of our savior Jesus Christ is almost non-existent in the majority of the human race. However, this does not mean that Satan has control over all mankind. Adam was a rebellious fool like we all are at certain points in our fragile lives, but he never proclaimed Satan as his god or authority.

What Satan did, as we often do when we turn from God, is say, "I will be like the most High!" This is stated through our actions of independence and doing things our own way apart from the plan of God. An English poet named William Ernest Henley, in his Invictus wrote about the cry of Adam toward God the Father: "It matters not how strait the gate, How charged with punishments the scroll; I am the master of my fate, I am the captain of my soul."

Remarkably expressed by this poet, his foolish attitude is so obvious when the Truth of the Angelic Conflict is staring back at you. What this poem states is that I am the leader, I am deity and master of my soul. "Only a fool says in his heart, there is no God" (Psa 14:1). Neither a man nor an angelic creature can bring all people, circumstances, and all in the atmosphere into perfect harmony, only a divine and all-powerful God can do that. Yet we have people and angelic creatures that claim and even attempt to do so throughout history.

There is a second tier or deeper layer of the Angelic Conflict because man has now rebelled and struggles against the Creator as well. Two separate battles are now raging because Satan stood against the Father and Creator of all things and said, "I will be like You!" Satan started out with a thought of discontent and became ungrateful, and now we have a mess we call planet Earth where a visible and invisible conflict is running rampant. Man is a rebel and rebels against his own flesh and people, he rebels against Satan's program and more importantly against the Lord. A Rebel is a proper description of most people we see every day of our lives. There is no satisfying the restless craving of the man without God. The words of Augustine expressed it perfectly, "Oh God, Thou hast formed us for Thyself; and our souls can know no rest until they rest in Thee."

The last segment of this chapter should answer the questions, just how far did man fall? How deep was the pit? How far off the path did man step when he chose his will over God's? To answer these types of questions we must always go back and look at Adam, the father of the human race. It is through his DNA that the sin nature is passed down. Some left wing "Humanist" groups might say that man did not fall, but is on his way up. Some branches of Protestantism hold the thought that though man fell, he still has the will to choose to get back up if he wishes to exercise it. Others believe, as is the Truth of the Bible, that man fell into a deep and inescapable pit (spiritual death). No works, efforts, or positive outreach program can assist him out of the pit, or even help him truly understand God. Man in his flesh cannot please God, or make amends with God, we are not capable in any realm. Anyone thinking that they can rise above the spiritual death issue apart from belief in our Lord and Savior Jesus Christ is very worldly—minded, their arrogance is so thick that they are completely blinded! A naturally-minded man cannot understand or accept the things of God (1Co 2:14). A mind set on the flesh is hostile toward God (Rom 8:7-8). Rom 3:11-12 says, "There is none who understands, there is none who seeks for God; all have turned aside, together they have become useless; there is none who does good, there is not even one."

These verses in Romans are so clear that ALL have fallen and that NONE can fathom or gain acceptance with God, that it should be simple to see that a works program by a fallen man cannot save him. The Bible does say that we are all sick in the head (Jer 17:9 and Isa 1:5-6), but I am sure that it will not sink into many sick heads and deceitful hearts who see these verses. The Bible is one of the least publicized books, and yet it is the most important book on the planet. The plan of Satan for human history is hard at work in this area, so many will not even take the time to study it at all. God wants to make it clear that we are helpless and hopeless creatures (angels and humans) without Him. After we discover this, the second part of God's plan is to get us removed from that pit (born again and saved) by His work and His plan. Phase three of God's battle plan, grow up spiritually and get into the battle! Yet Satan is having great success in blinding the human race and even believers about the whole issue of the Angelic Conflict. In Rev 12:9 it is said that Satan deceives the whole world. 2Co 4:4 says, the god of this world has blinded the unbelievers' minds (Greek word apistos = those without doctrine), that they might not see the light of the gospel of the glory of Christ.

How often do the media, school systems, or the general public discuss or promote the word of God, especially a subject like the Angelic Conflict? If you cannot see that this is the devil's world then you certainly have been blinded by him. If you were a military leader trapped in a long drawn-out battle and your troops were fluctuating in their dedication toward the cause, would you not use every trick in the book to keep them on your side? Now add to that, your opponent is a military genius with vast resources and has a great cause that he is battling for, would you not keep your troops blind to your opponent's cause and strengths? We have a battle going on and one leader is weak, but an expert at guerilla tactics and covert actions, he is ruthless and deceptive in his approach. The other leader is open, honest, has superior fire power, and will fight to the death for his troops. Who are you willing to fight for?

Adam was destined to fall and the fall would be deep and the repercussions would carry on throughout human history. This was the battle plan laid out in eternity past, but there was an escape route given from the pit! The Cross would implement the action for all who desired to be lifted up, to be rescued and saved. If you are a born again believer and are ignorant of the route, it is due to a lack of priorities and nothing else. Yes, there is a sin problem for the human race, but the problem has already been solved by a loving God who is always prepared and victorious in His efforts.

As a believer, part of your mission in this conflict is to understand and preach this Word of His Truth. The Greek word for preacher is kerux, used by the apostle Paul (1Ti 2:7 and 2Ti 1:11), also misunderstood in our day and age. The word is to be a title for someone who is faithful and represents the Word of God properly. The following definition came from an article written in January 1963, by Victor Paul Furnish in a magazine entitled Interpretation:

"A kerux was someone who had important news to bring. He often announced an athletic event or a religious festival or functioned as a political messenger or as a bringer of some good news or command from the king's court. He was to have a strong voice and proclaim his message with vigor without lingering to discuss it. The kerux's most important qualification was that he faithfully represents or reports the word of the one by whom he had been sent. He was not to be original, but his message was to be that of another."

Chapter 12

How God is Glorified in the Angelic Conflict.

We cannot see our enemy because we are entangled in an intensified stage of battle. Invisible gas, invisible chemicals, and invisible weapons that do not appear on radar are the most difficult and dangerous on any battlefield. A flesh and blood soldier charging at you is an easy target to pick off, but the sneak attack, and the invisible chemicals that pierce the air, are deadly in combat. We currently live in this intensified stage of the invisible conflict, a period (dispensation) referred to as the Church Age. The pastor-teacher should be qualified, prepared and filled with the Holy Spirit in order to teach and arm the Christian soldiers. The gift of pastor-teacher is not given out like candy on Halloween, it is a special gift with which God touches certain souls.

This present dispensation is a divine power experiment from God. Satan's angle is to discredit God, to point to the lie of God as unfair and unjust, and to promote independence from God and accept what he offers from this current world. The pastor-teacher has been designed as a chef to serve the meal of Truth to a hungry flock. Study and teach, then study and teach some more is the job description. The teacher of Truth is not described as a referee for quarrels, or a counselor of worldly relationships. He is not to be a weeping do-gooder who occupies his time involved with political agendas. He is to feed the flock, teach, study, and then teach some more. He is to be a dedicated student of the original Scriptures and to decipher the Word accurately.

> "For this reason, I Paul, the prisoner of Christ Jesus for the sake of you Gentiles—if indeed you have heard of the dispensation of God's grace which was given to me for you;" (Eph 3:1-2)

This dispensation here (Church Age) is a demonstration of the grace of God and unveils the fallacy of satanic lies, because we see the grace of God in offering fallen creatures, with negative attitudes and evil deeds, opportunities for change. Grace gives an opportunity to wash it all clean, put it in the past and move forward with no long term, eternal repercussions. A great example of this grace in action is seen in many prisons when a hardened, death-row criminal finds the Lord and is born again and saved before he is put to death. At no time in human history has this much power ever been released toward meritless objects for the fulfillment of the plan of God. Grace is the only substance that can fill the huge gap between divine perfection and human imperfection. As Paul has stated in Eph 3:2, this dispensation is all grace, no merit. Nothing can be earned, no one can compete and be a better human being to gain God's favor. You can look at the Heroes of Faith hall of fame in Hebrews 11 and come up with names like Moses, Abraham, King David, Sarah, or Rahab, and not one had a better position than you do right now. They had no better opportunity, power, or position than any believer of this modern-day era.

The fact is that we have more power available to us! In 2Co 6:9 we are called invisible heroes because winner believers of the Church Age are unknown (invisible to the world) yet well known (heroes in the Angelic Conflict). The history books of the world may never put your name in a paragraph but the angelic history books will speak volumes on winner believers in the Church Age. The phrase in the Bible that says "the last will be first and the first will be last" is also a reference to just how important the invisible hero is in the angelic community. Those devoted Christians that try to stay in the plan of God will certainly be considered the last on this earth but will be first to receive crowns in heaven. Paul goes on to explain a certain mystery not revealed by Old Testament scriptures, but by divine insight given to him as a chosen teacher of Truth in Ephesians 3.

> "To be specific, that the Gentiles are fellow heirs and fellow members of the body (in union with Christ), and fellow partakers of the promise in Christ Jesus through the gospel, of which I was made a minister, according to the gift of God's grace which was given to me according to the working of His power." (Eph 3:6-7)

The mystery doctrine that Paul is presenting was not something ever discussed in the Old Testament. Did any of the Old Testament saints say they were in union with Christ? Did they speak about the Holy Spirit or God living within their souls? The Church Age is very unique when you begin to see the power experiment that God implemented after the work on the Cross was completed. In Ephesians 3:8 Paul proclaims that he is the very least of the saints, yet he was hand-picked by God to bring the message to the masses and again he brings forth the mystery that is unfathomable, incomprehensible, and baffling to the human race.

> "... and to bring to light what is the administration (oikonomia = dispensation) of the mystery which for ages has been hidden in God, who created all things." (Eph 3:9)

Now as you get into verses 10 and 11 it notes the Angelic Conflict and its resolution.

> "In order that the manifold (many levels) wisdom of God might now be made known through the church to the rulers and the authorities in the heavenly places (angels). This was in accordance with the eternal purpose (God's plan in the conflict) which He carried out in Christ Jesus our Lord." (Eph 3:10-11)

Without a pastor-teacher who is well versed in the original language and filled with the Holy Spirit there is no possible way a believer could understand in what direction Paul was going and what the verses were pointing out. The communicator of Scripture has to be accurate and, more importantly, chosen by God. The world system will not offer you classes in angelic warfare, invisible heroes, and mystery doctrine because the devil has done a wonderful job of muddying it up, keeping it vague and mystical like a fairy tale instead of cold hard facts and the Truth that it is. This is why you should keep those teachers of Truth in prayer.

Paul asked for prayer, in Eph 6:19, "for teachers of the Word to make known with boldness the mystery of the gospel, and speak boldly, as they ought to speak." In 2Ti 4:2 it says that a pastor is to be ready to teach at all times, in season and out of season, to reprove and rebuke with the Word of God. Today we have men behind the pulpit who have no clue about the mystery doctrine or the Angelic Conflict, they are more concerned with popularity and putting "rear-ends" in the seats. This is the subtle work of the kingdom of darkness, using covert actions, like political activism and community projects that many teachers of the church get involved in.

The successes that Satan can brag about today are the small distractions and details of life that occupy a believer's time and distract from focusing on Truth. The teachers that do not have the gift, or if they do, do not make time to study because they are involved in personality conflicts and programs in the church that are nothing more than a dog and pony show, are among the many victories of Satan. Huge crowds and baskets full of money do not bring forth Truth that is vital for growth in the spiritual life. This all suits the kingdom of darkness just fine and is a portion of their battle plan where they can proclaim a victory. Anything that can detract from the Truth of the Gospel, distort it, or keep it murky is a direct hit from the demon army in this conflict. Most people will spend two minutes a day praying, and 8 hours working, and then 4 more hours watching a TV screen, this is certainly a victory for Satan in many respects. God is not being glorified and Jesus Christ is not being preached in that person's life.

Victory for the kingdom of darkness is not what a Hollywood movie depicts. Burning cities and evil babies born to conquer the planet are very graphic and fun to watch, but are not in the satanic battle plan. Satan prefers to work in the invisible realm to attack the Gospel and the Truth of the Word of God in any way possible. The apostle Paul had to undergo great tribulation during his time on earth. Adversity was around every corner for him, yet he kept studying and preaching the Word. Satan probably had to give personal attention to a teacher like Paul because he was such a force to reckon with in his Christian walk. Paul would even tell his congregation that they should not worry about him.

> "Therefore I ask you not to lose heart at my tribulations on your behalf, for they are for your glory." (Eph 3:13)

Paul is warning them not to grow weary and distracted by problems because it is part of the spiritual path he had to walk. The apostle Paul became a target of hostile pursuit by angelic demons and legalistic people so he was attacked on both fronts, the spiritual and the natural. The apostle Paul had people turning against him and leaving him as noted in 2Ti 1:15 and in 2Ti 4:11 where he wrote that only Luke had stuck by his side. Any pastor who teaches Truth as Paul did will eventually expose the kingdom of darkness, and the bull's eye is put upon their back after that. In 2Co 12:7 Paul realized he had a demon assigned to him to buffet or abuse him. This word in the original language is kolaphizo, meaning to use a form of violence and foul language when attacking someone. The scale of attacks for our Lord was much greater due to the very vital nature of His mission on planet Earth. But nonetheless when the Truth of the Word of God is shining bright (Eph 5:11) it illuminates the schemes of Satan and that will always bring the battle to your front door. We are told by Paul and below by Jesus Christ that it is not a source of worry or concern for any believer because we all have our own pre-designed plan and times of suffering as well as challenges to face. Our Lord said in Luk 23:28, "Stop weeping for me, but weep for yourselves and for your children."

It is God's intention or battle plan that His children learn the mysteries and become aware of the conflict, the invisible strategies, lest we fall on the battlefield and taste the dust of defeat like Satan. The simple fact is that until your relationship with God begins to flourish and the light of Truth comes into your soul you will be an easy target and victim of the depression and confusion that this world injects into daily human life. Many people believe happiness and contentment are two separate things that are related; however, the Bible shows that true happiness is contentment! Cosmic happiness is fleeting and does not guarantee contentment. The apostle Paul made this clear by stating, "I have learned to be content in whatever circumstance I am." And he goes on in Philippians 4 to say it is learned from Bible doctrine.

> "I know how to get along with humble means, and I also know how to live in prosperity; in any and every circumstance I have learned the mystery of being filled and going hungry, both of having abundance and suffering need." (Phi 4:12)

What Paul is saying is that he has studied and applied the doctrine and mystery of the Church Age and is a well-rounded student. Paul learned that in life the conflict we are in is designed for challenges, and that problem-solving by using doctrine brings both growth and blessing over time. Many Christians think that if they maintain a positive attitude that all things will work perfectly to their advantage. The perfect mate will suddenly appear, the career will skyrocket, and blessings will drop in their lap at each and every turn, and this is not the case. Not even the Old Testament saints had it that easy.

Abraham failed in marriage more than once and Sarah was far from perfect as well. David (a man after God's own heart) was known as a womanizer and made some terrible decisions as a king that cost people their lives. Jacob was a manipulative man and was always scheming with his own little agenda. We can assume that their old sin nature was hard at work during these difficult times, but also that the kingdom of darkness was working overtime in their lives as well. Yet, they all turned out to be Biblical heroes in the end. The word we keep referring back to in this book is "conflict", and meanings of this word include "quarrel," "fracas," and" battle." Words like tension or dispute or clash all define the word "conflict." So how is it you find true happiness or contentment in the midst of that? Again we can look at the best Bible teacher that the human race had after Christ physically left the earth: the apostle Paul.

> "I can do all things (endure all tests) through Him (Christ) who keeps on pouring His power into me." (Phi 4:13)

What you must realize is that our time on earth is the war and the time to grow up spiritually, because when we face death that battle is over and the war is complete. You are not looking to get an A+ on a Bible test at the end of your life, you are seeking growth and the strength to endure the battles ahead of you. Man cannot manufacture that kind of contentment, it comes from strength deep in our souls, within our thinking patterns, that is only developed through the intake and application of the Word of God. It is not an overnight process or weekend retreat that gives you this type of endurance and knowledge, it is a day to day workout schedule with the Lord Jesus Christ, it is His mind that has the power. Our minds must be renewed daily as the Bible often points out, repetition and continual practice is what makes a great warrior. This is why the military drills over and over again. What they initiate during basic training are fundamentals that are repeated and pushed day in and day out for weeks until a recruit can operate in those basic functions without any real thought. Our minds have a similar quality to that of a computer. It is a programming issue, if garbage is taken in then garbage comes out. The world bombards us with negativity and anti-God principles everyday, and when you have no time for God during your busy week what programming principles will stick and how many will be doctrinal?

Jesus Christ taught daily during his ministry and the apostles became fervent students of the Word. There comes a time when you finally realize the truth and depth of this invisible warfare and what is really going on. This is when you step up to the challenge and make God a priority, or you fall by the wayside. At the Judgment Seat of Christ your mastery of His word and your spiritual maneuvers during this conflict all come to light. That is when the Lord and all the beings, angelic and human, will see what you did with your time here on planet Earth. There are levels of spiritual growth and testing: evidence testing, testing for blessing, testing for growth, spiritual childhood, spiritual autonomy, and finally levels of maturity that will equal a high rank in eternity future. You cannot bring glory to God by maintaining a status of spiritual childhood for 20 or 30 years. That would be a statement of selfishness and arrogance, spending that kind of time in the spiritual life without having taken at least a few baby steps forward in the plan.

Your mastery of doctrines like the Angelic Conflict and the mystery doctrine of the Church Age makes you a competent warrior, ready and able to stand in the gap against the demon army. A good question to ask yourself is, could you take a major hit or loss in your personal life and still remain faithful to our Lord? Job is always brought to mind in consideration of Biblical questions like this and he is the prime example of real evidence testing in the conflict. His tale was one of brutal and gut-wrenching tests that God probably used as the extreme example and not the norm in spiritual warfare. Job lost wealth and health, family and friendships, his reputation was in jeopardy and he was struggling and stumbling to get through it the whole time. He was given over to Satan himself, and that is the most severe test and also the highest honor in this heavenly court case.

The tests could have lasted months, or a few years, but in the end he was given double portions and better blessing than what he had at the start of the test. Is the faith and endurance needed for such testing in your soul right now? If not, God cannot use you on the front lines just yet. Will your testimony aid in putting the fallen angels in a permanent and fiery prison cell for eternity, or are you one of the spiritual babes that wants to hide behind the safety of the mature warriors on the front lines? The Angelic Conflict is so profound that it must be revealed in increments. Our frail minds could not handle the magnificent plan that God has designed in pre-historic eternity past. So we are told to study and grasp a little at time, to grow at our own pace by daily learning and application of the Word of God. That is why finding the right pastor and submitting yourself to regular teaching under his ministry is so important.

> "For it is precept upon precept, precept upon precept, line upon line, line upon line, here a little, there a little." (Isa 28:10)

The Angelic Conflict is not just a doctrine about Satan, it is more of a doctrine of human history and our lives. The majority of the Christian community understands some concept of Satan but has a distorted view of the mission he is on and do not understand the human function in all of this. The erroneous Christian view is centered on marching at abortion clinics, building Christian schools, operating a successful Christian book store, or getting a Christian politician elected. The core of our real mission here on earth is to grow up in the spiritual realm and to glorify God when the time arises in our life. The verse we noted earlier in this chapter (Eph 3:10), when Paul used the phrase "that the manifold wisdom of God might now be made known through the church . . ." is stating emphatically that now (Church Age) is the time to preach and learn as well as to apply the mystery doctrine. The term for manifold in the Greek is polupoikilos referring to God's being of many levels and dimensions, all multi-faceted. This is a word that would also mean beyond human comprehension or any comparison to something here on earth. If you have not realized it by now, you cannot put God in a box and assume He will do B or C because you did step A.

No creature has God all figured out and knows the complete plan and result that God will obtain at the end of any situation. He is so versatile and beyond the genius realm that when we use the term omniscience to describe Him we sometimes lose sight of the fact that He made that word up to begin with! God may have you halfway through a situation that appears to be going in one direction, when He suddenly drops you off to a different result, but obtains all the required perfection and effects that were designed to happen in eternity past. God's end results never leave you in confusion, it is just that most times we cannot fathom what is happening until a much later date.

The Old Testament spoke of a king who was coming, yet a carpenter showed up with no physical crown or worldly or royal trappings. At first glance we would have never seen Him as a king, no matter how spiritual we think we would have been in that day and age. The Cross is a wonderful example of the multi-faceted God we have. In Gal 6:14 the Cross is the means of glorifying Christ and is also the means of propitiating God the Father (Heb 12:2). God gets several things done with one act, it is all done, complete and set in stone a million years before it happens! We cannot wrap our insignificant minds around something like that. Not only does the Cross serve the purpose of the Father and Son within the Trinity, it also offers a weaker creature redemption from the sin issue (Col 1:20). The Cross bridges the gap for mankind to become filled with the Holy Spirit by believing upon the completed work that took place upon It, and just for icing on the divine cake it also resolves the Angelic Conflict (Col 2:14-15).

The Cross achieved so many solutions, both angelic and human in nature, that we could spend eternity learning of a new one each day!

When Jesus Christ was born in His humanity there was something beginning to be revealed that even the angels with all their rich history of being around the Divine Creator in eternity past did not understand. The Church Age was a mystery being solved, unfolding each day to the wide-eyed surprise of the angelic community. Angels watched the Lord become human. They saw a lower creation and then witnessed the Creator become one of those creatures.

> "And by common confession great is the mystery of the unique spiritual life: He (God) who was revealed in the flesh, was vindicated in the Spirit, beheld by angels, proclaimed among the Gentiles, believed on in the world, taken up in glory." (1 Ti 3:16)

It is only when you live the unique spiritual life that God has so graciously designed for you, that you truly bring glory to God in the Angelic Conflict. In Eph 3:10 we are told that the angels are watching, and this is not the only verse in the Bible that points to the world as a stage for the conflict to play out on. Yes, angels can and are supposed to learn from us! The lessons they learn are from the radical changes that took place at the birth of the Church Age. The universal shift in the whole conflict began at the Cross and the angels must have been awestruck at this scene.

Within every generation there is a group, a pivot of believers that make the difference. The house of Noah highlights this pivot pretty well as God used them to re-start a generation after the debacle that took place between angels and human beings back in Genesis chapter 6. A positive group, or even a scattered batch of positive believers, can make the difference between national disaster and Godly blessings. This pivot refers to the invisible heroes highlighted in this chapter, but if you are looking for recognition in the worldly realm you do not understand the concept of this angelic warfare. There are relatively few in any generation that will make a difference pertaining to angelic or human history. The angels are blown away when a weaker creature, under difficult circumstances, withstands attacks and confusion, relies on God and applies His Word to keep pressing forward. This is a powerful and deadly artillery shell on the battlefield of angelic, invisible warfare. This is the statement on the witness stand that proclaims God is righteous, just and fair, a loving and compassionate authority figure that you can trust.

Problem-solving with the Word of God is your artillery unit during heated combat. As you may be aware, in the military, ground troops use artillery to advance as well as to cover themselves from oncoming attacks. Precision artillery can lay down a wall of explosions to support the foot soldiers in a deadly exchange. Artillery is the destructive force that is responsible for eroding enemy strongholds and fortresses. You cannot operate and fire a howitzer without proper training and repetitive firing drills. The time to learn that is not seconds before the battle but years in advance so that you are an expert at placing those deadly shells. Most believers are not prepared and fall apart during the stressful events and challenges that occur in their lives. The angels are then shown the failure of a believer in Christ instead of the awe-inspiring victory of the Word of God in action. Most believers react with cosmic emotionalism instead of responding with doctrinal weaponry during a time of pressure. The fact is that most Christians are no better off, or no more prepared than the common unbeliever of this world. They are easily sidetracked, shaken up, and shattered during any form of an attack.

A flawed creature that uses the problem-solving devices from God is astonishing for angelic creatures on both sides of the fence to witness. The believer who is trained, prepared, and humble enough to apply God's plan for their life is in the minority, but is a part of a powerful pivot that makes all the difference in this conflict. These invisible heroes will be applauded in the angelic realm. They are the ones in Rev 3:5, who are called winners and are acknowledged before God and all the angels. The sad portion of this lesson is that since the beginning of the Church Age the world has become a breeding ground for pastor-teachers who wish to be popular and well known in the cosmic sense, but neglect Truth and the true Gospel of Jesus Christ in spiritual warfare. This is because it is not popular or profitable to teach real doctrinal principles. It is more popular to scratch the surface, or even worse, to just teach another gospel, another truth, and a misleading message for the sake of gaining great numbers in their church. The fame and fortune that comes from most T.V. evangelism and popular teachers is nothing more than smoke and mirrors designed to gain fortune and to find themselves some worldly acknowledgment. That type of teacher may become a celebrity in the world but has proved nothing in reference to the Angelic Conflict and what God has designed for born again believers. The fact is that Satan uses men like that to cloud the Gospel and to mislead believers. This is just another angle of satanic attack on the ego and arrogance within man to be recognized.

> "... for they loved the approval of men rather than the approval of God." (Joh 12:43)

What becomes evident over the years since our Lord finished the work on the Cross is that Satan has never had enough control to organize mankind on one solid religious front, nor has he been successful in leading the entire human race astray from the Word of God. There has never been a moment of world peace throughout the planet, no perfection or one world order, no religious solidarity reaching out across all the lands. That simply tells us that the prince and power of the air has failed and is still in operation "Change the World" mode. He has not succeeded in being like God and is in a forward battle stance still pressing the issue and seeking his rebuttal victory. There was a song written by John Lennon that was used by over a hundred representatives at a recent Olympic venue, they all held hands and sang the following verses:

"Imagine there's no heaven, it's easy if you try. No hell before us, above us only sky. Imagine all the people, living for today. Imagine there's no countries. It isn't hard to do. Nothing to kill or die for, no religion too. Imagine all the people, living life and peace. Imagine no possessions. I wonder if you can? No need for greed or hunger, a brotherhood of man. Imagine all the people sharing all the world. You may say I'm a dreamer, but I'm not the only one. I hope someday you'll join us, and the world will live as one."

We all know the writer, the original talent that put this piece together, and I have no idea if he was a Christian or an atheist, but it is certainly a song that the kingdom of darkness must enjoy listening to because it holds many of their core values within it! The one guarantee I can give you at this point is that the world will never come under such terms as this song describes while Satan is still actively operating in the Angelic Conflict on this earth. Something to keep in mind is that Satan's fall—just like the fall of man—was so deep that he cannot (nor can man) climb out on his own power, with his own will and his own schemes. The two words for any fallen creature are best stated as helpless and hopeless. Rom 3:23 tells us that all have ultimately fallen short, and in Rom 3:10-14, "There is none righteous, not even one; there is none who understands, there is none who seeks for God; all have turned aside, together they have become useless; there is none who does good, there is not even one. Their throat is an open grave, with their tongues they keep deceiving, the poison of asps is under their lips; whose mouth is full of cursing and bitterness."

The Greek word translated in the Bible as "asps" is "aspis" which means a small and most venomous serpent, the bite of which is fatal unless the part that was bitten is immediately cut away. It speaks to the fact that every time you listen to gossip or slander, judging and criticism, you are allowing the bite of the serpent to destroy some part of your life. To gain further insight into God's opinion of wretched mankind, follow the next few verses:

> "Their feet are swift to shed blood, destruction and misery are in their paths, and the path of peace they have not known. There is no fear of God before their eyes." (Rom 3:15-18)

Rom 9:15-16 states that God will have mercy upon whom He sees fit, meaning that it does not depend on man's human efforts or which way he runs, only that God is the author of mercy and grace, not fallen man. We are not able to manufacture grace and mercy of the divine nature, certainly not from the flesh of our old sin nature. As we have noted earlier in the book, the naturally-minded man cannot understand God and the entire human race is sick (Isa 1:5-6), nothing good comes from us and deceit is our very nature (Jer 17:9). The Angelic Conflict clears up any notion that a creature would have divine power or anything good within him that could rise or fall on his own talent or merits. God must do everything for man that is to be done to bring him back to his position before his fall, yet even more than that, as we will see, to a place above that from which he fell.

The overall strategy that God has put into action offers three possibilities for hope as far as mankind is concerned. The fallen angels have gone beyond that point and can now only play out the hand they have dealt themselves. The three possibilities for the human race concerning hope are God, self-reliance, or the devil's world. There is not a fourth option or another avenue for mankind to choose. What God is accomplishing among a hundred other results by introducing this invisible warfare is displaying that created creatures cannot live successfully independent from their Creator. Nor can a created creature find happiness and true contentment away from a loving God. What God did is not only to create a lower species than His first creation to prove this, but also for the most part He uses the weakest of that species to do so.

> "For the word of the cross is to those who are perishing foolishness, but to us who are being saved it is the power of God. For it is written, 'I will destroy the wisdom of the wise, and the cleverness of the clever I will set aside.'" (1Co 1:18-19)

God will use the foolish ones and scum of the earth to confound the wise and popular ones of this world. God does not always put the obvious person in a position of authority. In fact, in many cases such as with David or even Jacob it was the least of the crowd that became the leader and blessed one. David was a scrawny teenager who stepped out ahead of his older brothers and many grown men of the tribe to challenge the fierce giant Goliath. Jacob was a momma's boy who was manipulated into a situation of blessing by a strong mother. Paul was an enemy of the apostles and yet became their leader and perhaps the best teacher of them all!

> "Where is the wise [referring to both angelic and human creatures, in the original language], where is the scribe? Where is the debater of this age? Has not God made foolish the wisdom of the cosmic system? For since in the wisdom of God the world through its wisdom did not come to know God, God was well pleased through the foolishness of the message preached to save those who believe." (1Co 1:20-21)

1Co 1:20-26 points out that the Jews asked for signs, the Gentiles considered it foolishness, the Greeks were seeking greater wisdom. So even during a time when Christ was still fresh upon their minds, the concept of the work upon the Cross was a stumbling block for most people outside of the apostles and those dedicated believers. They did not understand Him, His mission, what the Cross represented, and what God was calling them to do. This type of statement points directly to the so-called wise and elite leaders of the ancient world and it is just as widespread and maybe even more so today!

> " . . . but God has chosen the foolish ones of the world to shame the wise, and God has chosen the weak of the world to shame the things which are strong. And the base or unknown ones of the world and the despised, God has chosen the things that are not, that He might nullify the things that are, that no flesh should boast before God." (1Co 1:27-29)

Human history is the record of the attempts of mankind and Satan to do something for man. Therefore, when asked why an omnipotent (all-powerful) God permits the holocausts of human history, the answer from the Word of God must be that He permits them in order to demonstrate to the universe that neither Satan nor man can do anything for themselves or for each other. If it were otherwise, these forces, which are at enmity with each other and both against God as their common enemy, could say either separately or together: "We have done it! We have established a kingdom without God and have no need for Him or any of His plans." It would be a declaration of independence of the worst kind. Created creatures have arrogance, pride, ego, and lusts so deeply rooted into their DNA that whenever they come together to create something perfect, it usually ends in some type of suffering or disaster, far away from God's blessing. Creative, highly intelligent people have always come out with theories and statements that sound so profound and true that the masses simply cannot resist their appeal. That is why Hollywood sets trends and most people follow their lead, no matter how stupid and immature it may appear.

We are made up of a majority of foolish followers who put great stock in this world. These types of people are suckers for flash, sparkle, and charm. Most leaders are elected on the basis of looks and charm, not substance and integrity. H.G. Wells once made this ridiculous statement and to this day his name brings awe and great respect in many intellectual circles. His statement was "Faced with what we see around us in the world, we are forced to conclude that either God has the power and does not care, or that God cares but does not have the power." That is logic to a naturally-minded man. Yet we know it to be the exact opposite of what is true when the Angelic Conflict is studied in depth. The world simply does not take the time nor even have a genuine interest in Truth. What the study of this invisible warfare reveals is the truth that God does have the power and most certainly does care, but He has a unique invisible plan that has yet to be totally completed. The plan demands man's failure and ultimately chaos to demonstrate to all that help is to be found in Him and Him alone. God has the power to alter any terrible situation, but will not do so today because of His greater purpose. This greater purpose clearly shows, even screams, that if mankind is left to his own means and methods, catastrophic destruction is certain. God's plan will show that the world is easily shaken and assurance and security that gives mankind confidence is only found underneath the realm of our Lord's blessings and grace.

> "Therefore, since we receive a kingdom which cannot be shaken, let us show gratitude, by which we may offer to God an acceptable service with reverence and awe; for our God is a consuming fire." (Heb 12:28-29)

So God cares tremendously, enough to send His Son to Calvary to die for the whole world. His care can only be manifest today to those individuals who have accepted the principle that they are helpless without divine help. They are the ones who admit the principle of their spiritual bankruptcy and have turned utterly to the Lord Jesus Christ as God's one and only answer to their problems. The world has a sense that God does not care; however, like Mr. Wells, they are without spiritual insight. The injustice and cruelty of mankind are at every corner of the world, and without a true knowledge of the Angelic Conflict, and who and what Jesus Christ is to the universe, we may never see the compassion God has for all of us. God is unchangeable, unstoppable, and will not yield once He has set a plan into motion, because He knows the outcome is worth the collateral damage along the way. There is a war on, a war leveled against God, against His character and integrity, and it will run its course and it will reach His ultimate goal.

What Satan wants is a complete defeat and takeover of what God designed from eternity past before he was even a twinkle in the Lord's perfect eye. There must be an unconditional surrender and annihilation of enemy forces so it will not happen again. When all scrimmages have been won, when all falsehoods are exposed, when all the smoke and dust settle and God knows that the time is at hand, the conflict will come to its end. In the meantime the battle rages on and the enemy is operating with a full-attack strategy and an onslaught of lies.

> "And by common confession great is the mystery of the unique spiritual life: He (God) who was revealed in the flesh, was vindicated in the Spirit, Beheld by angels, proclaimed among the Gentiles, believed on in the world, and taken up in glory." (1Ti 3:16)

Since our Lord was taken up in glory, there is a new realm of doctrine noted in 2Co 4:4, the gospel of the glory of Christ (the mystery doctrine of the Church Age). The Church Age is new and inspiring to the elect angels and a serious threat to the fallen angels. To many believers it is of little concern, yet it is of the utmost importance in the grand scheme of the overall conflict. Satan's main concentrated attacks are at pastor-teachers who teach grace and Truth. Satan is always busy misleading and confusing the issue of this dispensation of grace to other teachers and religions. Satan is the author of confusion, division, and discord within the Christian community. Other religious organizations that do not focus on Christ as God and Savior have long since been infiltrated by demonic teachings, and in fact probably have been developed by Satan himself. For the angelic community to learn God's grace they would need to do an in-depth study of maximum grace in action and that is exactly what human history offers them.

We are the objects of maximum grace, there could be no better explanation or no better example than fallen, depraved mankind. Here again we see

God's multi-faceted design as grace is being put on display, at the same time a resolution to a rebellion from eternity past is being addressed. While simultaneously the angels observe and learn about grace from undeserving, spiritually dead creatures like us, God is being glorified. As human history progresses, God's wisdom, grace, mercy, and righteousness become more apparent to even the most obstinate critic of Christianity.

As stated earlier in this chapter God has chosen the weak to confound the strong, the foolish to shame the wise of this world. This reference is speaking to angelic and human arrogance and to those that have said, "I will be like the Most High!" In the human realm, we say this every time we ignore God and choose an earthly solution, a cosmic viewpoint, and make a mockery of the Lord Jesus Christ and what He accomplished upon the Cross by neglecting Him. For the positive believer, we are the weak, the ones viewed as foolish by our peers. It is the minority of the positive pivot that is used to bring shame upon the majority of the arrogant in the cosmic system. What God has done is set apart the positive believer; a positional sanctification occurs at the initial baptism of the Holy Spirit. Believers (positive and negative) are set above the angelic community. Your position is set and the end result is that you are a new creature, higher in rank and position in eternity and recognized in time by the heavenly community. We have stepped into a permanent position within the Royal Family of God.

When we chose our salvation through faith in our Lord Jesus Christ a change took place that is only visible in the angelic realm for now. Regeneration of a dead species is what took place at the moment of salvation. This is not a re-birth of old flesh but a brand new species, designed, developed, and set apart as special in the eyes of God. Believers are designed to live the unique spiritual life of freedom instead of an independent life of slavery. The born again, regenerated member of the human race is positionally higher than any angel. We are perfect and righteous because God sees the end results and not the current situation as to who and what we are. This heavenly position, eternally united to our Lord Jesus Christ, only happens in our dispensation (Church Age). All other dispensations reach their climax in this dispensation as a direct result of the ultimate victory our Lord won on the Cross!

> "God, after He spoke long ago to the fathers (ancestors) in the prophets in many portions and in many ways, in these last days (Church Age) He has spoken to us by His Son, whom He has appointed heir of all things, and through whom He has designed the ages (dispensations). And He (Jesus Christ) is the radiance (flashing forth is the humanity of Christ) of His (God the Father's) glory, and exact representation of His nature (deity of Christ); and He upholds all things by the word of His power. When He had made purification of sins, He sat down at the right hand of the Majesty on high." (Heb 1:1-3)

At this point our Lord Jesus Christ became not only the victor, but King of Kings and Lord of Lords, and the conflict shifted into a higher gear. Our Lord was an inferior creature to angels in human form but became superior to all at this point, this is the similarity we have within our state of salvation. This is highlighted in the next verse of Hebrews where it states that He became greater than angels, inheriting an excellent and royal title. An interesting point is that God never made this claim to any angelic creature. The next verse speaks of the Second Advent when Christ returns and the angels will worship Him, proving His position above and beyond any creature, and we share that position with Jesus Christ because we are in union with Him. Angels are created beings just like the human race, and they were given special powers and insight that the human race will not be able to gain until the judgment of the world is at hand. But we have been given the rock solid guarantee from a perfect Father that we have inherited much more than any angelic race ever received once we have accepted Christ as our savior.

Our Lord completed His mission on the Cross and was given His title and honors, and so will the positive believer who completes his mission (Pre-designed Plan) here on earth and receives his rank and authority in heaven. Heb 1:8-9 says, "But speaking of His Son, He (God the Father) says, (reference from Psa 45:6-7) 'Your throne, O God (God the Father calling the Son, God) is forever and ever, and righteousness will be the scepter of Your kingdom (Second Advent, Millennium and eternity). You loved righteousness and hated evil (perfection of Jesus in the flesh); Therefore God (Father), Your God, has anointed You above your associates with ceremonial oil of happiness.'" This is what we as born again believers share in with Jesus Christ. The born again believer who reaches maturity has much to gain. There are crowns and authority given to them beyond the average believer who simply made that one-shot decision believing that Christ is the Savior. Positive believers do have rank and special privilege and these verses that God the Father speaks to God the Son are for our benefit, because Christ is our connection to the Trinity. These verses also reveal that God the Son is one and the same as God the Father and God the Holy Spirit.

> "And (reference to Psa 102:25-27) in the beginning, O Lord (Jesus Christ), You laid the foundations of the earth, and the heavens are the work of Your hands." (Heb 1:10)

God the Father continues to speak toward God the Son in verses 11 and 12 stating that Christ will remain forever in His current state (hypostatic union) and will reign in eternity at the right hand of the Father. This is what the believer shares in because Jesus Christ is our link, our relation to the heavenly places, we are in union with Him forever. God has never told an angel, "You will sit down at My right hand and I will make a footstool out of your enemies" (Heb 1:13). God was speaking to the humanity of Christ which is also indicated toward believers. Until you gain the knowledge and confidence that Jesus Christ is in you and you are in Him, you will always lack the inner strength to push forward in this conflict. The end result is completed, you are righteous and perfect in God's eyes. You as a believer are part of the winning team, the victory is right around the corner! In Eph 2:6, God has made it clear that we are seated with Him in heavenly places. We cannot take advantage of our position if we are ignorant of the plan of God for our life. This pre-designed plan was completed and placed in your account in eternity past, so it is up to you to grow up spiritually, to take advantage of it, and to participate in the victory. This is truly the way to glorify God within this angelic battle.

Chapter 13

Free Will in the Human Race Perpetuates the Angelic Conflict

One of the false teachings that has been perpetuated by the kingdom of darkness is that mankind does not have a free will. The root of such teaching can be traced back to a man called John Calvin and those who followed his teachings. Calvinists (Hyper-Calvinists) did not compare scripture to scripture and dig into the original language, but actually took scripture out of context to come up with this principle.

They promoted a teaching that highlighted God's choosing man over the fact that man can make a conscious decision to choose God. This led to a teaching of selection, meaning that God would handpick some and neglect others. This principle basically says that all human beings do not have equal opportunity and equal privilege to choose for or against God. This would mean that free will holds no value in the grand scheme of the Angelic Conflict. This principle is false, and has disturbing consequences concerning the Angelic Conflict, consequences that would affect the justice and righteousness of God. The core of this teaching is that God pre-destined some to be saved, and some to be cast into the lake of fire! That is a direct attack on the character and nature of God. David describes the condition that all human beings were born into in Psa 58:3. He states that all were born wicked. All have gone astray since birth.

> "Behold, I was brought forth in iniquity, and in sin my mother conceived me." (Psa 51:5)

David, who wrote these Psalms, was no fool. In fact, he was a wise and doctrinal man, a man after God's own heart. We were born in sin not by choice. Our free will could not have chosen sin at birth. This is not an issue of negative volition on the part of newborn babies. 1Co 15:22 states that all died in Adam. We have a union with Adam (old sin nature) just as we have a union with Christ (new creature).

> "Through one man sin entered into the world, and death through sin, and so death spread to all men, because all sinned, when Adam sinned." (Rom 5:12)

Paul referred to all of us as creatures of wrath (Eph 2:3), he states that it is in the human nature itself. After the sin in the garden, every member of the human race was then born into sin. Our original parents, Adam and Eve, willfully sinned and that sin was passed down to us. Every member of the human race since then has been born into sin without their consent. Therefore, if God sent them to hell because they were born sinners, He would be unjust in doing so! The human race is not responsible for imputed sin.

Now in some sense mankind does not have a free will, and by that I mean that there are consequences to our decisions. These consequences are beyond our knowledge and control until they happen. However, we do have choices that are completely free on our part. The choice between heaven and hell in eternity is one of the few choices we do have that turns out exactly as we have been told it will. The Bible is full of the statements that Jesus Christ took away the sins of the world. The Lamb of God (Christ) took away the sins of the entire world, not a select few. The whole world is offered the salvation that He brought forth.

> "The next day he (John the Baptist) saw Jesus coming to him, and said, 'Behold, the Lamb of God who takes away the sin of the world!'" (Joh 1:29)

God did not take on the form of a human being, to be tempted, then endure extreme suffering and be crucified to save only a select group of people. Everyone has the opportunity to become born again and saved, even the children who die before the age of accountability (2Sa 12:20-23). Children who die before they are offered salvation, along with those people who do not have the mental capacity to make the right decisions, are offered a grace salvation.

> "So that whoever believes will in Him have eternal life. For God so loved the world, that He gave His only begotten Son, that whoever believes in Him shall not perish, but have eternal life. For God did not send the Son into the world to judge the world, but that the world might be saved through Him. He who believes in Him is not judged; he who does not believe has been judged already, because he has not believed in the name of the only begotten Son of God." (Joh 3:15-18)

This is an open offer. Nowhere in the Bible does the Word of God point to a select few that believe upon the work of the Cross. Nowhere in the Scriptures does it suggest that the whole world is not offered opportunities for believing upon the Savior Jesus Christ. He is known throughout the Scriptures as the Savior of the world, not just a select few. There in chapter three of the Gospel of John you can plainly see that it is the sin of unbelief and not sins that send a person to the lake of fire. Another false teaching is that only the Jewish race is destined for heaven. They are chosen and blessed, but not singled out for salvation alone upon this earth, it is offered to all unbelievers.

> "... and they were saying to the woman (of Samaria), "It is no longer because of what you said that we believe, for we have heard for ourselves and know that this One (Jesus) is indeed the Savior of the world." (Joh 4:42)

This is stating the whole world and not a certain population or select group.

> "I am the living bread that came down out of heaven; if anyone eats of this bread, he will live forever; and the bread also which I will give for the life of the world is My flesh." (Joh 6:51)

> "I have come as Light into the world, so that everyone who believes in Me will not remain in darkness." (Joh 12:46)

In Joh 12:47, Jesus Christ says again that He came to save the world. There is no other way to translate it from the original language except by referring to the whole world. In Romans 5:6, it says He came to save the ungodly, in Rom 11:15 it states that God reconciled the world unto Himself. This continues on in so many scriptures that simply cannot be translated any other way except that the whole world and all people who have been born into it are part of God's original plan of salvation. 2Co 5:19, 1Jo 4:14, and 1Ti 2:4 all state that God desires all men to be saved and Christ came to save the whole world. 1Ti 2:6 says that He gave a ransom for all! Heb 2:9 reveals that the Lord tasted death for everyone. Jesus Christ is the propitiation not for our sins only, but also for those of the whole world, clearly shown in 1Jo 2:2. So to teach that a select few or any one race are the chosen ones for salvation is not only incorrect but it is blasphemous toward the work on the Cross. The free will of man does apply specifically to salvation above all other decisions that the humans are responsible for throughout their life time. Pre-destination is a word that applies to believers only.

> "For those whom He foreknew (eternity past), He also predestined to become conformed to the image of His Son, so that He would be the firstborn among many brethren; and these whom He predestined, He also called; and these whom He called, He also justified; and these whom He justified, He also glorified." (Rom 8:29-30)

Eph 1:11 clearly states that the believer is pre-destined for inheritance through our adoption into the Royal Family. No one has ever been pre-destined to hell. Eph 1:5 says that we are sons when we become believers and that was the Father's will and intention from the beginning. Again we can see pre-destination occurring before the ages (eternity past) in 1Co 2:7, where it also speaks of the mystery of God's wisdom, knowing that before we were created some would be believers and others would not accept the offer, but the offer was put forth for all. People go to hell based on their own volitional decision, not upon the act of immorality and mental attitude sins as noted in Joh 3:18.

In the first half of this verse in Joh 3:18, "He who believes in Him," to believe is the present active participle of the Greek word pisteuon. In the active voice it means that mankind makes an individual willful decision to believe in the Lord Jesus Christ. Now the last half of the verse, "has not believed," is a perfect active indicative of the verb pisteuon which is pepisteuken, and in the active voice it means that he has refused to believe. The perfect tense means that they had the opportunity, and the indicative says that this is a dogmatic reason why they will be judged. So there is no such thing as double pre-destination, as is presented in some false teachings. We can consider pre-destination as a printout from the sovereign will of God and it applies to believers only!

> "The Lord is not willing for any to perish but for all to come to repentance." (2Pe 3:9)

How much clearer can that statement be, that God does not wish for any of His creatures to perish? Yet we see many teachings like Hyper-Calvinism pointing to a select group that were chosen by God. What they say is that you were elected to believe in eternity past and not offered an opportunity in the present. This is satanic in its core because it attacks the character and nature of God. So their teachings may not come out directly and attack God's nature, but they do have subtle ways to point out this false doctrine to their congregations. The Presbyterian Church makes the bold statement that the selection has already been made by God and this is what they teach regularly, much to the delight of the kingdom of darkness I am sure. You cannot ignore the portion of the plan of God that points to free will and volitional responsibility.

> "You did not choose Me but I chose you, and appointed you that you would go and bear fruit, and that your fruit would remain, so that whatever you ask of the Father in My (Jesus Christ) name He may give to you" (Joh 15:16)

The first verb in this verse is the word choose; this is the aorist middle indicative of the Greek word ekegomai. This middle voice tells us that God did not choose us based upon His volition only but also based it upon our response to His initiation. The middle voice refers to two wills in action, the will of God to save us and the will of mankind to respond. This responding is a system of non-meritorious perception called faith. Without the knowledge and effort to study the original language it becomes easy to interpret a verse in the wrong context, or to derive a different meaning from what God intended. Joh 15:19 is stating that the elect and non-elect are taken out of an existing aggregate or mixture of beings when it states, "I have (chosen) elected you out of the world." But it is these exact types of verses that are misused to promote the principle of limited atonement (that Christ died for some sinners but not all).

The mistake that many Hyper-Calvinists make is that they have no concept that the sovereignty of God and the free will of man coexist in human history by divine decree. Joh 15:19 states that you (the believer) are not of this world, but God has chosen you out of the world, therefore the world hates you. This verse uses the same verb (eklegomai) in the middle voice stating the action of two wills, namely, God's will and our response to it.

This study, if done properly, proves that God initiates the response, but it takes an action (thought) which is positive within the other party to set it into motion. There is a misunderstanding or a complete ignorance of the Angelic Conflict that will lead many teachers and students of the Bible astray on key principles of the Word of God. This is intentional on behalf of the kingdom of darkness to keep mankind in darkness pertaining to God's grace and how to glorify Him during the conflict. The fact is that no unbeliever is said to be elected or pre-destined to the lake of fire. The Unlimited Atonement (Christ died for all sinners) is the demonstration that the sovereignty of God desires that no one should perish. Personal sins were removed from the table when Christ completed His mission on the Cross, and so was the one sin (unbelief) that remained. We were given a solution for both with one act of grace. Both of these two issues concerning sin are dealt with on God's end of the conflict. It was then put into our laps as to what we will choose to do on our end of the conflict. God cannot do any more than He has already done without violating free will.

> "At the acceptable time I listened to you, and on the day of salvation I helped you." (2Co 6:2)

We have been given all that we need in eternity past, and equal opportunity has been laid out for the human race. However, human volition is naturally set against what God has put in motion in the beginning of the Angelic Conflict. In Joh 15:16 where it states, you did not choose Me, it gives us a sense that many will not make that choice. But looking at 2Co 6:2 we can see that He has helped us when we do. That it is not an effort or work that is needed, He simply listens to us make a positive decision, and then He does the work to accomplish our salvation for us. Joh 1:12 states that God gives the power to become His children when we believe in the Lord's name. It does not go into a detailed works program or say that it gives that power to a chosen few or to the ones who did some special act. It does not even hint that some were already picked out in eternity past. This verse actually points to the fact that you can do it now as you read the verse! It is a highlight of God's grace in continual effect. It does not say to speak a certain set of words or a prayer, it does not point to a guilt-ridden soul, weeping or pleading to become born again and saved. It simply says to believe in His name. To believe in His name means to believe that He is what He claims to be: the Word of God, the King of Kings, the Lord of Lords, the Lord our righteousness, Emmanuel, God with us, wonderful counselor, the mighty God, the everlasting Father, the Prince of peace, the great I AM, the Lord of ALL!

> ". . . who were born, not of blood nor of the will of the flesh nor of the will of man, but of God." (Joh 1:13)

Just as you did not earn or deserve your physical birth you also did not earn or deserve your spiritual birth. "Not of blood" refers to hereditary characteristics. The blood that runs through your veins does not matter, the parents that you were conceived from does not matter, family status or church affiliation within your family has no consequence on becoming a believer. No one on this earth can make you a Christian, not by walking down an aisle or being dipped into water, no sacraments or prayer from outside forces brings you to the point of becoming born again and saved. This is between you and God, a one-shot decision that is positive toward Jesus Christ as God and Savior of all. God has done all the work, we merely respond. No one is born a Christian nor becomes a Christian by any other means except the full acceptance of Christ as the only Savior and King. It is faith alone in Christ alone for eternal life!

Mankind does have a free will and is the one responsible for what he or she chooses. If God chose us we would have nothing to do with it; therefore, it would be unjust, unfair, and would be an agreement with the kingdom of darkness. The human race is born into sin and God would be cruel not to offer a solution to this severe dilemma. The existence of free will in the human race perpetuates the Angelic Conflict in two areas:

First of all there is evangelism within the Angelic Conflict. Mankind as a free agent in the devil's world can believe in Jesus Christ and have eternal life, or he can reject salvation and have eternal condemnation, sharing the judgment of Satan and his fallen angels.

Secondly, the existence of free will in the human race perpetuates the Angelic Conflict in the Pre-designed Plan of God for the Church Age.

As a member of the Royal Family of God, every Church Age believer can execute the plan and glorify God as a part of the system of victory in the Angelic Conflict. Or the believer can live in the cosmic system and remain ignorant of the relationship with God that is offered, therefore becoming a part of the enemy camp in time. As we have noted, this type of independence is nothing more than the trend set forth by Satan himself in eternity past. Every believer in the Church Age is given a maximum amount of divine omnipotence to execute the plan that God has established for that believer. When there is a rejection of Christ (unbeliever) or a rejection of the plan of God (believer), this is a direct path toward a choice for Satan's plans and Satan's schemes. The range of Satan's plans and schemes covers everything from emotionalism, arrogance, religion, legalism, socialism, and many forms of worldly viewpoints and independent thinking. God believes in freedom in many aspects, and the greater the freedom, the greater the inequalities, and this is true in the spiritual realm as well as within the worldly realm. The sovereignty of God makes the decision and the omnipotence of God provides the fantastic power for us to accept or reject it! God wants you to have fellowship with Him, but He never pushes or guilts you into that relationship. What better example of freedom than an all-powerful God who could easily snap His fingers and have an army of obedient robots, but instead allows us to go astray, to make our own decisions, to pick and choose when and if we want that relationship with Him.

Be it a positive or negative lifestyle God will still get the glory. We cannot hinder the outcome of His plan, only our own life becomes hindered from our negative decisions. In failure or success God will get the glory and the result will remain in His favor when the last day of human history arrives. It all comes down to what you do with the time you had: will it mean blessing and authority in eternity, or failure and regret at the Judgment Seat of Christ? Heaven is a perfect place but there will be great inequality there as much as we see in the world today. The difference is, there will be no cruelty, unhappiness, or pain because the old sin nature will be dead and perfection will be in order. But a certain rank and authority, a chain of command will exist in the heavenly realm.

Many people use freedom to live independently from any form of authority as often as possible. It can and will catch up to them when they cross over boundaries and lines that society has drawn. But the fact is that true freedom offers us the option for bad decisions and criminal behavior. There will be a minority of believers that will use their freedom to succeed in the plan of God. They will use divine power and live the spiritual life while other believers will become independent and use worldly solutions and human power to gain a measure of success in time. The difference within the success of each group will be the eternal value of one and the fleeting, temporal value of the other.

The result of a believer choosing the plan of God in the Church Age is three-fold and happens in three phases. The first phase is the gift of salvation offered to anyone who chooses to believe in Jesus Christ. The second phase is the unique spiritual life that is translated from the Greek word eusebeia, meaning godliness (experiential sanctification). The third phase is the position believers obtain as they become superior to the angels. To help understand and truly resolve any questions about the three operational phases and results it is best to break it down and do a brief study. The following points will hopefully be direct and condensed enough for anyone, believer or unbeliever, to understand:

1) Salvation: In choosing the plan of God at salvation through faith in Christ, regenerated man becomes positionally superior to angels through the baptism of the Spirit and the resulting sanctification (see

Heb 1:1-14). Not only becoming a member of the Royal Family of God, believers also become a new spiritual species that was never offered to Old Testament saints or angelic creatures. We are then free to live the unique spiritual life instead of an independent life of slavery to the flesh. At the moment of salvation, your position within the heavenly realm has skyrocketed above angelic creatures, you are in union with Christ at the right hand of the Father. So your guardian angel is truly your employee and not a divine being that you should be in awe of. In fact, it is the exact opposite, the guardian becomes in awe of you!

> "Are they not ministering spirits, sent out to render service for the sake of those who will inherit salvation?" (Heb 1:14)

2) Experiential Sanctification: The Greek word eusebeia means the godly life and that is what is in view with this definition. The believer not only receives his or her escrow blessings for time, but is able to glorify God in the Angelic Conflict because God has given the believer the power and problem-solving devices to do so. This is the believer living in the plan that God has designed for the individual's life and who is tapping into the power of the Holy Spirit and fellowship with God. This is done through His Word while defeating Satan in the small battles and stumbling blocks that his system will surely throw at positive believers. As we do this we display to all the angels that we are with Christ, in union and preparing ourselves for greater battles by becoming spiritually mature.

3) The position we obtain at salvation: The believer's resurrection body will be visibly and physically superior to those of the angelic population, but what you must realize is that right now in time your position has been secured and the power and authority is yours. You see, if we were given our resurrection bodies in time the conflict would be resolved by physical means instead of by means of faith, and truth be told, it would be unfair for the kingdom of darkness. During the seven years of the Tribulation period right up until the Second Advent of Christ, only Church Age believers will be in their resurrection bodies. During this period the demon angels will see that their position from the beginning was wrong. We are there as proof positive to the conflict being in God's favor all along! This is why they aggress so strongly during the

Tribulation attacks that display their fury and power, but it still ends with the righteousness of God in a triumphant victory.

> "Do you not know that we shall judge angels?" (1Co 6:3)

The Greek word judge used here is the future active indicative of krino which means to make a decision for, to conclude, or to approve, as well as being used for a term to govern or rule. So you can see that the fury of the powerful fallen angels is justified as lowly mankind rises above to rule and judge over them. What God is displaying here is that a creature (the human race) that was designed weak and frail, compared to powerful angels, is the one to come out on top. The problem with most positive believers is that they do not realize their position and that the end result is a position of such great power and authority that it would melt their minds to truly perceive it.

> "Now I say, as long as the heir is a child, he does not differ at all from a slave although he is owner of everything, but he is under guardians and managers until the date set by the father." (Gal 4:1-2)

The analogy that Paul is using is very instrumental in comprehending the position a positive believer has in this Angelic Conflict. Paul is getting at the fact that a slave and the heir are exactly alike while the heir remains a child or a minor. They are both in a position under greater authority and very limited in power within the landscape of the mansion, or the kingdom in which they reside. The heir in his youth has very little difference in authority and power than the house servant. The heir, being a minor, may not even realize the future power or recognize and appreciate what belongs to him. The heir may have a wonderful and rich portfolio of investments on his behalf but does not see himself as being any different from the house slave. The point Paul is trying to teach is that born again believers who have not reached adulthood and do not understand the divine solutions and assets are no different from the unbelievers of the world. In fact, there is really no difference between the lifestyle of the born again believer who is carnal, and the unregenerate individual who is an unbeliever.

> "And I, brethren, could not speak to you as to spiritual men, but as to men of flesh, as to babies in Christ. I gave you milk to

drink and not solid food; for you were not yet able to receive it. Indeed, even now you are not yet able." (1Co 3:1-2)

Paul went on to say that they were fleshly, jealous, and causing strife among one another, walking like men of the world. This is a great description that covers believers who reject the plan of God. Most born again believers walk like the men and women of this world, and do not recognize the gifts and blessings that God has designed for them in eternity past. This type of attitude stems from a belief that the kingdom of darkness promotes that there is something to gain in the cosmic system. That there is some form of grandeur and happiness, a sense of great accomplishment, a euphoric relationship or experience just around the next corner. It is the carrot that always dangles from the stick, just out of reach. When it is obtained it never brings the contentment that it promised. What the majority of believers do is very similar to what unbelievers do and that is to conduct their lives on the basis of human solutions. They do not even realize that they are heir to at least forty grace gifts given at the moment of salvation. We are joint heirs with Jesus Christ, we have been adopted into divine royalty (Gal 3:26). This adoption principle is also clearly presented in Gal 4:1-7.

"Therefore you are no longer a slave, but a son; and if a son, then an heir through God." (Gal 4:7)

An heir has a radically different lifestyle than a slave. Until a believer begins to grow and gain momentum in the plan of God they cannot reach forward to the stages of spiritual maturity that offer them the ability and knowledge to operate in their royal adoption. Once a believer grows up he will have a personal sense of destiny and the power of Biblical problem-solving devices to set him apart from the slave lifestyle of the world. The Bible has many scriptures referring to the maturity and growth needed to succeed in the plan of God, but this verse in 2 Peter chapter 3 says it best: 2Pe 3:18, " . . . grow in the grace and knowledge of our Lord and Savior Jesus Christ."

You can certainly know that you have reached the first stage of spiritual adulthood when you begin to develop that personal sense of destiny that you know the plan that God has for your life. At this first stage you have a sense that God is working in your life, guiding and calling out for you in a certain area. You begin to use Bible doctrine as your problem-solving strategy. The priorities in your life shift from self and personal desires to God and His Word becoming a staple in your life. A carnal believer is experientially like an unbeliever. When a believer does not fit God into his or her schedule, with priorities centered instead on family, career, and wealth, it is no different from the unbeliever who is consumed with worldly viewpoint and treasures. Both categories of people are under satanic viewpoint and casualties of angelic warfare. There are those who use the terms and loud chatter of Christianity, but cannot solve a problem using God's solutions in their lives. The pious attitude and "Praise the Lord brother!" shouts fall on deaf ears when they reach heaven. God does not recognize nonsense and lazy attitudes. By lazy attitudes I simply am pointing to the majority of believers who talk the talk, but do not walk the walk. They have the terms and language down, but do not have time to study, apply, or dedicate their time, talent and treasure to a doctrinal ministry.

God sees right through to the heart of a matter as well as the intent within a person's soul. The attitude of "I have my own relationship with God" and "Jesus and I have an understanding" is something God can look right through with a divine transparency that mankind does not even fathom. A good pastor-teacher knows that the bulk of his job is to assist in the believer's growth, to get the believer from the experiential stage of slavery to the experiential stage of heirship. To help lost believers find their liberty and spiritual freedom through the teaching of Truth.

> "It was for freedom that Christ set us free; therefore keep standing firm and do not be subject again to the yoke of slavery." (Gal 5:1)

Bible doctrine is the food we need daily to survive in the Angelic Conflict. Until we learn to metabolize (digest) the Word of God and the problem-solving devices that God has laid out for us we will be a slave to circumstances. We will be like the unbelievers who are tossed to and fro and controlled by circumstances, people, and emotions. True stability comes from the Word of God, but if it is not prepared and taught properly it is useless to try to apply it to your life. Without divine solutions in life you are nothing more than a slave to this cosmic system. You may question the need for all of this in a book about the Angelic Conflict, but it is invisible warfare so why would you think that your weapons would be tangible in the human realm?

There is a great difference between a Christian and an unbeliever, there is just as much or more of a difference or a gap between angels and humans. Yet, if we take a closer look at fallen angels and unbelievers there is less difference and a smaller gap between these two categories of creatures. Take a good look at this quote from Lewis Sperry Chafer taken from volume 7 of his Systematic Theology:

"God has four classes of intelligent creatures in His universe—angels, Gentiles, Jews and Christians; and there is more difference to be observed between Christians and either Jews or Gentiles than between angels and Jews and Gentiles. Should this statement seem extreme, it must be because the true and exalted character of the Christian is not comprehended. No angel is a son of God by actual generating birth from above, nor is any angel made to stand before God in the pleroma or the fullness of Christ, which fullness is the fullness of the Godhead bodily."

You will notice that he is highlighting the "son-ship" and union we (believers) have with Jesus Christ, the unique relationship. Angels are not given this unique relationship at any point within their history, past, present, or eternity future. When looking at the independence of fallen angels, the anger and bitterness toward God and His plan for their lives, the unbeliever has the most in common with them. The unbeliever goes to his or her own systems and merit programs to resolve issues much like the fallen angels do because they have cut themselves off from God. The unbeliever has a barrier between self and God, a self-imposed barrier but nonetheless very similar to the fallen angels. The spiritual combat we face takes spiritual weaponry that only the Truth from Bible doctrine can supply, and it takes practice and repetition to use these weapons effectively. The greatest pressures we face in life come from the invisible realm. It is the unique spiritual life that our Lord Jesus Christ has lived that is our example and blueprint to follow.

> "Be strong in the Lord, and in the strength of His might. Take up and put on the full armor of God, that you may be able to stand firm against the schemes of the devil." (Eph 6:10-11)

The armor of the Word of God is in view in this scripture. Until you learn to live in and utilize the full armor of God there will be no difference between you as a believer and the common man on the streets who is an unbeliever. This is what sets you apart from not only unbelievers but carnal believers. Eternal salvation is a huge divide between even the unbeliever and the loser believer but that gap widens over time when you grow up spiritually. Shuffling around human priorities in this life is the expertise of the agents of the kingdom of darkness. This is where they strike most often in our life, especially a born again believer's life. Satan has developed ways to intimidate, coax, and manipulate believers away from doctrinal teaching. The local assembly is a provision supplied by God, and it is a target for the cosmic system and those who run it! Satan loves the mind-set of "Look how I am being blessed without God!" Or "What do I need church for? I am doing just fine." And the kingdom of darkness can bless people with certain promotions and material items, maybe even a relationship, but never can Satan match the blessings of God! This goes back to the counterfeit principle we learned of earlier in this book.

There are cosmic evangelists, they are the ones who promote that kind of mindset mentioned above. If you were to talk long enough to an intelligent atheist, eventually the conversation would become intriguing and would probably begin to sound like it makes some sense. These types of people seem very sincere at times and they are, they are sincerely wrong! The reason this negative promotion is allowed to run rampant upon this earth is the whole point we have been dealing with, free will. Mankind's freedom of choice and the fact that Satan is the captain of the ship is the answer to any questions about negativity toward the Word of God.

So we can deduct from this chapter that the mystery doctrine of the Church Age is the means by which ordinary people can become invisible heroes and glorify God as a witness for the prosecution against Satan. Hey positive believer, wake up and recognize the gifts, power and impact you have on the Angelic Conflict! Satan was able to blind so many believers and unbelievers throughout human history, starting in the garden, that it is no surprise he has foot soldiers even in human form. These human foot soldiers are manipulating Truth within the churches today. In Act 20:28-29 there is a warning against those that come to devour the flock. There will always be attacks against the Truth, be it directed at the pastor-teacher or at positive believers, and these attacks will always come against the Truth. One of the attacks comes in the form of preconceptions concerning the messengers of God i.e. making judgments because you think you know something to be true, or becoming familiar with the teacher so his messages have very little meaning to you after a period of time. There have been evil generations since the days of John the Baptist that try to stop Truth from being brought forth. In Matthew chapter 11, we can see John the Baptist in prison when he heard the works of our Lord Jesus Christ and the mutual respect between the two was very deep and not at all familiar or judgmental.

> "And . . . said to Him, 'Are You the Expected One, or shall we look for someone else?' Jesus answered and said to them, 'Go and report to John what you hear and see:'" (Mat 11:3-4)

Jesus Christ went on to talk about all the healings and preaching of the Gospel that He was doing, as well as speaking highly of John the Baptist (Mat 11:7). As true friends do, John had first spoken about Jesus with great reverence, and Jesus did the same. In Mat 11:7 the Lord asked the crowd, "What did you go out into the wilderness to look at? A reed or a stalk of a plant shaken by the wind?" This is a metaphor for a person who wavers or sways, someone who vacillates under the pressure of difficult circumstances. This was not meant as a description of John. If those who went out to see John in the wilderness expected to see someone who buckled under pressure, that expectation was bound to be frustrated. The people of that day were used to the Scribes and Pharisees as the authorities of all things spiritual and the ones who taught the Bible. In Mar 1:22-27 the Bible records the fact that people were astonished by the authority and wisdom with which Jesus taught. They were amazed at this new, fresh style of teaching and how it did not sound like the same thread of teaching that came from the Pharisees. It was teaching that went against the grain of what had been the religious norm for that time period. John the Baptist did not fit the mold they expected either, he was not the gentle or delicate man that some might have expected.

> "But what did you go out to see? A man dressed in soft clothing? Behold, those who wear soft clothing are in kings palaces." (Mat 11:8)

John the Baptist certainly did not fit the preconception of the clergy of that day and would be considered too gruff and harsh for the delicate Christian minds of many believers right now. The women of our day and age would probably consider him a Neanderthal and he would certainly rub a few feminists the wrong way if he were up behind a pulpit right now. Most people today would be too shocked to sit and learn because of his attitude and appearance, yet he would be the type of teacher that could bring you into spiritual maturity.

The clergy of the Old Testament wore expensive robes with tassels and extravagant designs upon them. John the Baptist had a camel hair covering and leather belt to hold it up! What many people thought they knew of John the Baptist was that he was being disciplined by God at the time when Christ was speaking about him. They saw him as imprisoned and defeated, a loser in many people's eyes. What Jesus Christ was telling them was so different from what they had believed to be true. This is one example of not judging a person or situation but giving it over to the Lord because no one knows all the facts except Him.

One of the truths of the Word of God is that lessons on real Truth are unpopular especially pertaining to the Angelic Conflict. Believers will come into times of great perplexity and adversity as the apostle Paul did. Paul faced a shipwreck, he was beaten many times, three times he was beaten with rods, he was imprisoned, and he was stoned to death once. One of the beatings Paul had withstood was a lashing that consisted of thirty nine strikes. He was exposed to the elements and nearly died. Paul had sleepless nights and was starving many times on his journeys. Phi 1:29 and 2Ti 3:12 both point out to the suffering and persecutions that all believers who live for Jesus Christ will have to endure.

The loser believer does not want to know about this and has the attitude that it is not realistic or it does not pertain to this modern age. There were those who simply came out to the desert to see who this John the Baptist was, and it came from a place of curiosity, not humility and eagerness to learn about God. True humility is not a shy demeanor and quiet attitude, it is something deep within the soul that is connected to a person's relationship with God. It is integrity and character that will display your humility. A humble person could be loud or shy, but that is not at the core of the humility within that person. There is a false concept that is perpetuated by arrogance within the cosmic system that says that a pastor or church leader has to be a certain type of individual or personality to be in that role. This concept focuses more on personality than on content. This attitude was promoted centuries ago and was what the Pharisees and Scribes tried to project very early on, purity or an appearance of humility that is outward and a façade. Some of the most arrogant people on earth may have a very quiet demeanor. However, Moses or John the Baptist had this outward, rough exterior and a very commanding or authoritarian presence, yet they were both very humble men of God.

The apostle Paul had an unpleasant way about him at times, not the most attractive or soft-spoken teacher on the circuit at that time! Stereotypes have been around since the early churches of the Old Testament and they are nothing more than show, an outward display to impress mankind because they do not impress God. He sees right through the nonsense into the soul. A teacher or spiritual leader who lacks knowledge, or is too lazy to study the original language, will substitute Truth with emotional messages and outward appearances of being godly. This type of teacher points us to morality and charity work as the key to spiritual growth. But morality and charity are the results of growing up in the spiritual life, not designed as a works program to get you there. This is usually all wrapped up in a sweet presentation or a kind personality. Sweet personalities and the issue of living a morally pure life are superficial concepts of what it means to be a Christian, yet it is that aspect that many people focus on.

There is no special personality that a pastor or church leader has to have. The apostles were all very different in the realm of passions and personalities. Sweet personalities might be needed for politicians, but not so for a pastor-teacher. There are pastors behind the pulpit today that shout and demand attention with such dynamic personalities that it is hard to ignore them, but they have very little content or messages of Biblical Truth. There are those soft-spoken men that appeal to the nursing home crowd and tender-hearted believers, but can give their congregation nothing but milk to grow upon. It is content that matters. Truth is always the final factor when it comes to teaching the Word of God, not political correctness or social justice, not sweet personalities and works programs. Stereotypes become a huge stumbling block in social relationships but even more so in the church. The problem arises when a pastor strays from the Truth to fit into a mold for his congregation. The congregation is usually the one putting the squeeze-play on their pastor, watching his every move, judging his lifestyle and personality, dictating to those in positions of authority how the church should be run. The proper way a church should be run is from the top down: God, then the pastor, and then the deacons or those in authority. The congregation or body of the church is there to first learn Truth and grow spiritually and then to support and operate in virtue within the church. If a congregation member is unhappy or has a problem responding to the authority in the church they should find the nearest exit so they can remove that awful burden from themselves. The wrong way to handle a problem with authority is to gossip and undermine the authority. We have seen the first example in history of undermining the authority figure in the beginning of the Angelic Conflict itself!

A funny illustration of the pastor personality issue is shown through this example:

A famous preacher who was not the most personable man but a great teacher passed by some people in the hallway, and shortly after the preacher made his way to the pulpit, two of the young men got together. The first young man said, "The pastor finally spoke to me!" The second man was excited and said, "Really!" And the first young man stated, "Yeah, I saw him coming in and heading toward the pulpit." The second man anxiously asked, "Well what did he say?" The answer from the first man was, "He told me to get out of the way!" The point is that they had made such an issue out of the man that his message meant very little to them.

I would also like to note Lewis Sperry Chafer on this issue. The following quote is from his writings (Systematic Theology volume 4, page 223):

Warning against false Prophets, "Beware of false prophets which come to you in sheep's clothing, but inwardly they are ravening wolves. Ye shall know them by their fruits" (Mat 7:15-20). The warning to the children of God under grace is against false teachers who are to be discerned by their doctrine concerning Christ (2Pe 2:1, 2Jo 1:7-11): never by their lives; for outwardly, false teachers are said to be directly under the power of Satan who himself appears as an angel of light (2Co 11:13-15). The attractive personality of the false teacher affords great advantage as a background for the appeal he makes for his doctrine."

People have preconceived notions about the personality and demeanor of those involved in the ministry, but there is no prescribed personality for the pastor or the prophet of the Old Testament. Amos was a farmer, Daniel was a scholar, and God used both these men to bring forth His message. Ezekiel was a gruff and harsh character, Isaiah was an ambassador for a king, Jeremiah was very young when he was called to the ministry and he tended to be emotional at times because of his patriotism. In fact, the Lord Jesus Christ was actually considered to be a reincarnation of Jeremiah by some Biblical scholars due to the fact that Jesus wept over Jerusalem and the loss of status of the client nation. Others refer to a comparison of Jesus and Elijah because He (Jesus) would be on fire at times and blasted the daylights out of the Pharisees as in Matthew 23. As for John the Baptist, he was accused of demon possession in Mat 11:18 because of his abnormal eating habits, and that he would sometimes fast and he lived alone in the desert. He was accused of being anti-social which led them to say that he was possessed or a sociopath. Then along comes the man called Jesus who drank good wine and ate the best food. He would dine with sinners and prostitutes. He even took money from women (Luk 8:3). That is when statements calling our Lord a glutton or alcoholic would be thrown about. Jesus Christ certainly did not fit into the pastor-teacher mold much less the Son of God mold of any day and age.

> "The Son of Man came eating and drinking, and they say, 'Behold, a gluttonous man and a drunkard, a friend of tax

> collectors (similar to modern-day mobsters) and prostitutes!'
> Yet wisdom is vindicated by her deeds." (Mat 11:19)

They could not figure out our Lord, and when they judged, as is almost always the case, they judged Him wrong! Jesus would use opportunities at public places where some criminal element or sinners would gather so that He could touch their hearts and teach them the Truth. He went to places that the religious crowd would never frequent.

> "But to what shall I compare this generation? It is like children sitting in the market places, who call out to the other children, and say, 'We played the flute for you, and you did not dance; we sang a dirge, and you did not mourn.'" (Mat 11:16-17)

John the Baptist came and they played a flute and a happy tune, then they said that he did not dance but acted like he was at a funeral! Then they played a funeral dirge, and Jesus Christ laughed and basically said that you can never judge or appraise a spiritual man. Trying to scrutinize someone's spiritual growth or spiritual gift is impossible for anyone but God.

> "But he who is spiritual appraises all things, yet he himself is appraised by no man." (1Co 2:15)

The fact is that we do not even know ourselves as well as we think we do, for it is God who created us and God is the only one who truly knows our heart. David put it nicely in Psa 19:12 when he stated, "Who can know my errors and faults?" And the apostle Paul said it is the Lord who examines us not mankind (1Co 4:4). We all surrender some of our thoughts, fears, and deep secrets in marriage or an intimate friendship; however, nobody really knows your whole heart except God. The same holds true for the authority figures within the church, they do not take responsibility for your decisions out on the street. No one behind the pulpit knows everything about you, and they should not be involved in your day to day decisions and social affairs. You should always have freedom in a grace ministry.

> "Therefore no one is to act as your judge in regard to food or drink or in respect to a festival or a new moon or a Sabbath

day— things which are a mere shadow of what is to come; but the substance belongs to Christ." (Col 2:16-17)

The pulpit is not a place for spiritual bullying or a place to manipulate people through guilt. The pastor should teach Truth even if it is unpleasant, unpopular, or offends someone's gentle nature. The pastor is a teacher. As a chef, he prepares a meal with the best ingredients and skills that are gained from being filled with the Holy Spirit and with long hours of study, then he serves it to you. It is your choice to eat it, digest it, and survive on it. The pastor is not a politician or community activist, nor is he the neighborhood counselor or sex therapist. In fact, the pastor should remove himself from giving too much personal advice because his focus should be on the Scriptures. He does not have all the facts to provide answers that are behind the scenes of a personality conflict or community issues.

John the Baptist and Jesus were never partial or played favorites with anyone in their congregation. John was not afraid of the repercussions of teaching Truth and even reminded King Herod that it was unlawful to sleep with his brother's wife (Mat 14:4). There was a time when he was baptizing people and the Pharisees came out to see him. John noticed the Pharisees and Sadducees approaching (Mat 3:7) and said to them, "You generation of vipers, who warned you to flee from the wrath to come?" These were respected and powerful men of that day and John was at odds with them, much like the Lord who was completely rejected by and at odds with the religious establishment. This is why it is so important to have your focus be on Jesus Christ and the message, not the man or religious system behind a pulpit. Even in the early Church they had problems with preconceptions and iconoclastic arrogance in which Paul and Peter, as well as Apollos, were proclaimed by certain parties.

"For when one says, 'I am of Paul,' and another, 'I am of Apollos,' are you not mere men? What then is Apollos? And what is Paul? Servants through whom you believed, even as the Lord gave opportunity to each one. I planted, Apollos watered, but God was causing the growth." (1Co 3:4-6)

This was said because of the division some people caused by getting caught up in the personality game, showing favoritism toward one teacher over another. Paul's teaching was too rough and to the point. Apollos had a more polished oratory style, whereas Peter could be temperamental and harsh at times. The kingdom of darkness loves to blind people from Truth, and one way is to get people concerned about personality and to promote some form of expected stereotypic behavior.

This is simply a distraction from the teaching of the Truth that we need in order to be victorious in our role in the Angelic Conflict. This is why our free will is so important during this conflict. We must grow up and get beyond judging and petty personality conflicts, for any form of distraction from the Word of God is a direct strike from the devil.

Chapter 14

The Angelic Conflict Observation and Opposition in Human History.

The elect angels observe human history while the fallen angels are designed to oppose human history. Elect angels rejoice over the salvation of one person (Luk 15:7, Luk 15:10). Luk 15:7 says that there is more joy in heaven over one sinner who repents, than over ninety-nine righteous persons who need no repentance. The Lord was willing to go to any lengths to reach those that needed to be saved during His ministry on planet Earth. As we covered in the last chapter, personality and reputation were never an issue with the Lord Jesus Christ because to save sinners was His real priority.

> "Now all the tax collectors and the sinners were coming near Him to listen to Him. Both the Pharisees and the scribes began to grumble, saying, "This man receives sinners and eats with them." (Luk 15:1-2)

The Lord went into a very interesting parable after that statement. It was a parable about a lost sheep, one lost sheep out of a hundred, and the Lord said that the shepherd would leave the 99 to find the one. And when the lost sheep was found the shepherd would pick it up and rejoice.

> "And when he comes home, he calls together his friends and his neighbors, saying to them, 'Rejoice with me, for I have found my sheep which was lost!'" (Luk 15:6)

This is when the Lord lets them know that the angels rejoice in the very same way for one sinner saved by grace. We lose sight of the fact that there is a daily observation and conversation about our choices here on earth. This courtroom trial is not in the fleshly realm and because there is a spiritual veil even the most stringent believer loses sight of this fact at times. The Angelic Conflict is not in our face every day in the sense that it is visibly in front of us. However, with the steady intake of Bible doctrine it becomes hard to neglect the conflict because with the right teaching it will be refreshed in our memories.

In the dispensation of the Hypostatic Union, angels observed every part of the first advent and incarnation of our Lord: 1Timothy 3:16 says that He was "Beheld by angels." In the dispensation of the Church Age, angels observe members of the Royal Family of God in their failure or success in executing and fulfilling the Pre-designed Plan of God. In 1Co 4:9 the apostle Paul states that we are a spectacle to the world, referring to both angels and humans observing us. Eph 3:10 also makes mention of the angelic community watching and learning from us. It is the same in 1Pe 1:12 where it says that angels long to look into the Truth we have revealed to us!

The Greek word for spectacle is the nominative neuter singular of theatron, giving us the English word theater, and it means a visual theater, a place for public shows, a play, or a place for dramatic representations. There are so many things that God's people take for granted that the angels desire to see.

> "I solemnly charge you in the presence of God and of Christ Jesus and of His chosen angels, to maintain these principles without bias, doing nothing in a spirit of partiality." (1Ti 5:21)

When the Bible says that angels long to see, it is from the word epithumeo, meaning to set your heart upon or have a strong desire for something. What you have to realize is that the angels have stimulated our very existence and are part of our daily lives. Angels have guardian roles and messenger roles within the history of mankind as well as observational roles.

> "See that you do not despise one of these little ones, for I say to you that their angels in heaven continually see the face of My Father who is in heaven." (Mat 18:10)

In Luk 16:22 angels escorted the believer Lazarus to Paradise when he passed away. It is said that angels observe the attitude toward authority that we have here on earth as highlighted in 1Co 11:10, referring to the role of authority in marriage and how a woman respects her husband. The role they take is part of the judgment as well, which was mentioned earlier (1Co 6:3). The word for judge is the future active indicative of krino, meaning to conclude or make a decision, to govern or preside over. This is all in reference to elect angels because the fallen angels have their role as enemy combatants, not operating under any of the principles we just covered other than getting to see us in action. They are in attack mode, disruptive and angry. Frustrated and manipulative is a better description of their current attitude toward mankind.

Satan has a vast and powerful demon army, and though aspects of it may be beyond his control, it is nonetheless a deadly force of evil against evangelism, Truth, and the fulfillment of the Pre-designed Plan of God for believers. Satan is still the leader and there is a measure of great fear and respect among his troops.

> "Be of sober spirit (attain spiritual self-esteem), be on the alert. Your adversary, the devil, prowls about like a roaring lion, seeking someone to devour." (1Pe 5:8)

Though we have examined that the cosmic system is a growing empire of lies against God that has existed since mankind spread out on this earth, the two-fold operation that Satan truly spearheads falls under these two objectives:

1) To blind the minds of unbelievers so they will not accept Jesus Christ.

2) To hinder the function of those who accept Jesus Christ by using distractions and confusion to keep them in the dark.

This is an army, organized, assembled and prepared, one that sees mankind as a bug to be squashed! Believers are the true target and the ones who get plenty of heat from this demon brigade. Unbelievers are much more compliant and docile in the grand scheme of the cosmic system, they are basically on board with Satan's initial program. Most are part of the battle plan and do not even realize it. Satan as commander in chief has several functions that fall directly upon him to oversee. In the area of believers, the function that he holds true authority over is the worldly plan we can label as cosmic one and cosmic two, for these types of believers. This is a simple reference to the two directions that lure many believers. One is the ways of the world, the party crowd who live for self and pleasure, but still cling to a belief in Jesus Christ. The other is the legalistic crowd that is involved in works and self-righteous arrogance. Both directions lead a believer far from what God has designed them to do in life. The party crowd is simply too busy living in a false sense of freedom and self-centered lust to care about a plan that God has. The legalistic crowd is involved in the wrong aspect of the Church Age plan. In fact many of the legalistic believers do not even know what dispensation they live in! They are the ones who blow up abortion clinics and spend weeks and months at a time on political campaigns that promote false Christian values in the world. They judge and gossip about the failures of those in their community, never once looking in the mirror of Truth about their own pride, arrogance, and failures, past or present.

Satan has another function or direction that he has to approach when dealing with the unbeliever, who is his enemy as well, but it is an enemy that he can manipulate and use to his advantage. The approach that he oversees is more of a blinding technique or the smoke and mirrors type of illusion that projects the work on the Cross as an unsolved mystery, and the salvation offered by Christ as a dark and cloudy subject. We see it in the educational system and media just as much as in the scientific community. Evolution and promoting Jesus as a man that was simply a prophet are two key elements to the attack Satan has developed. Removing doctrinal teaching from pulpits, replacing it with emotional nonsense, and spiritual tolerance of another god other than our Lord are two other methods of assault on unbelievers. Ignorance to the saving ministry of Jesus Christ is the singular goal that Satan developed thousands of years ago for all unbelievers.

> "Those beside the road are those who have heard; then the devil comes and takes away the word from their heart, so that they will not believe and be saved." (Luk 8:12)

2Corinthians 4:3 refers to the gospel being veiled to unbelievers, saying someone or something covers it up!

> "And even if our gospel is veiled, it is veiled to those who are perishing, in whose case the god of this world has blinded the minds of the unbelieving so that they might not see the light of the gospel of the glory of Christ, who is the image of God." (2Co 4:3)

The unbeliever is kept in the dark, and that is sufficient for the majority of them as far as Satan is concerned. But even the ones who may take a moment to look at Christianity, what they find is confusing or it is filled with guilt-riddled messages that are blindly followed by ignorant people that promote legalistic works programs. So it is no wonder that an unbeliever is turned off from the Gospel. Think how often you have seen on television a minister, hopefully of the male persuasion (women do not teach Bible doctrine), and he lays hands on someone and they collapse into a blubbering pile and claim that they are cured. The other one you see often is the seed of faith or the magic cloth that is blessed. The seed of faith is you sending money to a preacher who is doing nothing but getting wealthy off your guilt and ignorance of the Word of faith. Every ministry needs gifts in the financial realm to survive, and a good pastor-teacher should be compensated, but the nonsense that is going on in many ministries is a shame! If your pastor's message is more centered on finances than on Truth within the Scriptures you may want to look elsewhere to gain your spiritual growth. Grace is how the pastor and church should operate, not selling every book, pamphlet, or CD that comes from their pulpit. In fact the Bible says that "freely you have received, freely you should give," in Matthew 10:8. This is why a believer is such a great enemy to the kingdom of darkness, because they have the ability to learn about grace and faith, and then operate in it, teaching others and leading people to Truth.

> "So that no advantage would be taken of us by Satan, for we are not ignorant of his schemes." (2Co 2:11)

> "Submit therefore to God. Resist the devil and he will flee from you." (Jam 4:7)

The word resist in that last scripture is one of the greatest ways to combat satanic distraction. Many pastors that have the gift to teach can get distracted from what the Spirit is saying to the Church. Distractions and confusions can enter into doctrinal ministries when the pastor gets too involved in the personality conflicts within the body. This often happens when he is counseling and social networking with everyone in the congregation. In 2Co 11:3 it states that the serpent can deceive us like Eve was deceived and lead us astray from the simplicity and purity of devotion to Christ. It is always best to stay alert and aware of the petty distractions because they always lead to the bigger issues that can become stumbling blocks for believers and teachers of the Word of God. The body (Church) is to remain strong, determined to go forward, not petty and divided on issues. The Church is an enemy of the kingdom of darkness and an extreme sore spot for Satan since the early days of Christianity. In Rev 2:8-10 it refers to the body of Christ (Church) and points out the struggle and suffering it has to endure due to satanic attacks throughout history. It is a highlight of the hindrances and persecutions that Christianity will suffer from demonic attacks.

> "Do not fear what you are about to suffer. Behold, the devil is about to cast some of you into prison, that you may be tested, and you will have tribulation for ten days (Referring to periods in life of suffering and challenges). Be faithful (Reach maturity) until death, and I will give you the crown of life (Rank and honor in heaven)." (Rev 2:10)

You see, the true enemy has nothing to do with the earthly creatures around us. It is not a flesh and blood issue, rather a spiritual one. Take your eyes off personalities and the flaws and failures of people and keep the focus on a warfare that is invisible. Never forget that our struggle is not against flesh and blood, but against Satan and his demon army (Eph 6:12). In Rev 2:13 we see a believer killed by the kingdom of darkness, taken home to be with the Lord, this is an example of a casualty of war. Warfare is never a perfect design or a precise art, only if God is in full control would it have laser accuracy and no human casualties. The fact is that God is allowing angelic and human creatures to carry on this entangled and deadly conflict. The Bible itself represents an enemy force to the kingdom of darkness, that book alone is the master key to all weaponry used by fallen mankind.

> "When anyone hears the word of the kingdom, and does not understand it the evil one comes and snatches away what has been sown in his heart. This is the one on whom seed was sown beside the road." (Mat 13:19)

As you go deeper into Mat 13 and get to verse 39 it distinctly points out that Satan can sow that seed, and any seed he has sown is false. The Word of God, when properly taught and then applied is a tremendous weapon that builds an arsenal against the lies promoted by Satan. Satan considers Israel his nemesis as well. We can research this by looking into the original language and interpretation of verses in the Bible such as in Revelation.

> "And his tail swept away a third of the stars (angels) of heaven and threw them to the earth. And the dragon stood before the woman (Israel) who was about to give birth, so that when she gave birth he might devour her child (Jesus)." (Rev 12:4)

> "And when the dragon saw that he was thrown down to the earth (Satan being kicked out of heaven during the Tribulation period), he persecuted the woman (Israel) who gave birth to the male child (The Lord Jesus Christ)." (Rev 12:13)

This verse notes the one Man (Jesus) that was born of a woman who can and will defeat Satan in the end. As you delve into Rev 12:14-15 the references are all about Israel and Satan's attack upon that region. Satan has been against the Jewish race since the time of Abraham, the father of that race. That race was also the bloodline of Christ, and Satan has tried to damage, corrupt, or destroy it since ancient times.

The dispensation of the Hypostatic Union has been the enemy of the kingdom of darkness as well as all the nations. The fallen angels, and those that they seek to destroy or rule over, are the two sides. There is not a nation or people that Satan considers a real comrade within this conflict.

The kingdom of darkness has always been the sworn enemy of the dispensation of the Hypostatic Union, and always the invisible foe of all the nations. The fallen angels are the enemy of the whole human race, for they only seek to use, destroy, conquer, and rule over them. There is not a nation or people that Satan considers a real comrade within this conflict.

There are foolish people who claim to worship Satan that are just as hated as any believer or nation by the demon army. These are the type of people that are more of an embarrassment to Satan than a source of pride or assistance to his cause. The deceptive concepts and ideas that have been promoted about fallen angels and Satan in general are so far from the truth that it has to be a source of humor, even a source of great victory for the devil and his legion.

> "And the great dragon was thrown down, the serpent of old who is called the devil and Satan, who deceives the whole world; he was thrown down to the earth, and his angels were thrown down with him." (Rev 12:9)

The kingdom of darkness will prolong the battle for as long as they can, because they realize that the end is not going to fall in their favor. For them it makes sense to extend the conflict for as long as they can, to get the point across that they can be independent from God and that God is unfair and His creatures are just better off living without Him. Satan and his fallen angels are the chief antagonists of the extension of the Angelic Conflict into human history. The two chapters that highlight mankind being lower than angels just like Jesus Christ was, until He went to the Cross, are Hebrews chapters 1 and 2, which also explain why God would consider us to be higher than angels when the mission is complete. These chapters are all speaking on human history that is intertwined with angelic history. The two are linked and were permanently bonded as one history coexisting in time, designed in eternity past. The application of the omnipotence of God to Satan as our great enemy is found in verses like 1Jo 4:4, "Greater is He (the Lord) who is in you than he (Satan) who is in the world."

So the challenge is out there every day in the cosmic system we live in, but we do not have to bow down to it. Our mind needs renewing and strengthening and it can only gain that by the constant intake of Bible doctrine. If something you cherish gets dirty almost every day, would you not wash it, and do the upkeep needed to preserve it? Do you cherish your soul? Is your mind important to you? Wash it clean with the Word of God to keep the thought patterns running in doctrinal "sync" with Truth. The angels observe your choices, they watch how you keep yourself thinking and applying God's Word in a world filled with evil and confusion.

Chapter 15

The Angelic Conflict in Human History Answers the Basic Questions About Life.

If you have reached this chapter and still do not understand why the human race was created, simply put: man was created to resolve the pre-historic Angelic Conflict. The second part of that answer would have to be that man was created to glorify God within that conflict. If you have gained those answers from this book then so far you have comprehended a basic but important principle about your life. It is one of purpose. There is a divine plan that is not just haphazard or tossed together by a series of chemical accidents or a fluke of nature.

> "For this reason (Angelic conflict) we must pay much closer attention to what we have heard, so that we do not drift away from it." (Heb 2:1)

The perfection of the Lord Jesus Christ as being greater than the angels is drawn from the Old Testament, and the completeness and perfection of this demonstration is revealed by the seven references to this in Hebrews 1. As we noted earlier, He (Jesus) has inherited a more excellent name than the angels (Heb 1:4). He will be worshipped by them (Heb 1:6) as the firstborn. Jesus is said to be anointed higher than any angel and sits at the Divine throne (Heb 8:1). In Heb 8:10-12, Jesus is said to be the

Creator of the universe, immutable and eternal. These are all quotations from the Old Testament, so it clearly reveals that Jesus Christ is Deity, the Savior and God of all. It is not in one section or a brief mention in the New Testament, it is throughout the Scriptures.

The warning then becomes crystal clear that the human race should not reject Jesus Christ as Savior. The Bible leads us to conclude that all have fallen including the angels. None are considered worthy, and this is truly interpreted as every created creature, angel and man. So this also points to the fact that the angels, in eternity past, had to have been offered a form of redemption or salvation at some point, because not all angels are with Satan today. Though it is not defined how the angels could return to God, it is hard to find a scripture in the original language that says that only some have fallen short or failed at some point. The human race is warned that a certain group of angels chose against God at some point and did not repent. This is revealed for our example, so we will not be thrown down to the lake of fire when the end comes, as is the case for the fallen angels (Mat 25:41).

When we are told to pay much closer attention in Heb 2:1, it is from the present active infinitive of the Greek word prosecho which is prosechein. Pros means "face-to-face", referring to looking at someone directly. Echo means to have and to hold. Therefore, the verb means to apply the mind to something, or to concentrate on the subject which is the doctrine that is being taught! This is in the present tense, meaning to keep concentrating until you see the Truth, to keep paying attention to what you study or hear. This is in the infinitive mood, telling us that God's purpose for the unbeliever is to hear it before the judgment comes. As we have already noted, grace always precedes judgment. This scripture, as with all of the Scripture, has been designed for today, as well as the Truth it held during a certain period in ancient history, and this verse in Heb 2:1 was a gracious warning to Jerusalem. They were about to be destroyed in three years. Pay attention to what we have heard, which points out the doctrinal lessons and messages that you do not want to let drift by you. In the original language it describes the words flowing by you without your grasping them. This one verse points out many of the problems that unbelievers and believers have had for thousands of years, ignorance toward the Word of God. There are no excuses for those of us who have reached an age of accountability and have no mental or physical disability that would hinder our intake of Truth.

It comes down to three volitional decisions that people make that account for their ignorance of the Gospel or ignorance of advanced doctrines. The first is refusing to hear the Word, not even giving it the time or effort to listen. Also, they may listen occasionally, but refuse to have the consistency to gain any momentum.

The second decision has to do with concentration upon the Word of God and being filled with the Holy Spirit. Some believers make a feeble attempt to take in a message or to sit under a pastor, but never focus on the teaching and do not understand the power of the Holy Spirit. Without the filling of the Holy Spirit a message can be lost.

The third decision that keeps people ignorant of doctrinal Truth falls under the metabolizing of Bible doctrine. This is the digesting process in a person's soul once they have absorbed something, so it becomes part of their system of thinking and ready for application. If they do not fully accept it, and then apply the principles, it soon becomes lost. This last principle really brings us back to Heb 2:1 and is a great example of how doctrine drifts or flows past you.

But all three of these are common methods of ignorance used by mankind to remain deaf, dumb, and blind toward the Word of God and any form of spiritual challenge or growth. If we do not remain steadfast and focused on what the Spirit is saying to the Church we will surely drift away. It is always a subtle, slow process when someone begins to drift away from his or her intake of Bible doctrine. It is very rare for someone to go from dedicated student to becoming a complete stranger to the Word overnight. Perseverance in the faith and continuance in His word are the primary prerequisites for the disciple or student of doctrine.

> "But encourage one another day after day, as long as it is still called "Today," so that none of you will be hardened by the deceitfulness of sin. For we have become partakers of Christ, if we hold fast the beginning of our assurance firm until the end." (Heb 3:13-14)

The Angelic Conflict

This scripture is telling us to hold fast or we may not be partakers of the divine nature. This is not a scripture that says anything about the loss of salvation, because that is never the case. The entire epistle of Hebrews gives us warnings and reminds us not to be distracted, drawn away, or sidetracked from the Truth. In Heb 10:25 we are told not to forsake assembling together as a church. Heb 10:39 says the positive believer does not shrink back into destruction. In Heb 10:23 it states that we need to hold fast without wavering. God takes no pleasure in witnessing a believer who operates as a coward or a quitter. The only ones who enjoy that scene are those in the kingdom of darkness. Looking back again at Heb 2:1, it is a serious statement that warns of doctrine drifting right through your system of thinking, and having no substance or stability in your mental attitude.

> "For if the word spoken through angels proved unalterable (this is a first class condition meaning it did), and every transgression and disobedience received a just recompense," (Heb 2:2)

The phrase "every transgression" is the Greek noun parabasis which means every form of stepping over the line, basically violating God's perfect laws. The reference for disobedience in the original language is a word that points to neglect of a principle, allowing something important to go past you. In fact in the Old Testament the word obedience is described not as doing, but first hearing!

Angels were used to bringing forth doctrine to people (Act 7:38,53) at certain points in human history. But an angel could gift-wrap a wonderful scripture and deliver it to your door with the full explanation and meaning of that scripture, and you would get absolutely nothing from it if you were not filled with the Holy Spirit. The word for disobedience is also used as a term of refusing to hear something first as in Isa 28:12 when it states, "They did not listen." Again we see it in Isa 30:9 referring to rebellious people who refuse to listen.

This is an interesting quote from Kenneth Wuest on the subject of disobedience: "The nature of the sin of Adam was a careless indifferent attitude towards the commands of God." Notice the attitude is careless and indifferent. The state of mind, the thought process and mental focus, the motivation is all starting to boil down to this. If your motivation is to get rich, all of your energy, time, and thoughts will be devoted to schemes to gain more wealth. An active addict will spend about 70% of their day on thoughts, actions, and methods of trying to get to the next high. That is where their motivation lives. The act of disobedience that Adam lived in is still a common thread within all of us.

The word parakoe is the word used for disobedience. It points out the meaning to disobey, but it also hints at a failure of concentration. It actually has a meaning that a principle is taught and you have avoided the path of its message or content. This is the careless attitude that the lesson being taught is not that important. Even though it is God's will for you to learn and to grow in His grace and knowledge, this attitude is a statement of defiance and your will over God's will. This following verse uses the same term within it:

> "For as through the one man's disobedience the many were made sinners, even so through the obedience of the One the many will be made righteous." (Rom 5:19)

There are many people within your social circle that think that they will have time for God later, or they believe that it is not important right now. However, the Word of God will become scarce when the end times begin to unfold in human history. When God's plan and His Word are continually rejected in a believer's life or in their nation in general, it is then that God brings in the famine.

> ""Behold, days are coming," declares the Lord GOD, "When I will send a famine on the land, not a famine for bread or a thirst for water, But rather for hearing the words of the LORD. People will stagger from sea to sea and from the north even to the east; They will go to and fro to seek the word of the LORD, But they will not find it." (Amo 8:11-12)

The world we live in today has shrinking resources as far as real doctrinal teachers are concerned. It is the Muslim belief and atheism that are spreading faster than Christianity in our day and age. So, we should never become too familiar with the Word of God. We should not only be eager to listen and to learn, but to physically and financially support good pastors who teach the Bible the way it was designed to be taught. We see this in the invisible realm as another strategy of the devil, another military ploy to gain ground in the conflict. It is the cosmic system and the temptations and deceptions within it that keep the human race focused on everything else but a relationship with God.

We can actually see the Angelic Conflict in action in a verse like Heb 2:2 when the end of the verse points out "just recompense." This is directed toward the angels and can be noted in Mat 25:41 as well. When this verse in Hebrews speaks about the transgressions and disobedience receiving a just recompense, it is talking to the fallen angels right now and warning the human race in the future. As mentioned earlier in this book, God can accomplish many things with one action or one verse in a way that is too vast for the human mind to follow. Without a thorough study of the original language, the comprehension of line upon line teaching, and a clear understanding of dispensations, as well as matching scripture with scripture, all powered by the Holy Spirit through your pastor-teacher, you will never scratch more than the surface of the Word of God.

The recompense in Heb 2:2 is just because it is from God, and the fact that it is directed toward fallen angels—and human history now and in a future tense—would be lost on the average Bible student. Many men that claim to be Bible teachers are confused with this type of Truth, they do not have the gift or ability to dig that deep. God owes the lake of fire to the fallen angels, but that is not what is happening in the present. It is a future event, a retroactive wage or debt that will definitely be paid. So, we can see that having a careless attitude toward the Bible or just neglecting to grow up spiritually will leave you lost and confused. Bear in mind that we are also covering believers in this book, not just the unbelievers of the world.

Neglect is another word that covers this careless attitude. This is an aorist active participle of the word amelesantes, meaning to take something lightly or to make light of something important and is used as a word for disregard as well. It is used in the following verse of Hebrews.

> "How shall we (human beings) escape if we neglect so great a salvation? After it was at the first spoken through the Lord (Jesus spoke about it first), it was confirmed to us by those who heard," (Heb 2:3)

What is being described beneath the surface of these scriptures is the rejection of the plan of God and any salvation He offered to fallen angels, and the just recompense is eternity in the lake of fire! We (the entire human race) are being warned not to disregard the salvation offered by Jesus Christ. In fact it states "so great a salvation" giving the implication that what is provided for the human race cannot be compared to any type of salvation offered to fallen angels. Christ on the Cross cannot be compared to any other event in the universe!

The apostles were the ones who carried these messages forward and were given authority to teach and even given a gift of spiritual powers to prove that they were the messengers of God. When you read further into Heb 2:4 it speaks of bearing witness and having various signs and wonders, the gifts imparted by the Holy Spirit. This was God's credit card or stamp of approval upon the apostles for a period of time so that they could perform healings and miraculous wonders. These gifts are not given out in our day and age, though we have phony healers and so-called miracle workers in the churches. They are not working under the power given to the apostles. Again this falls under the proper teaching and understanding of dispensations and the design of the Church Age. If they truly are healing and showing off miraculous wonders it may not be from God, but rather from the god of this world. This message we must not pass by is new after the resurrection of Jesus Christ. A new era had begun and the teaching was not found in the older scriptures (Old Testament).

So the apostle had to be established and given greater authority for a period to bring the new Church Age into the future and to push it forward for future generations. It also became a time when the fallen angels would have a more predominant role and the invisible warfare would accelerate and begin a new phase of intensified battle. So we can truly say that the Church Age is the domain of satanic ruler-ship more so than the Old Testament. But in the future, angels do not rule or have control in the Millennium, humans do!

> "For He (God the Father) did not subject to angels the world to come, concerning which we are speaking." (Heb 2:5)

The ultimate triumph of man occurs in the world to come (Millennial reign of Christ) where Jesus Christ reigns for a thousand years. This will be a period of winner believers (Old Testament and Church Age) who rule with the authority given directly from the Lord. Luk 19:17-19 proclaims that winners will have authority for they are the ones who remained faithful. The issue out there in the churches today becomes Truth. Is it emotional nonsense that the believer is being fed or is it a politically correct agenda or is it Truth? Because you (the believer) are accountable for sitting under a teacher who teaches Truth from the Bible, not mixed messages and confusing analogies. Sitting under this type of nonsense will certainly leave you lost and apathetic in the long run. A great example of understanding the original language comes up in this next verse.

> "But one has testified somewhere (David testified in Psa 8:4-6), saying, "What is man, that thou remembers him? Or the son of man, that thou art concerned about him?" (Heb 2:6)

There is actually some divine sarcasm within the verse because it was directed toward the so-called Jewish scholars of that day. And the "son of man" reference is pointing toward the descendants of Adam when normally it speaks to the Lord Jesus Christ. The word for concerned within that scripture is a present middle indicative of the word episkepte which refers to medical comfort or to go and see the sick, to relieve those who are ill. (In my own sense of sarcasm, I wonder if the average believer could have figured all that out just by reading the book of Hebrews. Not sure my sarcasm was divinely inspired!) This was a word used in ancient times for the local doctors making house calls. When we see the medical comfort of that word we have to think of the universal doctor who heals all patients and that is the Lord Jesus Christ.

> "But when Jesus heard this (why is your Teacher eating with tax-gatherers and prostitutes?), He said, 'It is not those who are healthy who need a physician, but those who are sick.'" (Mat 9:12)

In Mar 2:17 Jesus said again, "It is not those who are healthy who need a physician, but those who are sick; I did not come to call the righteous, but sinners." The only doctor that can address the pain and wounds from the Angelic Conflict after the fall of man is our Lord.

One of the misconceptions that comes from many pulpits is that the fall of mankind or even your own mistakes has some profound effect upon God. As if God is clueless as to how something happened or what would happen next in any given situation. Satan did not win the war when Adam and the woman fell in the garden. God did not panic and change plans as though He was caught off guard. We do not have the ability to set back God's plan, nor does the kingdom of darkness. Actually what we can see is greater grace being placed upon the scene after the fall of mankind. God always has a way to turn a curse into a blessing (Deu 23:5), and it is done in eternity past before the creation of man, before the curse ever existed.

In God's grace, mankind is made lower than the angels for a period of time, which keeps the Angelic Conflict fair and just and gives us the ability to become winners and to live in eternity in a perfect environment. In Heb 2:7-8 it first makes mention of Adam, and then in verse 8 it speaks upon the second Adam (Jesus Christ). The principle is clear then that all creatures are subordinate to Jesus Christ. This occurred after his resurrection. In His deity, Christ is the creator of angels, and in His humanity He spent time lower than the angels. Since Christ is our leader, our example, and we (believers) are in union with Him, this puts us in the same category. For a little while we are lower than the angels! The first Adam failed miserably (1Co 15:45), but the second Adam is triumphant. We can safely say that only two members of the human race came into the world with no old sin nature, Adam and Jesus. The first Adam lost it all for mankind, but the second Adam regained it all back plus He provided salvation and even more!

> "However, the spiritual is not first, but the natural; (Adam who was first) then the spiritual. The first man (Adam) is from the earth, earthy; the second man (Jesus Christ) is from heaven." (1Co 15:45-46)

In verses 48 and 49 it states, as is the earthy, so also are those who are earthy. This is pointing out that Adam was dead in sin and therefore all his ancestors follow the same genetic path. It then goes on to tell us that we inherit or bear the image of the heavenly: this is the new nature that we are given at salvation. So the only way we can become superior to angelic creatures is through union with Jesus Christ. We are going to be raised up with Him at the right hand of the Father (Eph 2:6). Our position as believers is secured and set at the right hand of the Father. This principle of our position is a major nuisance to Satan, who will always attempt to keep people blinded to the baptism of the Spirit and to our identification with Jesus Christ. Satan cannot stomach the fact that positionally there are those of us within the human race (believers) that have become superior to him. There will come a time when we will experience this permanent position we have been given, and this does not sit well with any of the fallen angels. Our resurrection bodies are said to be greater than angelic bodies in Phi 3:21 and 1Co 15:53, and this is one reason why the Church is first to go up in the Rapture because we will go to the bema seat judgment.

The first Adam was crowned with glory and honor, having no old sin nature and given perfection with his power. The Greek word for crowned is stephanoo, which is derived from the word estephanosas, meaning to adorn with an honorary crown or to receive the approval of God. That is the term used in Heb 2:7 which says, "Thou hast crowned him (man) with glory." When the word crowned was used initially about Adam it pointed to his creation. The aorist tense of that word was used to explain that God created and blessed Adam in the beginning. It is in the active voice meaning that God the Father has produced the action of the verb. God crowned the original man with glory and honor. The indicative mood says that God did the work and it is a fact. So perfection was given to Adam and he fell, he lost the perfect environment and blessings that God had bestowed upon him and his wife. The rest of mankind was then created to resolve the conflict, and all this was accounted for in eternity past. The perfection that we will receive in eternity future is even greater than the perfection that Adam had and lost in the Garden, since we are eternally in union with Christ! Moving on to verse nine is where we see another vital point.

> "But we do see Him who was made for a little while lower than the angels, namely, Jesus, because of the suffering of death crowned with glory and honor, so that by the grace of God He might taste death for everyone." (Heb 2:9)

Jesus Christ never lost His glory and honor. Jesus Christ built upon that honor given to Him. So the Lord's victory becomes our victory when we believe in Him. In Heb 2:8 the victory is highlighted as we see all things put under subjection to Christ. What we have is a position into which we were born, that is Adam and his bloodline, receiving the old sin nature. But a second position came along that wiped the first clear off the map, and that is a union with the Lord Jesus Christ. All that this position requires in order to be secure is a positive attitude toward the Savior, no works or special deeds are needed. During the Millennial Reign the saints will rule in resurrection bodies. Some will rule ten cities, some five, others may just run errands.

At the end of the Tribulation the Baptism of Fire in Mat 24:40-41 (taking up the unbelievers off the earth) occurs. All unbelievers are then taken up and baptized or identified with the lake of fire. You do not want to be the one taken up at this time! (This event is different from the Rapture seven years earlier, in which believers are taken up to Christ before the Tribulation.) At the Baptism of Fire event, the legions of demons will also be removed, and Christ at His Second Advent begins His Millennial Reign, this time not as a carpenter or teacher but as the divine authority over all. Just as the unseen forces of the kingdom of darkness have authority and power on the earth now, so too will winner believers step into the authority roles that the Lord will give to them. This will be a time of the ultimate role reversal. All those against Christ will be removed, and when the Bible says, "All things will be subject to Him," it means that the air, weather, water, and space, also including every being created by the hand of God, will be under His rule.

So we can see in the verses of Heb 2 that in verse 7 we touched on the past, the first Adam, and verse 8 recognizes the future with Jesus Christ, and verse 9 refers to the Church Age believer of today. The physical birth of Jesus Christ was a position lower than the angels, yet His victorious death upon the Cross raised not only Him but anyone in union with Him above angels. The crown of glory and honor also refers to the physical birth of Christ. But none of these scriptures and meanings will hold any value unless you have become a dedicated student of the Word of God. If you are not taught by a man with the gift of pastor-teacher who has the dedication to study original scriptures you will remain a clueless child of God, a babe in the spiritual realm. Salvation is the means by which The Lord Jesus Christ not only saves mankind but gains dominion over all. No angelic creature could give himself upon that Cross. Only a man could taste death for every man. The Cross saved mankind and won back the crown that Adam lost!

> "For it was fitting for Him (God the Father), for whom are all things, and through whom are all things, in bringing many sons to glory, to perfect the author of their salvation through sufferings." (Heb 2:10)

The word "for" is the Greek conjunction gar which is used to link the last sentence with this one. This conjunction points to the first verses' (1-9) being true. The words "it was fitting" have the meaning of an inner fitness, to be totally equipped or suitable. The imperfect tense of that statement describes the continuous habitual action that occurred in the past, referring to God the Father's character which is perfect and has always provided for us. This shows that God the Father always does what is appropriate, meaning that His plan is perfect, and guess what? God does all the work.

We see that by the statement "bringing many sons to glory" this is God doing the work for His people (believers). Everything depends on God's character and God's ability, and that is why it was fitting for Him to bring many sons to glory. The Greek word eprepen is the word used to translate "it was fitting," also emphasizing God's perfect design. Any plan or design by God is complete and perfect, and anything a creature adds to it takes away from its state of perfection. This is a prime example of why legalism coming from the Christian community is so damaging to the plan of God. Sins cause less damage than a works program or Christian legalism and self-righteousness ever does concerning God's work.

Satan cannot possess a born-again believer. He may have degrees of influence on a negative believer, but not possession. This is why false doctrine and legalistic teaching are such powerful weapons within the devil's arsenal. This type of teaching then becomes an influence of evil in the negative believer's life. This concept may be difficult to understand because it is all that most churches and community programs teach. Human effort, good religious deeds and legalistic works programs all promote credit to the creature instead of the Creator; however, human good is devastating to the plan of God in a believer's life. It is the equivalent of being on the wrong road to an important destination, going further away from your goal, because your road map is a fake! Remember that the road to hell truly is often paved with "good" intentions of religion!

Improving the world system is really what Satan has set out to do. Anything that is independent from God and pushes us further away from His grace, His logistics, His will, is certainly not from our Lord. In Heb 2:10 there is a statement of victory when you study the word "glory" and it is the Greek noun doxan, meaning a form of dignity and honor.

So we see the victory in the Angelic Conflict given to us by God's grace. Also the word "author" in that verse is used only three other times within the Bible and refers to the humanity of Christ. The Greek word is archegon and it is a noun that points to a supreme leader, a ruler, or prince as well as an author. It is used in Act 3:15, Act 5:31 and Heb 12:2, where it always refers back to the humanity of Christ and to His glory at the right hand of the Father. The term "to perfect" is derived from a word that means to advance to completion or finish, which is exactly what the Lord Jesus Christ has done for every son (Church Age believer), and it will be completely finished when He and His bride are united. When Church Age believers unite with Christ it is the completion of the vows or the end of the ceremony.

As the verse points out it all came through sufferings, which is plural because Jesus Christ died and was judged for every single sin in the history of the human race! The fallen angels hate grace. They hate the fact that with proper teaching and a positive attitude any believer can realize what the work upon the Cross meant for mankind and this invisible warfare.

As the next verse (Heb 2:11) states it is Christ who sanctifies, which comes from the word hagiazon, a present active participle that means to make holy or purify, and this covers a physical and mental cleansing. This purification refers to overt sins as well as to mental attitude sins such as bitterness and jealousy or judging. Basically it is a full cleansing, allowing you to throw away the garbage that has darkened your soul. In Heb 10:10 and 1Co 1:2 it tells us that every believer is sanctified and set apart by God. It is not pointing out something to obtain or work for, but it is a state in which we begin our Christian life. The present tense says the Lord keeps on setting apart those who believe through the baptism of the Holy Spirit. The active voice is saying that the Lord Jesus Christ does the sanctifying through God the Holy Spirit, who is an agent and the reason why we are in union with Christ. The term "those who are sanctified" is a reference to the Church Age believers and the participle denotes the purpose of the Cross.

We see positional truth illustrating the Father's plan, and a believer must understand his or her position, otherwise you can be led astray by guilt and legalistic teaching. At the end of Heb 2:11, "sanctified" is the present middle participle of the word hagiazomenoi, and this is the middle voice, meaning to receive holiness and to be set apart. Believers receive, they do not earn or purchase it themselves!

Without the knowledge of your position in Christ you miss out on fantastic implications concerning the Angelic Conflict. So the current condition in which you see yourself has no consequence compared to the position in which God sees you. God chooses to look at us in our union with His Son, even though He can see the thought and intent of the heart. He can see through the thick, ignorant skull of the human being.

> "And there is no creature hidden from His sight, but all things are open and laid bare to the eyes of Him with whom we have to do." (Heb 4:13)

Keep in mind that if God kept a record of sins and mistakes there is no one that could stand (Psa 130:3). If all your sins and flaws were put upon an overhead projector for everyone to see, would you feel shame, or embarrassment? I would guess that most people would answer yes to that question. Only the arrogant would deny the awful feelings that this kind of projection could press upon their soul. And we are talking about the mental attitude and not just the overt. We are talking about the times when you cut corners or cheated, lusted, or lied and only you knew about it. This also would display your motivation for doing something, be it good or bad. How about some of the nasty thoughts or hidden selfish motives you had this past week? I hope you are getting the drift because God sees it all: past, present, and future sins and iniquities.

Now when you view that from the human realm it is rather humbling to think that God does not feel shame or anger toward you in any capacity. Think about the times you sat next to a so-called loser in church and you felt some type of embarrassment or shame. The Lord has nothing but compassion and love for that same individual, there is no embarrassment toward His people. One reason is that the Lord Jesus Christ is in union with every believer and cannot harbor such feelings for Himself. We are an integral part of Him. Heb 2:11 says that He is not ashamed to call you brethren!

The verb for that word "call" is a present active indicative of kalien, meaning to simply call or to name. The present tense says that He is never ashamed of us. Satan hates that fact and is happy when we have feelings of shame and guilt and do not operate in our position. So Satan can do what he loves to do over and over again, which is to make accusations against members of the Royal Family of God. Satan is a genius, so he knows better than to make things up and to put that type of nonsense on display in front of an all-knowing God. But our Lord is never ashamed of us, even if the accusations are true!

Saying (Jesus Christ is declaring), "I will proclaim your name (name of the Father) to my brethren, in the midst of the congregation I will sing your praise." And again, "I will put my trust in him." And again, "Behold, I and the children whom God has given me." (Heb 2:12-13)

This is the Lord Jesus Christ who is speaking and proclaiming. And how does He announce and declare these things to us? He does it through the mind of Christ (1Co 2:16), the Word of God or the Bible.

When the Bible uses the term "Behold" it is the verb idou, speaking upon an important subject, meaning to focus your attention on it. And in Heb 2:13 He is actually commanding all creatures, including angelic ones, to pay attention and to follow the command. "Behold, listen, I and the children God gave me," is what is truly said.

The gift that God gave Him is the children (believers) as a reward. This means that at the completion or the finish line it is already determined that we are in union once we have crossed that barrier of salvation. It is like entering a race and knowing that you are already the winner and that the trophy is yours once the course is complete, nothing can take it from you. You could run a slow race and still come out with the trophy!

The Cross neutralized Satan and has made him powerless. This is why we (positive believers) are absolutely public enemy number one on the kingdom of darkness' hit list. We cannot damage the outcome of the race or the glory of God. God's plan is never compromised by creatures. In Heb 2:14 it states that Satan has the power of death over us, but it is only God who can permit Satan to bring death to a human body. The power of death is referring to the powers that Satan does hold over humanity as we should not forget he claimed the earth when Adam fell.

One power Satan clings to is the fear of death, which is removed from a believer's life once he understands the end result of the conflict. Fear of death is a form of slavery, one of the many forms of slavery Satan holds over the human race.

Speaking upon this form of slavery, Heb 2:15 says "might deliver," which is an aorist active subjunctive of the word apallaxe, which points to freedom or a deliverer, setting someone free. The aorist tense is without reference to duration or completion. The active voice says that the Lord delivers anyone who believes. The subjunctive mood is saying that the potential is there, that free will is involved.

This fear of death is a basic satanic doctrine, and the human race has been inculcated with it since the early ages. The slavery of the human race is intertwined with the old sin nature, the influence of the kingdom of darkness, and the arrogance of self, which has many doctrines like the fear of death. It is all bottled up in a cosmic system guided by an infamous fallen angel, who would love to blind us from our Lord's final victory over death in 1Co 15:54-55!

Remember that there are at least five reasons why the Lord Jesus Christ had to become a member of the human race:

1. Jesus Christ had to become true humanity to do the will of His Father (Heb 10:5-10).
2. Jesus Christ had to become true humanity to become the one true Savior of the world (Phi 2:7-8 and Heb 2:14-15).
3. Jesus Christ had to become true humanity to become the mediator between God and man (Job 9:2, 32-33 and 1Ti 2:5-6). Jesus Christ is both equal to God and to mankind.
4. Jesus Christ had to become true humanity to become our high priest. A priest must be a man and can then act as the mediator between the parties. (Heb 7:4-5,14-17,21-28 and Heb 10:5,14).
5. Jesus Christ had to become true humanity to be a king and ruler forever. He had to fulfill the Davidic covenant and to be royalty from the line of David (As seen from the promises to Israel, 2Sa 7:8-16; Psa 89:20-37).

In Heb 2:16 it clearly says that He did not come to help angels but to help the descendants of Abraham.

> "Therefore, He had to be made like His brethren in all things, so that He might become a merciful and faithful high priest in things pertaining to God, to make propitiation for the sins of the people. For since He Himself was tempted in that which He has suffered, He is able to come to the aid of those who are tempted." (Heb 2:17-18)

The Lord was tempted in all things. He was tested constantly even by the devil himself! The phrase "was tempted" comes from the word peirastheis, meaning to approve for good or for bad, or to test someone to determine their character. The word for "suffered" is the present active indicative of the word peponthen, speaking about undergoing great punishment. But what we have gained is fantastic blessing from His sufferings and punishment.

The active voice in this word is referring to our Lord's choice to take upon Himself great suffering, and the indicative mood is the reality that the suffering had to take place to resolve the conflict. Some of the testing took place so that the kingdom of darkness could view His humanity, see the pain and struggle in His flesh. When this verse points out that Christ can come to the aid of those who are tempted it is in a present tense. As in Rom 7:25, He is always coming to our rescue!

"Those who are tempted" is the dative of advantage coming from that same word peirastheis. The verb is in the present passive participle of the word peirazomenois, again pointing to testing someone's character or qualifying an individual. The present tense indicates that the world will keep testing us. The passive voice says that we receive the tests to glorify God. The participle establishes that this will continue throughout our lifetime. The dative of advantage states that it is to our advantage to go through such testing. Again we are brought back to the point stressed earlier that we are on display, being watched by angelic forces. They all witness the believer who is applying the Word of God. They witness God's grace blessings. They see everyone's life playing out upon an open field.

So if ever the conversation arises as to why did God allow the fall or sin in the first place, the simple straightforward answer is that it was to resolve the Angelic Conflict. But most people (even believers) have little or no knowledge of the subject, so you always should be prepared to reach deeper to another level to bring forth this explanation. The next point you need to make is that God created all creatures with a free will, because He is just and fair, the perfect gentleman and loving God.

The free will of angels and mankind began the issue of sin and independence from the Father. The primary source of temptation is the old sin nature, but the source of sin comes from the volition. We saw the function of negative volition in heaven in eternity past, and then on earth in the Garden. There was only one specific prohibition within the Garden: "Eat from any tree, but from the tree of the knowledge of good and evil you shall not eat." This was the one command that was emphasized. Satan was able to take that one rule, twist it and turn it to his advantage because he was well aware of free will and that all created creatures experience a temptation toward some form of arrogance.

> "Indeed. Has God said, 'You shall not eat from any tree of the garden?'" (Gen 3:1)

God actually had said any tree but one. Notice the subtle difference? Satan is a master at misrepresenting the character and giving of God. No wonder religion misrepresents who God is on such a massive scale to this day! Satan knows that without our eyes fixed on who God really is, creatures are doomed to fall to one temptation or another.

The grace of God has given us all free will and the ability to spend a certain amount of time living just as we please; however, the omniscience of God, motivated by His infinite love and perfect justice, developed a plan to resolve both the fall of man and the entire Angelic Conflict!

If God allowed created creatures like angels or mankind to fall and just continue on in arrogance and lust patterns of the soul indefinitely, eventually anything that God had created would be destroyed. In that case, He would have had to watch all His creatures, whom He loved infinitely, eventually destroy themselves.

So the all-knowing Father allowed the angels to begin a rebellion and to set the wheels of anarchy into motion, and then He determined to resolve it permanently after the conflict had played itself out completely. Once the rebellion occurred in eternity past, God could not have brought a new creation upon the scene and given them more power, or Satan in his appeal trial would have cried out that it was a mistrial. Satan would have cried that those creatures' greater power was what enabled them to follow God faithfully, instead of their free will accepting all that the grace of God gives. And if God even removed the issue of free will from a new creation, making them obedient robots, yet again Satan would cry foul and have a valid point in the end.

So, to resolve the conflict there was a need for a creation that was weaker, less skillful, and still had a free will to choose for or against God. Any other scenario would have left questions about the fairness of the appeal trial and would have gone against the nature of God.

However, God's plan still went forward even with the curse of sinful mankind, turning what appeared to be a curse into a blessing, because at the Cross all human sin was judged while human good was rejected.

> "He saved us, not on the basis of deeds which we have done in righteousness, but according to His mercy, by the washing of regeneration and renewing by the Holy Spirit," (Tit 3:5)

This is why the efficacious saving work of Christ on the Cross is the basis for the strategic victory of the Angelic Conflict (Col 2:14-15; Heb 1-2). The Cross was the place where God expressed His perfect love, justice, and righteousness. And the answer to any accusation made e.g.how can a loving God cast His creatures into a lake of fire? Then picture the fact that the same loving God poured out His wrath on His only Son to save us all from that fate. The Father allowed the Son to be beaten, humiliated, and treated as an outcast, then allowed Him to suffer pain beyond description for all the sins of the whole world upon that Cross. Satan could not even come forth with an accusation once the Cross came into view.

This is why the phrase, "the Cross broke the back of Satan" is so pertinent. Satan had used every distraction and trick at his disposal to stop the act that took place upon that Cross. Satan used humans, kings and leaders, temptations and lies to try to stop Jesus Christ from first being born and then to try to stop Him from completing the work that God had given Him. The kingdom of darkness used people to shout out statements that would tempt Jesus to come down off that Cross. In Mat 27:33-37 they gave him wine to drink to ease the pain, yet He refused it because He was so focused on His mission that He turned down any distractions, even if they would ease the pain. In their thoughtless rejection of the Messiah, they even bid upon His clothing as He hung naked. They placed a sign that read, "This is Jesus the King of the Jews" above His head.

Mat 27:39-42: "And those passing by were hurling abuse at Him (blasphemeo meaning to speak evil or to vilify), wagging their heads and saying with sarcasm, 'You who are going to destroy the temple and rebuild it in three days, save Yourself! If You are the Son of God, come down from the cross.' In the same way the chief priests also, along with the scribes and elders, were mocking Him and saying, 'He saved others; He cannot save Himself. He is the King of Israel; let Him now come down from the cross, and we will believe in Him.'"

In Mat 27:43 they shouted, "He trusts in God; let God deliver Him now!"

Satan has difficulty trying to attack the character of God, because at the Cross that same character of God condemned His own perfect impeccable Son while bearing our sins. Christ became the issue in the Christian way of life, not sin or human good! This combination has left Satan and his legion in a perpetual state of frustration and anger.

The emphasis within the conflict is first the issue of salvation and then human volition. There are certain divine rules of establishment and divine standards, yet creatures with free will and plenty of room to act out have violated these principles; therefore, we have the answer to our question. A perfect, loving God does not cause sin or the fall of an entire race. He allows it when He operates in His character and nature by creating a free will and by offering freedom.

This creation of free will combined with the principle of freedom now points us to the answer for chaos within this world. Chaos and evil are nothing new and will never be completely removed until Jesus Christ returns and the conflict is complete. 1Co 14:33 clearly states that God is not the God of confusion but of peace. Creation will not experience true peace on earth until the Millennial Reign of our Lord Jesus Christ!

Satan does not have the power or ability to control all inhabitants (human and angelic), nor the ability to produce a perfect environment. You see, this is the goal of beliefs such as communism or socialism, to infringe upon people's rights and to manipulate freedom so that it will supposedly cause a greater good for all creatures. It is a debilitating form of control imposed by a few to manage the majority. When you begin to cut into people's rights and to tailor their "freedom" to suit everyone else it always turns out in disaster! God never designed any creatures to be completely identical with all the same strengths and weaknesses. The only time there is equal opportunity and equal privilege is in the invisible realm of our spiritual walk. During our spiritual walk all believers have equal chances to grow or to move forward in God's plan. Outside of it there will always be weak and strong, authority and subordinate, rich and poor in some realm.

Satan would love to have more people think that chaos exists because he is making it happen rather than its being a result of his lack of power and control. He wishes to hide his embarrassment as the ruler of this world for the mess it is in today! So he promotes religion, legalism, and the belief that God is angry and taking it out on the people of this world.

Now this brings us to a very confusing fact in Christianity i.e. so-called good deeds and acts of Christian activism. Most of Christian activism is a blind, ignorant movement to clean up the devil's world. There is a tremendous emphasis among evangelical Christians today to enter into activism, to practice social and political engineering. Social engineering means trying to force biblical principles on society via laws. Political engineering means trying to control the government with principles from the Bible. If you do a close study of our Lord Jesus Christ's ministry here on earth you will find that He was not involved in anything like this. This arrogance manifests itself in the fact that most Christians do not have a clue about the Christian way of life. Christians are famous for sticking their nose into other people's business, intruding on the privacy of others, violating constitutional rights, and even violent acts like blowing up an abortion clinic. In fact, to outlaw a certain segment of society because they do not adhere to someone's view of Biblical principles is a disaster.

We have no right to judge, imprison, or cause people misery and grief for their personal beliefs. Any cult or religion has the right to their opinion just as much as any Christian group in the free society God has put into place. Jesus Christ anticipated this problem even in the early Church. The Pharisees tried trapping Him from any religious angle many times (Mat 22:15-21).

In Mat 22:16 they sent their own disciples out to question Christ, starting off by saying, "We know that You are truthful . . . You are not partial to any." Then they went on to question giving taxes to Caesar. Jesus Christ knew this game too well.

But Jesus perceived their malice, and said, "Why are you testing Me, you hypocrites?" (Mat 22:18)

Jesus asked to see the coin for the taxes, and when they showed it to Him, He pointed out the picture on the coin and asked, "Whose likeness and inscription is this?"

They said to Him, "Caesar's." Then He said to them, "Then render to Caesar the things that are Caesar's; and to God the things that are God's." (Mat 22:21)

They quickly went away in awe of Jesus Christ once again. So the believer's responsibility is a dual role but does not include activism. "Render unto Caesar" is in reference to respecting the laws of the land and divine establishment principles, being a good citizen. "Render unto God" is Jesus Christ telling them to execute the plan of God for their life and to stay out of the political nonsense. Christian activism becomes tantamount to the Church Age believer who is involved in the temporal solutions to the problems of life when spiritual solutions are available. Satan cannot improve on the laws of divine establishment, he has no hope of duplicating God's predesigned plan. What he does have is an army of ignorant Christians that are working overtime to represent him in this world, attempting to clean up and chase away all the bad stuff so we can try to have a perfect environment.

Satan is the original counterfeiter. He has no influence to provide real, lasting provisions for anyone, nor has he compassion or power to offer grace to a fallen creature. He only has fakes and phonies lined up that have no fortitude. Everything he offers is either hollow or it comes with strings attached. Arrogance is his main ingredient, selfish pride and gluttony, lust, lies! That is why the world appears in such chaos at times, as he does not have the ability to pull it all together under his control. He probably has many rebellious angels under his command who scoff at him behind his back and run rampant in certain areas. Do you realize that one of the worst times in human history was the Middle Ages, because religion was in charge! Crusades of morality or chaotic activism, socialism or human good are all rooted in the satanic plan, not the divine plan. We cannot even call it a plan because Satan is obviously failing to "BE LIKE THE MOST HIGH!"

Satan has been trying for centuries to duplicate the coming Millennium and failing miserably. Every satanic program and attempt to bless mankind in his kingdom always results in some form of evil, human good, crusader arrogance, social engineering, socialism, communism, religion, plus all the folly of rulers.

So the question must arise as to whether Satan is really happy with all the resulting evil in the world, manifest in degeneracy, since Satan is trying to prove that he is good and that he can come up with a system as good as God's good. The inevitable consequences of man's involvement in Satan's cosmic system is chaos. We can see it in many realms: psychologically, socially, personally, nationally, and internationally.

Man's folly in rejecting God's plan, first at salvation, then in the PPOG, brings chaos, unfairness, evil, and disaster into the world from both believers and unbelievers. With the angels observing it is imperative that positive believers not be caught up in the details of the devil's world. The Angelic Conflict is moving forward with or without you! When the believer grows up spiritually and can function in the Pre-designed Plan of God for their life it nullifies Satan's power and punches holes in his cosmic game plan.

The believer must understand the power of the Holy Spirit, the need for doctrinal Truth, and must avoid the Christian nonsense that fills the world. A believer who never grows up or one who remains faithful to the ways of the world is nothing more than a disciple of Satan, and those that get involved with the legalistic aspect of Christianity are equivalent to foot soldiers for the kingdom of darkness.

The issue of human suffering is always difficult to explain even to a positive believer because when it is personal, like a parent or friend who is suffering an illness or facing death, the Angelic Conflict could be the culprit in some cases although not all suffering points directly to the kingdom of darkness. The free will decisions of people throughout their lives have a great deal to do with medical, emotional, and financial suffering that occurs in mankind. The human body is not designed for flawless performance year after year, and it is going to age and go back into the dust of the earth, so that explains many medical and death issues that arise in the human population. Negative volition toward the Word of God can also bring about the sin unto death and can cause believers and unbelievers great mental and physical pain when they stray too far from God. There are consequences with every decision in life, many consequences take years to catch up to us. In the long run, negative lifestyle choices lead to negative endings! God is the perfect gentleman and steps back from our negative choices because we are saying in essence, "I don't need you Father; I will do it my way." There are some consequences even God will not touch or alter after they have been set into motion.

This all comes under the umbrella of freedom and free will. God can and will turn a curse into a blessing when a believer begins to turn things around, but it does not mean that the results of your bad decisions are automatically removed. There is suffering associated with sinful lifestyles, and it is a reality of our free society and realm of life. Ignorance is no excuse though many will claim it after the suffering or pain begins in their life.

Evil, injustice and unfair treatment all come with the package of freedom and free will that God has given us. Both immoral and moral evil bring upon the human race a great deal of pain and even death. Self-righteousness is a fine example of moral evil, and many self-righteous people bring suffering and judgment and even act out in violence toward people they believe are wrong.

> "If therefore the light (moral evil) that is in you is darkness, how great is the darkness!" (Mat 6:23)

Many times morality is nothing more than a façade for self-righteousness and legalism. Suffering can be a challenge in two realms:

1) Under the law of volitional responsibility and divine discipline, suffering is designed to orient us to the reality of sin and failure, and the need for recovery.
2) Under undeserved suffering or suffering for blessing, the believer is challenged to use the problem-solving devices, like the faith-rest drill, virtue-love, doctrinal orientation, a personal sense of destiny, and occupation with Christ, in order to grow in grace, to orient to the plan of God, and to advance to spiritual maturity where we can glorify God in the Angelic Conflict.

Under the first realm we see suffering arising due to a series of bad decisions, and if we are humble we can learn from it. The term "reaping what you sow" has a great deal of truth to it. There is a doctrinal principle that comes from the law of volitional responsibility that is called self-induced misery. This simply means that you cause your own problems and emotional breakdowns due to a lack of spiritual maturity. Lack of doctrine in the soul allows cosmic system viewpoint to find a home, and therefore leaves a person unstable and a sucker for bad decisions in life. In Jer 2:19 it says "Your own wickedness will correct you, and your apostasies will reprove you."

"When your dread comes like a storm, and your calamity comes on like a whirlwind, when distress and anguish come on you. Then they will call on Me, but I will not answer; They will seek me diligently, but they shall not find Me, because they hated knowledge (doctrine), and did not choose respect for the Lord." (Pro 1:27-29)

The next verses in Proverbs state that they would not accept counsel and that they shall eat of the fruit of their own way. God is speaking to stubborn believers and ignorant unbelievers about their free will choices. When God adds divine discipline to the negative decisions and the emotional state of a person it truly becomes overwhelming. Most of the time we have become a danger to ourselves and to those around us because of negative decisions before God finally drops the hammer. The grace of God will give anyone a long time to wake up and to return to Him before bringing in a crisis to try to reach them and to call them home. So this is the first and most common form of suffering in the Angelic Conflict. The second realm of suffering falls under suffering for blessing. This is the type of suffering that brings glory to God and is a strategic part of the conflict. There are three types of undeserved suffering or suffering for blessing which relate to the plan of God for your life.

1) Preventative suffering, which is added to spiritual self-esteem (first stage of growth) and is usually short term suffering that can propel a believer forward to another stage of growth, gaining more independence in God's plan (spiritual autonomy).

In Psa 119:71 it talks about affliction being good to help us grow and learn more in the plan of God. Not easy to understand, but God does allow problems, testing, and suffering for our own benefit. You learn the power of applying the Word of God and the meaning of faith when adversity arrives on your doorstep, not when you just won the lottery. Even Jesus Himself learned the application of doctrine through the things that He suffered (Heb 5:8), not during peaceful times! Many times we do not understand what God is doing or why certain situations are allowed in our life, but we can fall back on the fact that He is faithful. Solomon who is considered to be among the wisest men in Biblical history said something interesting upon this subject.

"In the day of prosperity be happy, but in the day of adversity consider—God has made the one as well as the other so that man may not discover anything that will be after him." (Ecc 7:14)

If we change our view on adversity and realize that God is at work, then we submit to it, make the mental adjustments, and gain the benefit from it. Preventative suffering can be to learn obedience, humility, self-discipline, and to make changes in our lives. When we speak on humility it can mean that it is genuine or enforced as this point reveals. Though suffering is usually designed to build spiritual strength (2Co 12), many people become weaker afterward because they did not apply and make the appropriate changes. Suffering either leaves a person better or worse, it never leaves any of us the same!

Preventative suffering is designed to prevent a believer from becoming arrogant, not to push him or her deeper into arrogance. Arrogance can creep into a believer's soul as the individual grows and gains a little knowledge. Maybe they believe that they have everything figured out and begin getting themselves puffed up with knowledge. God makes war against the proud and arrogant so this is not something to take lightly. It can be very intoxicating to have people be in awe of your knowledge or show you a certain level of respect that they do not display toward others. God will sometimes allow attacks upon your reputation or inner circle of friends and family, that is all designed to focus our eyes on Him instead of ourselves! The sad part is when other so-called loving Christians rejoice when you are suffering or being humbled by God. The apostle Paul gives a good example of personal suffering at this first stage of spiritual growth:

"Because of the surpassing greatness of the revelations (Paul in spiritual self-esteem), for this reason, to keep me from exalting myself (Paul had great knowledge of mystery doctrines), there was given me a thorn in the flesh, a messenger (angel) of Satan to buffet me—to keep me from exalting myself!" (2Co 12:7)

The word "given" in this scripture is an aorist passive indicative of the verb edothe, and in the passive voice it means that this was given for a blessing and a benefit. It may not feel good, but it is good for you! We know that Paul was often persecuted by people wherever he traveled, and this may have come from the kingdom of darkness, but it certainly was a tool used for his growth because he applied doctrine to it. God allows the kingdom of darkness insight into your areas of weakness or even avenues to assault you, for your own growth. It is a part of the plan for your life to be allotted areas and times of suffering and weakness. In fact a positive and powerful believer like Paul is a threat to Satan, and Paul could easily have become arrogant with all the knowledge he had gathered by the grace of God. So we can see suffering in the sense that it is sometimes an attack from satanic forces, but it is permitted by God for our benefit as this appears to be the case for Paul.

"Concerning this (thorn in the flesh) I entreated or appealed to the Lord three times that it might depart from me." (2Co 12:8)

The kingdom of darkness is given a license by God to poke, prod, and torment a positive believer (see book of Job). One key element that the modern day Christian uses to try to remove suffering is prayer, and prayer was never designed as a problem solving device. What God does not remove He intends for us to bear. We see that prayer was not answered for the apostle Paul in this situation, and it is a good example for us to learn from.

In 2Co 12:9 the term "And He has said to me" is a perfect active indicative of the verb eireken. It is saying that Paul remembered something that the Lord had taught him. What is in view here is recalling doctrine, not God failing to respond to prayers. How are we to grow up and fulfill the plan of God if at every difficult twist or turn we are rescued by our Father? Then think in terms of the accusations that Satan could throw upon the divine courtroom: "Look, You saved another one; they are treated like babies and protected by You! Of course they will choose You over me." This is the reality of the conflict we are in and the type of statement that the kingdom of darkness would love to use. Remember Satan's statement in Job 1:9-11 that Job only follows God because God puts a hedge of blessing around him!

What Paul then realizes is that in his weakness he can be strong, because then the Lord can work through him (2Co 12:9). God's grace is sufficient for us! Paul even states that he will gladly boast of his weakness, in order that the power of Christ may reside in him. Our Lord when He was here on planet Earth lived in spiritual maturity. And we have His viewpoint in time, right now within us, to sustain and problem-solve using the mind of Christ. Everything necessary to fulfill the plan of God is laid out for us, it was provided in eternity past. So God supplies the solution before the problem, which is a common doctrinal principle that every Christian should know.

Suffering could be viewed as a spotlight on talent! The angels are watching believers under pressure and the outcome does matter. Your mental attitude and your words and actions under pressure are pertinent. Suffering for blessing focuses on God's grace and God's power. It is the invisible hero who shifts the focus off of self and glorifies and worships God instead. It is not boasting to glorify self but boasting of (rejoicing in) the dynamic mental attitude of spiritual growth facing preventative suffering.

"Therefore I am well content with weaknesses (preventative suffering), with insults (slander and people testing), with distresses (thought testing), with persecutions (system testing), with difficulties (disaster testing), for Christ's sake; for when I am weak, then I am strong." (2Co 12:10)

This one verse covers four tests that may be expected in any believer's life in continuing to grow. When you begin to pass these types of tests using the doctrine in your soul, not murmuring, complaining, or trying to pray your way out of them, it is then that God sees that you are ready for the next stage. Reverting back to human solutions and crying your way through these types of problems only sets you back and you will be tested in the same area again.

2) Momentum testing is further testing which begins to put real muscle on your spiritual life. It highlights the unconditional love toward others in which all mature Christians should operate.

Any type of suffering displays the flawed and weak creatures we are, and this should push us closer to God and give us the chance to depend on His grace and divine solutions, not the world and human viewpoint. Suffering should put muscle on your faith, not develop a stronger sense of dependence on self or the world. The first type of suffering is to increase strength and get you focused on your personal love for God, bringing your dedication to Him to a new level. This next phase of suffering will build muscle on top of your new faith, bringing you even closer to

God, but it is truly designed for your journey in this world. Your faith will begin to have an impact on the people, situations, and environments you face every day.

Impersonal, unconditional love is very difficult to achieve even with some doctrinal intake. However, love is part of the Fruit of the Spirit (Gal 5:22-23), and if people continue in the Word of God and operate within the power sphere of the Holy Spirit, they can live in unconditional love on a consistent basis. The tests that reside in this stage are all focused on injustice, unfair treatment, uncomfortable settings, and chaotic environments outside your control. Basically what you can ask yourself is how do you treat people who treat you badly? That is the gauge or measure of where you are in the area of momentum testing and is the whole point of this second phase of suffering. In Mat 5:44 when it speaks of "love your enemies" it is using a term for unconditional love, not a personal love. Then it states to pray for those who persecute you, not an easy task if you have been deeply hurt by someone and the trust is completely gone.

" . . . so that you may be sons of your Father who is in heaven; for He causes His sun to rise on the evil and the good, and sends rain on the righteous and the unrighteous. For if you love those who love you, what reward do you have? Do not even the tax collectors do the same? (Mat 5:45-46)

It goes on in Mat 5:47 to say that if you greet or show kindness to your brother do not the unbeliever (Gentiles) do the same? Now when you begin to pass these tests and gain momentum you will have more capacity for life and a real contentment will settle into your soul, because you are reaching spiritual autonomy. This in turn brings on more happiness within you no matter what the circumstances. This is all a result of the combination of spiritual self esteem, providential preventative suffering, and applying the Word of God. You now have a strong entrenched contentment, which will not be disturbed by the arrogance complex or the attacks of the kingdom of darkness in your life. You see the imperfections, flaws, and old sin nature of other people as a speed bump and not a roadblock in your path. Mistakes, temper tantrums, and lies directed at you will no longer cause you grief or bring you out of fellowship so easily.

Impersonal love that God instills in your soul is the ultimate problem-solving device toward the human race. It is a build-up of virtue within your soul structure and that unconditional love from virtue is directed outward toward those in your periphery. You will have a whole new outlook on relationship issues and mistakes that people make that used to cause you misery. Never forget that if someone or something can get you out of fellowship with God, you become a slave to that person or problem.

Your capacity for love will grow by leaps and bounds when spiritual autonomy becomes a reality in your life. Impersonal love is also the tool needed to solve system testing which most times relates to people in authority in your life. Regardless of the relationship in your life impersonal unconditional love is the application that is needed. Impersonal love is the ability to apply doctrinal principles regarding human relationships and authority issues in your life. Thinking about loving someone unconditionally and applying it are two different things, as is the case with all doctrinal principles. Application is where you truly show your growth.

This cannot be faked or forced, it has to come from true growth within a believer who is filled with the Holy Spirit. As personal love for God reaches a greater height within you, then in turn, more motivation to learn and grow in the plan of God will be the result. This will give you strength to endure suffering with no complaining and without seeking worldly solutions. This stage of growth is assuring you that momentum is gathering in your spiritual life, and that you are able to stand up to the schemes of the devil, the trickery of the cosmic system, and the failures of human beings without losing your contentment and happiness in God. Spiritual momentum pushing you into spiritual autonomy is the insulation needed to ward off frustrations, human weakness, and flaws that come from yourself and especially others around you!

3) The final and highest type of suffering for blessing is evidence testing. Evidence testing is given for the mature believer to glorify God to the maximum in the Angelic Conflict.

This type of testing was what Job and the apostle Paul experienced, as well as, and primarily, our Lord Jesus Christ. In fact the Lord endured more attacks and pressure—as well as physical and mental pain—than any other being in the universe. This type of testing does not happen until a maturity level is reached and God can recognize that you are ready for it. There is no definite set of rules or regulations pertaining to spiritual tests, but the most common areas are your wealth, health, and personal relationships. These are the ones that are day-to-day challenges and tests that come from God and the devil's world.

Evidence testing, especially in the area of relationships, is best highlighted in the book of Job and also with the Lord Jesus Christ (Mat 4, Luk 4) who was tempted in His humanity (not deity). One test concerning relationships was a direct attack upon the fellowship of Jesus with the Holy Spirit in Mat 4:1-4. In light of the tests that our Lord withstood, the question then arises, do you rely on God the Father and the power of the Holy Spirit or on human solutions and worldly viewpoint? Do you trust in the strength of your flesh? Does it hold more problem-solving power than your relationship with God?

The second test that the Lord underwent was His relationship with the Word of God (Mat 4:5-7). Jesus relied upon the Word of Truth that He knew from the Bible, trusting in God the Father's words and solutions. Then in Mat 4:8-10 you can see the test of the relationship of Jesus' humanity to the plan of God, whether Jesus in His humanity would endure and follow through exactly as planned. Human beings have a tendency to step only so far down the path when it comes to faith and trust in any given situation and then they crumble, back away, or begin to devise their own agenda or plan.

Job was a man that went through extraordinary tests that most positive believers at any level will never have to endure. The chances are slim that any believer will be hit so heavily and with such intensity as the way that Job was struck down. There may be two or three believers out there reading this book that will come close, but the tests of Job reveal a vicious attack by Satan himself during a time in early human history. Perhaps Satan felt a strong, unrelenting assault was in order because the timing was right.

Perhaps he thought he saw a chink in the armor of Job's faith, or maybe Satan was getting agitated, slowly realizing that he was in a serious battle and was in way over his head. Either way the attacks on Job's family, health, and property were devastating. In the first chapter of Job we see the loss of prosperity, and then in chapter two the attack upon Job's health and social life begins. Job's personal appearance becomes very grotesque for a period of time due to skin boils that Satan was allowed to inflict upon him. Job's friends began to question and malign and accuse him.

All of this happens within a short period of time, perhaps as little as a few months. Bear in mind that Job lost his children as well! Job did not pass every test right away, and when he failed, he eventually recovered and rebounded back into the plan of God. Basically Job passed the first few parts of the test and failed the third part, but he did recover and ended up with double blessings in the end.

So for the questions surrounding suffering, there are several answers but all are embedded within the plan of God. One reason for chaos and suffering is that the cosmic system is operating on its own level away from a relationship with God, because Satan is the one in charge. Also the kingdom of darkness is entrenched in a battle with God, and the human race is being manipulated and used to resolve the battle by Satan and his troops, which points to another reason for suffering in the world. Because of the defeat of Satan at the Cross, we are in the intensified stage of the Angelic Conflict, and there will be tremendous hostility from the kingdom of darkness directed toward any advancing believer. Finally, there is a law of freedom and free will among all creatures that causes great chaos and suffering due to negative decisions and their consequences. We can also see the grace of God at work in crisis evangelism. God uses personal and historical disaster to reach people with the Gospel and their need for a Savior. Some of the greatest times of evangelism in history come through crisis!

So all of these were accounted for in eternity past and God was able to use these negative situations to fulfill His plan. Along the way He uses these situations as testing grounds and a spiritual gym where the human race trains, so that they can later display their skills and gain spiritual momentum in time and glorify God in the conflict. Suffering is an extension of the Angelic Conflict to see whether the believer will learn from metabolized doctrine and utilize the dynamic grace provision designed in eternity past.

There is another important question that needs to be addressed now that the question of human suffering and chaos has been dealt with: why the unique dispensation that is known as the Church Age? The Church Age, or the Royal Family of God, came into existence as a result of our Lord's strategic victory in the Hypostatic Union. The third royal title given to Jesus Christ is King of Kings and Lord of Lords, given as a result of His victory at the Cross and His resurrection, ascension, and session. This was a royal title or warrant; however, our Lord had no royal family. He is called the first Son of God and His royal family is God the Father and God the Holy Spirit. His second title is Son of David and His royal family is the Davidic dynasty or born-again Jews. So we can now recognize ourselves, Church Age believers, as His royal family under this third title.

God the Father interrupted the Jewish age with its ritual plan and substituted the Church Age with its predesigned plan. In this stage the conflict intensified after the strategic victory of our Lord on the Cross broke the back of Satan. The believer has the comfort of knowing that all the issues of this conflict are going to be resolved before the resurrection of the Church. Therefore the Church Age is the most challenging yet exciting time in human history. Never before in human history or after the Rapture has there been or will there be more divine power available than right now! Everything depends on the individual believer, which is unique as well. As goes the believer, so goes history in this dispensation. You cannot view the Church as an organization but as an organism. We are created individuals, but in the spiritual realm we are united into a body of one, not living for ourselves as separate entities. No believer is called to live as an island! In this dispensation every believer is in union with and is considered the bride of Christ.

"Though Christ appears to currently be absent in form, He is here within us and also the leader or head of the church." (Eph 1:22, Col 2:10) The Church or Body of Christ is the great weapon or power that stands against Satan during this phase of human history. Throughout history, Satan has successfully caused the Church to implode or splinter off into denominationalism, thus removing a layer of power from Christians, who are meant to understand the Body of Christ and the Church Age. This puts human power and good works on display and in the forefront of many churches or denominations. Human organizations cannot replace divine organizations. During the Middle Ages this is what happened, the denomination eventually became the state. All this is designed by Satan to distract believers from the power and plan available for our victory in this time. This time is so unique because the Lord Jesus Christ during the Hypostatic Union operated in the same power available to Church Age believers today!

> ". . . but you will receive power when the Holy Spirit has come upon you; and you shall be My witnesses both in Jerusalem, and in all Judea and Samaria, and even to the remotest part of the earth." (Act 1:8)

Jesus Christ also taught that we have an inner treasure (2Co 4:7) and power given from God not from our own strength. The Lord's work on the Cross terminated His time here on earth for a period and ushered in the current Church age. The victory was truly complete from God's standpoint, and it was now given over to believers to challenge Satan and to have a portion of the victory or glory in this battle. We have the potential to experientially attain the victory in the Angelic Conflict. Our victory occurs when a pivot of mature believers turns the course of history. If enough believers grow to spiritual maturity, there will be prosperity in certain portions of the earth. If Satan is allowed free reign to dominate because the majority reject doctrinal teaching, then two forms of power begin to govern.

1) Angelic power, manifest by a great deal of demon possession among unbelievers and of demon influence among believers.
2) Human power, organized for influence and control.
Therefore, Jesus Christ is represented by the Royal Family of God on earth. Our Lord will have representation on earth until the Second Advent when the devil's kingdom comes to an end. This is why it becomes so important to function as a Royal Ambassador in the plan of God.
Jesus Christ does not come down to planet Earth today to bail people out as He did for past believers in ancient history. After the cross the Church Age kicked into gear, and we were given the invisible assets and power through the Holy Spirit, our union with Christ, to deal with everything on our own. You do not need Christ present in human form or swooping down from a fluffy cloud to rescue you. That is more of an insult than assistance in the Pre-designed Plan of God. Asking and praying for miracles is blasphemous. It is the equivalent of a highly trained infantry soldier like an Army Ranger crying out when a few bullets whizz past his head during a firefight. What would you think if that infantry man never picked up his weapon to respond to the enemy but kept crying out for help and looking to other soldiers to rescue him? What a waste of training, talent, and opportunity to engage in a battle you claim to believe in. Either that or he got all the way through basic training, advanced infantry school, and Ranger training without learning a thing!

Jesus Christ was present many times throughout the Old Testament, including His incarnation which occurred in the dispensation of Israel. But today it is not necessary for our Lord to be here, because the provision for the Royal Family of God is infinitely greater than any grace provision of any other dispensation in history. The really interesting twist here is if just a few or even one believer can utilize the grace provision through metabolized doctrine, the prosecution can use this believer as evidence to prove that Satan's appeal is not valid. This puts us center stage in the Angelic Conflict. All the demon activity, wars, invasions, and violence of the Tribulation is absolutely nothing compared to your challenge in the Church Age. Your daily choices and lifestyle routines have impact right now and into eternity. In the human race it is positive believers who are the war heroes. It is you who demonstrate the important lesson concerning this prehistoric battle. As a winner believer you validate the divine sentence of the fallen angels!

All historical changes for great blessing and Truth exist because believers have fulfilled the plan of God and advanced to spiritual maturity. With the absence of Christ right now, we are to stand in the gap against the kingdom of darkness. By doing so we bless not only ourselves but those around us, and we can even reach out and bless or save a nation. The church was left here to challenge Satan and his schemes. Paul touches on this point somewhat in Eph chapter 3. He states that grace was given so he could preach to the Gentiles (Eph 3:8).

> " . . . and to bring to light what is the dispensation of the mystery (Church Age) which for ages has been hidden in God, who created all things; in order that the multi-faceted wisdom of God might now be made known through the church to the rulers and authorities in the heavenly places." (Eph 3:9-10)

Paul goes on to say that this is the purpose for the human race, that we may be bold in the face of adversity through our faith in Christ. In verse 13 Paul tells all believers not to lose heart at his tribulations or your own for that matter. The tribulations we all face bring glory to God, and it is through God that we are granted the power (Eph 3:16) by way of the inner spirit (Holy Spirit) and Christ who dwells within us! And it is only through doctrine resident in the soul that we may know the depth and height and length of our Lord and His plan (Eph 3:19).

> "Now to Him who is able to do exceedingly abundantly beyond all that we ask or think, according to the power that works within us, to Him be the glory in the church and in Christ Jesus to all generations forever and ever. Amen." (Eph 3:20-21)

Because of the power that God has given to the Church Age, this dispensation is the crossroads of history. Again, this is viewed as the intensified stage of the Angelic Conflict. Satan's power will be challenged by positive believers but will not be broken completely until the Second

Advent of Christ. The fact that the United States is declining today is a reminder that God has a purpose for your life in all this, and a spiritual challenge for you to grow up and engage in the battle. Your time on earth is a drop in a huge bucket compared to eternity. In eternity the negative believer will realize that the opportunity passed him or her by. It is a time of equal opportunity and equal privilege, so what will you do with your allotted time? You can never lose your salvation but you can end up at a much lower rank than God designed you to be in eternity past.

Things you may consider important right now like work, family, and your bank account will mean absolutely nothing at the moment of your death. Regret will be felt momentarily at the judgment seat concerning believers who have failed God's mission for their lives. Then there will be a loss of special blessings in eternity. However, divine happiness and contentment are guaranteed for every believer in the heavenly realm, as all pain, suffering, and confusion is permanently removed. Those unfortunate unbelievers will be separated from God and endure regret and suffering for eternity in the lake of fire.

When we touched upon the sin unto death for believers, we noted that, although they cannot lose their eternal salvation, instead of a victorious life and death on earth, their life ends in a very sad, painful, regretful state. This is where the agony of negative decisions plagues a person facing death. Bitterness and hopelessness set into their soul, and the act of facing death becomes overwhelming, instead of an act that you can face with courage in glorifying God right to the end. Most people never scratch the surface of having a real relationship with God, and they believe that their bank account, personal pleasures, and reputation are far greater on the scales of life than taking time for God.

Suffering for a mature believer becomes a form of pounding another nail in the coffin of Satan, imitating what Jesus accomplished upon that Cross. Two key elements within the battle of the fallen angels against God have to do with Jesus Christ upon the Cross and with the positive believer who operates in the plan of God. Both areas are a devastating and deadly blow to Satan and his army. Christ completed it and drove the final nail into the coffin, but we are invited to join the conflict and reap the victory with our Savior.

The strategic victory belongs to the Lord and the tactical victory can be claimed by those who advance in the plan of God. Suffering always offers the opportunity for growth and a purpose that was laid out in eternity past. However, if these principles are not recognized and then acted upon during the suffering, it becomes fruitless and frustrating to the flesh. This brings nothing but bitterness and confusion to the surface and is one of the main reasons why people get angry with God during times of tribulation. It is a time that will bring you closer to God or drive you further away, all depending on the mental attitude in your soul. This period of time (since the work upon the Cross) is the only time when the Trinity indwells all believers. Race, gender, or intellect do not matter. All believers have this divine power and indwelling. This is the dispensation of invisible heroes as well as of invisible warfare. The choice is yours to become a tactical soldier that can share in a portion of our Lord's tremendous victory. Is it the role of winner or loser that you choose after salvation? There are promises made to the winner, the ones who overcome in time.

> "Furthermore, the winner, even he who keeps My assignments (Pre-Designed Plan of God) until the end (endurance through all testing and tribulations); to him I will give authority over the nations." (Rev 2:26)

> "Furthermore I will give to him the order of the Morning star." (Rev 2:28)

> ". . . (To the winner) they will walk with Me in white, for they are worthy. He who overcomes will thus be clothed in white garments (uniform of glory);. (Rev 3:4-5a)

The Bible speaks of rewards and authority, of rank and privilege, and even of an honors list.

> "He who overcomes (the winner) will thus be clothed in white garments; and I will never blot out his title (becomes knighted at the judgment seat) out of the book of life; In fact I will acknowledge his title in the presence of My Father and before His angels (a formal presentation)." (Rev 3:5)

In Rev 2:17 the winner is said to be given certain escrow blessings, including a Royal title and a white pebble (God's final vote of approval for the winner believer) that no one would have been aware of during this present time because of the status of invisible hero.

> "The winner, I will make him a pillar in the temple of My God. Furthermore, he will never again vanish from history. Also I will emblazon on him the title of My God, and the name of the city of My God [this will be his pass to enter the eternal city, the New Jerusalem, a satellite city suspended above the earth in the atmosphere or in space], the new Jerusalem, which shall descend from heaven from My God; also My new title [King of kings, Lord of lords, bright morning star]." (Rev 3:12)

All winner believers are given great privilege and title above others, for all eternity. Part of the privilege is where and how you will move about in the heavenly realm, being involved in a great leadership role and having access to certain events or places that the average believer may never see! The temple of God contains the eternal record section of heaven. You the winner can enter and move about freely because of your authority and rank given to you above others. This is an eternal membership to a special club with gifts given to a select few.

In Rev 2:7 the winner is said to eat from the tree of life in the paradise of God. These winners enter the gates of beautiful cities and may even hold a position over the cities as a ruler (Luk 19:11-26). When the book of Revelation touches on entering the gates of the city, it speaks of the New Jerusalem (Rev 22:14). Revelation chapters 2 and 3 are full of rewards and blessings for winner believers that are actually beyond our ability to imagine or describe in time. This all comes down to free will, decisions, and lifestyle choices and nothing else. No human works or human trickery or a magic bullet, but a belief in Christ and then perseverance in growing up spiritually. Paul had a wonderful way of summing up so many doctrinal principles that it may be best to hand the last few sentences of this chapter over to him.

> " . . . that He would grant you, according to the riches of His glory, to be strengthened with power through His Spirit in the

inner man, so that Christ may dwell in your hearts through faith; and that you, being rooted and grounded in love, may be able to comprehend with all the saints what is the breadth and length and height and depth, and to know the love of Christ which surpasses knowledge, that you may be filled up to all the fullness of God. (Eph 3:16-19)

CHAPTER 16

Operation Footstool

The term "Operation Footstool" is based upon a principle that is found in many passages of Scripture. It is first mentioned in Psalms, but we need to be clear in our understanding of a "first mentioned" principle or doctrine in the Bible. The First Mention Principle in the Word of God means that the first mention of a subject reveals the truth about that subject as it relates to the rest of Scripture. This refers to the first occurrence of a word or phrase or principle in Scripture. It is the key expression of its subsequent meaning and a guide to the truth connected with it. The first time a subject or principle is stated in Scripture it brings forth a meaning that will carry over throughout the Word of God.

> "The Lord (God the Father) says to my Lord (Jesus Christ): 'Sit at My right hand, until I make Thine enemies (Satan and the fallen angels) a footstool for Thy feet.'" (Psa 110:1)

In this verse of Psa 110 we see the first mention principle of the Messiah's reign and His kingdom when He comes back to earth. Verses 1-7 say that the Lord will rule from the right hand of the Father. This description of the first mention principle holds true for most subjects in the Bible. A good example of this is the first time that we are introduced to Satan in Gen 3:1. Here he is described as subtle and crafty, and throughout the Scriptures when the serpent is mentioned the same characteristics of craftiness and subtlety are always attached to him. This prophecy of Operation Footstool is so important that it is quoted six times in the New Testament, four of the six under a rebuttal concept used to settle a Jewish controversy regarding Christ's identity as the Messiah to Israel and the dispute regarding the Hypostatic Union. When questioned by the Pharisees about the son-ship of Jesus Christ, our Lord quotes this passage from Matthew:

> "Now while the Pharisees were gathered together, Jesus asked them a question: 'What do you think about the Christ (not Himself but what do they think about the Messiah that they expected), whose son is He?' They said to Him, 'The son of David.' He said to them, 'Then how does David in the Spirit call Him 'Lord,' saying, 'The Lord said to my Lord, 'Sit at my right hand, until I put your enemies beneath your feet? If David then calls Him 'Lord,' how is He his son?'" (Mat 22:41-45)

Our Lord Jesus Christ was once again putting the legalistic leaders of His day in their place. The Pharisees were denying the fact that Jesus Christ was the Messiah and a member of the human race at the same time. Mat 22:46 reveals the Pharisees as dumbfounded by the wisdom of Christ, and they would not dare ask Him another question. We can see a similar situation with the Scribes in Mar 12:34 where Jesus had answered the Scribes intelligently and they did not want to ask any more questions.

> "And Jesus began to say, as He taught in the temple, 'How is it that the scribes say that the Christ is the son of David? David himself said in the Holy Spirit, 'The Lord said to my Lord, 'Sit at My right hand, Until I put Your enemies beneath Your feet.' David himself calls Him 'Lord'; so in what sense is He his son?' And the large crowd enjoyed listening to Him." (Mar 12:35-37)

Our Lord Jesus Christ again quotes Psa 110:1 in Luk 20:43 when the Sadducees questioned the resurrection. All three legalistic groups were dealt with through that one scripture. Then Peter (Act 2:24-36) gives the famous message on resurrection on the day of Pentecost also quoting from Psalm 110:1. And again it is quoted in Hebrews 1:13 and Heb 10:13.

Now the occasion for this prophecy is the death, burial, resurrection, ascension, and session of the humanity of Christ in the Hypostatic Union. Therefore this prophecy was fulfilled at the end of the dispensation of the Hypostatic Union. The Deity of Christ is omnipresent (everywhere present). This is why He could say to His disciples, "I am with you always, even to the end of the age (Mat 28:20)." Bear in mind that the humanity of Christ is limited to one location, and only the humanity of Christ could sit down at the right hand, Deity does not sit. The important principle here is that a lower creation, not an angelic one, is seated at the right hand of the Father. This is an important principle pertaining to Operation Footstool and the Angelic Conflict as a whole. The point is that at the right hand of God the Father is a human being, not an angel or a half-godlike being, but a flesh and blood man! This should give the human race great confidence and joy to know that we are allowed that privilege and will indeed be above angelic creatures in eternity.

At the Session, Christ received His third royal title based on the dispensation of the Hypostatic Union and the resulting strategic victory in the historical Angelic Conflict. The term "Session" is a reference to the humanity of Christ seated next to God in the highest place of authority in the universe. Operation Footstool is viewed as the pinnacle of triumph as He comes back a second time to establish His kingdom on earth. Operation Footstool has two phases, one at each end of the Millennium. Phase one is the Second Advent of Christ, following the Tribulation period, which is a time of great demon attacks. The Lord returns and puts His enemies under His feet as He lays hold of planet Earth. This will begin the 1000-year incarceration of the fallen angels (Rev 20:2-14). This triumphant return and its repercussions are also highlighted in Zec 13:2 and Jer 10:11.

As a part of phase one all unbelievers will be swept up and removed along with the fallen angels. The unbelievers who survive the Tribulation are collected into two groups, Jews and Gentiles (Mat 3:11-12) for their judgment, the baptism of fire. This distinction is made because the Tribulation is a part of the dispensation of Israel. Jewish unbelievers are removed from the earth and cast into torments, the compartment of Hades for all unbelievers since the beginning of time. All unbelievers remain in torments until their second resurrection, when "Hades delivers up its dead" as noted in Rev 20:13.

> "Then death and Hades were thrown into the lake of fire. This is the second death, the lake of fire." (Rev 20:14)

Also the Scriptures from Mal 4:1 and Eze 20:33-38 touch on this principle of Jewish unbelievers during the Tribulation period. All other unbelievers (Gentiles) are also thrown down to torments as noted in Mat 25:31-46.

> "And all the nations (these are the Gentiles) will be gathered before Him (Christ); and He will separate them from one another, as the shepherd separates the sheep from the goats; and He will put the sheep on His right, and the goats on His left. Then the King will say to those on His right, 'Come, you who are blessed of My Father, inherit the kingdom prepared for you from the foundation of the world.'" (Mat 25:32-34)

Jesus Christ goes on to tell the believers that they fed Him when He was hungry, gave Him a drink when He was thirsty, and when He was a stranger they invited Him in. Then our Lord looks to the unbelievers on His left and says, "Depart from me, accursed ones, into the eternal fire which has been prepared for the devil and his angels." He tells them the exact opposite of what He had just uttered to believers. They did not feed Him when He was hungry or help Him when He was in need, and He finishes the statement with this profound verse in Mat 25:45, "Truly I say to you, to the extent that you did not do it to one of the least of these, you did not do it to Me."

The separation of unbeliever and believer is also highlighted in Mat 24.

> "Then there shall be two men in the field; one will be taken, one will be left. Two women grinding at the mill; one will be taken, and one will be left. Therefore be on the alert, for you do not know which day your Lord is coming." (Mat 24:40-42)

In verse 44 of the same chapter, it says to be ready because the Lord is coming at an hour when you do not think He will come! The Millennium begins with believers only. Verses 40 through 42 describe unbelievers being scooped up and thrown into torments, and believers staying on earth for the Millennial Reign. At the end of the Millennium the unbelievers will be judged and cast into Gehenna (lake of fire). We can see many parables such as in Mat 13 also pointing out the baptism by fire during Operation Footstool.

> "Again, the kingdom of heaven is like a dragnet cast into the sea, and gathering (fish) of every kind; and when it was filled, they drew it up on the beach; and they sat down, and gathered the good (fish) into containers, but the bad they threw away. So it will be at the end of the ages; the angels shall come forth, and take out the wicked from among the righteous, and cast them into the furnace of fire; there shall be weeping and gnashing of teeth." (Mat 13:47-50)

There is also the parable of the weeds in Mat 13:24-30. This is where Christ said to allow the weeds and wheat to grow side by side until it is time for harvest, then pluck out the weeds to burn. Then the parable of the ten virgins in Mat 25:1-13. The fact is that they all point to the separation of unbelievers from believers during Operation Footstool, a time when our Lord will rule from His headquarters in Jerusalem (Zec 14). This encompasses an entire judicial sentence set in motion in eternity past: phase one will display the judgment of angelic creatures, phase two the judgment of human beings. The fallen angels face the abyss for a thousand years, and the unbelieving human beings of the Tribulation face a thousand-year sentence locked in torments. So this series of events will begin with the forming of the Royal Family in the air (Rapture) to meet the bridegroom (Christ). This is followed by the Tribulation, since God owes Israel seven more years, then the Second Advent and Operation Footstool will begin.

As was noted earlier Operation Footstool contains two parts or phases, one at the beginning of the Millenium (the judgment we have covered) and one at the end, which is noted by many scholars as the Gog and Magog Revolution (Rev 20:7-10). It is the end of the Millennium when

Satan is released, and he immediately starts an international conspiracy! He is joined by unbelievers who never came to believe in Jesus Christ, even though it was perfect environment and perfect blessings were available during the thousand-year reign of Christ.

> "(Satan) will come out to deceive the nations which are in the four corners of the earth, Gog and Magog, to gather them together for war; the number of them is like the sand of the seashore. And they came up on the broad plain of the earth and surrounded the camp of the saints and the beloved city, and fire came down from the heaven and devoured them." (Rev 20:8-9)

This rebellion is stopped and Satan is thrown down for good (Rev 20:10). Then the final judgment of mankind is held (Rev 20:11-15) which fulfills the judgment that was written about in Joh 3:18 and Joh 3:36. Both scriptures clearly state that he who believes in Christ is not judged, but those that did not believe have been judged already!

> "He who believes in the Son has eternal life; but he who does not obey the Son shall not see life, but the wrath of God abides on him." (Joh 3:36)

There are passages of scripture within the Bible describing this period and stating that the enemies of our Lord will be nothing more than a stool upon which to rest His feet. The book of Corinthians points to the relationship of the two phases of Operation Footstool.

> "But each in his own order: Christ the first fruits, after that those who are Christ's at His coming, then comes the end (the Second Advent), when He (Jesus Christ) delivers up the kingdom to the God and Father when He has abolished all rule (Satan) and all authority (dictators and demons) and all power." (1Co 15:23-24)

It is at this point that Jesus Christ supersedes Satan, brushes him off the throne and hands it over to the Father. The Father then gives full ruler-ship to our Lord and Savior as the last dispensation begins and Christ has the prize and victory of the Angelic Conflict.

> "For He must reign (1000 years) until He has put all enemies under His feet." (1 Co 15:25)

At this point Operation Footstool is very apparent to all who can read and comprehend, but studying doctrines of depth and divine knowledge is never an easy task for the common believer. That is why there have been gifts ordained within the Church, like teachers or pastors. A pastor has to understand isagogics (historical setting) within a passage, and he must match scripture with scripture, understanding doctrinal categories (systematic theology). He must also possess knowledge of the grammar and syntactical analysis of the original languages, known as exegesis. So anyone who looks upon this term or explanation of Operational Footstool as something frivolous or made-up could not be further from the truth!

A good pastor-teacher with the gift from God will relate to the ICE principle here, referring to Isagogics, Categories and Exegesis, all related to the in-depth study of the Word of God. If your church leader is not able to teach under this principle, he is not the right teacher for your spiritual growth. Anyone with emotional conviction can interpret a passage to say whatever they feel in the moment, but it may not be how the passage was originally meant to be construed. Therefore, you would gain nothing from it, and the opportunity for the knowledge you need to be victorious in this Angelic Conflict would be lost.

As we move forward in the study of Operation Footstool there is an analogy that would be lost without isagogics. In Colossians there is an analogy between the ancient Roman Triumphal Procession and the subject of Operation Footstool (Col 2:15). We first read in Col 2:13-14 that we were dead in our transgressions, but Jesus Christ brought us back from the dead through His work upon the Cross. All was forgiven at the Cross. The verse goes on to say that a debt was cancelled out, not by anything we did, but by what He did! It was nailed to the Cross and removed from our lives.

> "Having disarmed the rulers (demon leaders) and the authorities, He (Jesus Christ) made a public display of them, having celebrated a triumphal procession over them (Satan

The Angelic Conflict

and the fallen angels) by means of it (the work that He had done through the Cross)." (Col 2:15)

When we study the phrase, 'He made a public display over them,' we need to look at the main verb. The Greek word used here is the aorist active indicative of deigmatizo, meaning to display or exhibit the captives. The aorist tense is what is known as an iterative aorist, which means at a certain point in time He began to make a show of the fallen angels openly. Then we look at the words 'having triumphed' which is the aorist active participle of thriambeuo, referring to leading a triumphal procession. This also is a term used for a victory celebration or a triumphant parade, or even used to describe a special exhibition. You see, the custom after winning a war in the ancient world was that you brought back treasures and prisoners in a victory march. A triumphant parade through your own city, to show off the victory and the spoils of that war, then followed.

The Roman army would do this on a regular basis because of their military might and many victories on the battlefield. The Roman army had three categories of officers and all could be involved in the triumphal procession. Company grade officers were called centurions, field officers were called tribunes, and the general officers were called praetor or imperium. When the imperium was victorious, his army lined up and saluted him with a tremendous shout; "*Ave Imperator!*" So the victorious general was named an imperator, and the highest honor that could be given to an imperator was a triumph (triumphus).

This Triumph always included a parade or procession of some kind at the end of the victory and the return home. The Roman Senate would approve the triumph and a vote of a certain sum of money would be agreed upon to defray some of the expenses. This was treated as a holiday, and all Senate members and city dwellers would come out to see the victory parade. Everyone would find a spot to witness the procession. The streets and window ledges would be overflowing with excited citizens who wanted to partake of the victory celebration. The victorious imperator (general) would assemble his troops just outside the city gates, and a ceremony of honors and medals would begin for the homecoming war heroes. The general would deliver a commanding speech and honor the soldiers who fought bravely, then the decoration or medal ceremony would take place.

The highest honor or medal given was the corona, which is translated crown from the Latin. In the Greek this word for crown is stephanos. The soldiers were also given generous financial shares from the war campaign they had just launched. After all this was complete, the general would mount up onto his chariot, and then the military march would enter the city gates. They would first be met by the magistrates and senators of the city and welcomed in the name of the Senate and people of Rome or SPQR. This procession had a very definitive order and the captives or enemy combatants would be in front, in chains, marching on display for the whole city to see. If a king had been captured he might be sitting in back of the general's chariot and even be forced to hold his own crown up over the victorious general's head.

Our analogy is that this describes what will happen to the fallen angels when Christ comes back to claim the throne! This was a full-on parade and display of all the enemies that were now prisoners, and also of all the treasure and weapons as well as horses, jewels, and any items of value that the victorious soldiers had seized during their battle. All would be on display as it was marched through the city. In fact, Cleopatra said she would never be in a Roman procession because of the humiliation, the jeering and embarrassment of the whole scene. Cleopatra allegedly committed suicide by allowing a cobra to strike her, which was probably preferable as these victory processions could last two or three days if the plunder and captives were massive enough. Not to mention that they usually ended up in a dungeon with the brutal slaughter of many prisoners of war.

The procession would ascend to the Capitoline Hill, the highest of the seven hills of ancient Rome. Now all the while there were musicians playing and vendors selling goods, nothing but a frenzied party atmosphere surrounding the whole event. There were animal and prisoner sacrifices and gifts laid at the altar of Jupiter, to give thanks for the victory. All the prisoners were marched in chains in humiliation throughout the city.

Although it was a tremendous victory celebration, an incredible honor to the new imperator, two timely phrases would be whispered, in the general's ear only, during the entire parade. It is vital even in moments of extreme victory never to allow arrogance into the picture or into our souls! A slave would stand behind the imperator in his chariot, holding a jewel-encrusted crown. As the whole city cheered the triumphant general, the slave would continually whisper these two truths: "Sic Transit Gloria Mundi (the glory of the world passes away)" followed by "Look after yourself; remember that you are only a man."

This was a festive celebration like nothing we experience in a modern-day city, it was glorious as well as brutal. The prisoners were treated like cattle being led to a slaughter with no human rights whatsoever. When it was announced that the enemy leaders had been killed and the oxen had been sacrificed, the imperator took the laurel wreath he had been wearing and placed it at the altar of Jupiter, as the victory was now complete.

A public banquet would take place that could last up to 8 hours. During the banquet the imperator was given a large sum of money (gold) and a mansion called a Triumphalis Domas (the House of Triumph). Most victorious military leaders had statues built in their image and riches given to them and their families for years after the war. This was a great honor and it is no surprise that we see it mentioned at least eight times in the New Testament.

> "But thanks be to God, who always leads us in His triumph in Christ, and manifests through us the sweet aroma of the knowledge of Him in every place." (2Co 2:14)

Now it is at this point, when the Lord Jesus Christ was resurrected three days after the Cross, that He was on the earth for 40 days and then ascended to the right hand of the Father. He then heard the Father say, "Sit at My right hand, until I make Thine enemies a footstool for Thy feet!" The Lord Jesus Christ was the conquering general returning from the battlefield at this point. During His ascension it was quiet on earth because Satan and all the fallen angels had been taken as captives in the triumphal procession! So there was stillness, or a moment of calm in demon activity on earth, while Jesus Christ took His proper seat on the throne. The elect angels were parading the fallen angels in front of our Lord and Savior at this point of angelic history. After this, the fallen angels were allowed to resume the conflict as the court case had shifted dramatically into high gear.

The reality of Operation Footstool was now in plain view for the fallen angels, so the conflict began to intensify. The fallen angels now truly knew what was coming down the road for them after this humiliating procession took place. Satan and his crew know that the Second Advent is the time of final judgment, and that they are on borrowed time so to speak, which is why their anger and aggression reach new heights. The spiritual triumphal procession that will occur at the end of the Millennium will include Royal Family believers who can shout "Ave Imperator!" The Lord Jesus Christ will be recognized as the Lord of Lords and King of Kings, and certainly the top general among all generals! This second victory parade will be much more of a public spectacle, a larger festival than the first, which took place in the heavenly realm. It will take place upon the earth, and there is no doubt who will reign supreme.

> "and in that day His (Jesus Christ's) feet will stand on the mount of olives, which is in front of Jerusalem on the east;" (Zec 14:4)

> "And the seventh angel sounded; and there arose loud voices in heaven, saying, "The kingdom of the world has become the kingdom of our Lord, and of His Christ; and He will reign forever and ever." (Rev 11:15)

Just as we noted that in the Roman Empire the Senate would vote on a sum of money to defray some of the expenses for a declared holiday, with immense processions, so too we will see a procession that is even larger than any other witnessed in human history.

> "Behold, He is coming with the clouds, and every eye will see Him, even those who pierced Him; and all the tribes of the earth will mourn over Him. Even so. Amen." (Rev 1:7)

Just as the victorious general gathered outside the city walls and gave a commanding speech to his troops, we will see our Lord give a speech and decorations as well as honors to winner believers (Rev 3:5). This will be at the Bema Seat Judgment before He comes back for the Second Advent. Winner believers will be eligible to receive the crown of life or the crown of righteousness and rewards and rank for all of eternity, as did the soldiers and military leaders in the ancient world. These crowns are awarded to believers who overcame through faith during the difficult times in their lives. These are the ones who stuck with the plan of God and produced fruitful lives that were examples in the Angelic Conflict. The crown of life for example will be given to those positive believers who matured and moved forward in the plan of God despite the distractions and difficulties of the day-to-day battles of human life. The crown of life is awarded both to believers who lived for our Lord during trials, in Jam 1:12, and to those who died for our Lord as martyrs, in Rev 2:10.

> "Do not fear what you are about to suffer. Behold, the devil is about to cast some of you into prison, that you may be tested, and you will have tribulation ten days. Be faithful until death, and I will give you the crown of life." (Rev 2:10)

There is also a crown of glory given to the teachers and pastors who remained faithful and stuck to the Truth throughout their ministry (1Pe 5:4). The ultimate decoration is the Order of the Morning Star, given to a select few winner believers (Rev 2:26-28) who have reached an ultra-supergrace status and were able to maintain such high standards for lengthy periods in a lifetime.

> "Furthermore I will give to him the order of the morning star."
> (Rev 2:28)

The spiritual analogies are very easy to spot once you have done an in-depth study in this area of Operation Footstool. Winner believers are the soldiers who stepped up during combat. Maybe they were hit on the battlefield or felt some tremendous pressure during certain periods, but they pressed onward and fought the good fight! They will share in the spoils of war and receive honor and authority in eternity. Almost any positive believer will be guaranteed a place of honor, but those who went above and beyond the normal battles receive greater honor and greater authority for their deeds done in the Spirit.

Then when our general mounts up for the ride into the city, He (Jesus Christ) will direct us to follow Him as well.

> "And I saw heaven opened; and behold, a white horse, and He who sat upon it is called Faithful and True; and in righteousness He judges and wages war." (Rev 19:11)

This is the final ride or procession into the city to show everyone the victory that the Lord has won for us.

> "And the armies which are in heaven clothed in fine linen, white and clean, were following Him (Jesus Christ) on white horses." (Rev 19:14)

And the analogy continues as we ride into the city with our general Jesus Christ. Every eye will witness and every tongue will confess (Rev 1:7-8, Phi 2:10-11). This is like the people and politicians of ancient Roman times who were watching when the victory march took place within their city walls. There was a definitive order of the procession and this time it will be very similar. They had the musicians playing, animals and treasures on display, and the enemy combatants chained up in a line. So, we will see this same type of display with our Lord Jesus Christ on His white steed. The Old Testament saints will be raised from the dead and everyone will be in rank and file order like a military march. This is pointed out in 1Co 15:20-24, where it shows the battalion divided into four ranks.

> "But each in his own order: Christ the first fruits, after that those who are Christ's at His coming," (1Co 15:23)

So just like the Roman Triumphal Procession, the public display of the enemies chained and marched out in front of everyone will be a grand victory celebration for believers. Satan is cast down for a thousand years and winner believers will cast down his demons (Col 2:15, Zec 13:2). The imperator had a wreath on his head, a scepter made of gold in his left hand, and a laurel branch in his right. The victorious general wore a purple toga, embroidered with gold, so too we will see our Lord adorned accordingly.

> "And I looked and behold, a white cloud, and sitting on the cloud was one like a son of man, having a golden crown on His head, and a sharp sickle in His hand." (Rev 14:14)

There is an interesting side note here, seen in Joh 19:2. As Pilate and his soldiers put a crown of thorns on Jesus and a purple robe on His body, they did not know the significance of what they were doing at this moment in history, or how it would point to a future event! When we see the banquet that caps off the celebration related to the procession, we can note the spiritual analogy of the Lord Jesus Christ being honored at the marriage supper of the Lamb in Revelation 19:7 and again in Rev 19:17. When we compare the mansion (Triumphalis Domas) or house of triumph given to the imperator at the banquet we can say that the perfect environment (Millennium) ushered in by the Second Advent is certainly a mansion. The analogies are there, given for our benefit and personal growth, so that we will not be blind to future events and what the coming of Christ holds for human history.

The last portion of the chapter needs to highlight the salvation or saving ministry that was certainly offered to angelic creatures after they fell. A perfect God would not have designed a plan that excluded angelic beings that went negative toward Him. It is not in God's nature or essence to exclude any of His creatures from the possibility of eternal life. Contrary to what many may believe, God is not a punishing or brutal dictator that stamps His powerful finality upon creatures who go astray. But He is a judge that is righteous and definitive, and He will have a perfect beginning and ending to His plan. It will not be murky or questionable, rather it will have a final judgment that cannot be revoked, recalled, or repealed.

So when we look upon the subject of angelic salvation we must first recognize that all angels fell at some point, that none remained perfect. Please note that these angels had a free will like all of God's created beings. The statement that one third fell with Satan is not fully correct, although it is a fact that Satan took one third of the angels with him in his fall. All angelic beings have fallen short of God's glory at some point in time. All creatures have fallen short of God's grace, and that means all angels as well as all human beings. And the only perfect one ever is said to be the Lord Jesus Christ. So these statements can resolve the question right here, but for anyone with further questions, we will press on to the truth of the matter.

> "For it was the Father's good pleasure for all the fullness to dwell in Him, and through Him to reconcile all things to Himself, having made peace through the blood of His cross; through Him, I say, whether things on earth or things in heaven." (Col 1:19-20)

Jesus Christ on the cross reconciled ALL things to Himself, whether things on earth (man) or things in heaven (angels).

Do you not think that Satan would have one mighty case if only humans were offered forgiveness? God would easily be labeled unfair by the kingdom of darkness, and it would be hard to argue that point! In the Garden it was a clear case of choice for Adam when he ate of the fruit. The woman allowed herself to be deceived, but the first man was much like Satan in his choice to become independent from God. So now we have something that would not hold up in court. Why offer salvation to one set of beings and not to the other? You can look into the book of Job for more evidence that all angels fell.

> "Can mankind be just before God? Can a man be pure before his Maker? He puts no trust even in His servants; And against His angels He charges error." (Job 4:17-18)

We can see that even the angels who belong to God (His angels) have failed at some time. Do you really believe that a fair and just God would charge error against a few angels and if so why not say that only a few failed? In the Tribulation we can see that no one is worthy of bringing divine judgment or even discerning it, except the perfect One, The Lord Jesus Christ.

> "And I saw a strong angel proclaiming with a loud voice, 'Who is worthy to open the book and to break its seals?' And no one

in heaven or on the earth or under the earth was able to open the book or to look into it. Then I began to weep greatly because no one was found worthy to open the book or to look into it; and one of the elders said to me, 'Stop weeping; behold, the Lion that is from the tribe of Judah, the Root of David, has overcome so as to open the book and its seven seals.'" (Rev 5:2-5)

Look into Psa 89:5-8 and you can see similar references that no one is on the Lord's level of sinless perfection. In Rev 7:10-12, resurrected believers praise the Lord for salvation and angels join in. They join in twice by saying "Amen" in concurrence and agreement. It is a personal understanding of salvation. Jesus Christ is the unique holy one. Man is given the mandates to become holy, thus he is not absolute in experiential holiness. Angels are said to be holy, but it is important to understand that they became holy, meaning that they were not this way at some point.

Two key verses to note on the one and only Holy One are in Rev 15:4 and Rev 16:5. This holiness expresses the uniqueness of Jesus Christ and no other being. This version of it is used eight times in Scripture to describe The Lord Jesus Christ and points to an absolute uniqueness. It is used as His person in Act 2:27 and Act 13:35, and as a guarantor of blessings for the believer in Act 13:34. It is used to point out the Holy High Priest in Heb 7:26, a prerequisite for prayer in 1Timothy 2:8, as a testimony for believers in 1Th 2:10, and the goal for believers in Luk 1:75. It is used to point to the characteristics of the New Man in Eph 4:24; therefore, it is only the Lord who remains experientially holy. The angels are in fact called holy (the same word) in four verses, but it is used as an adjective.

> "For whoever is ashamed of Me and My words, the Son of Man will be ashamed of him when He comes in His glory, and the glory of the Father and of the holy angels." (Luk 9:26)

Rev 14:10 is another verse that uses this term holy for angels in the same sense. We have to realize that even animal sacrifices in Scripture are referred to as holy, but not in the same sense as the Holy One Jesus Christ. While other men, angels, or things are called holy, His unique holiness resides in the fact that it is perpetual, not merely present. Angels were made holy. That points to a status. Like Christians they came from a place of not always being holy.

When we look back into the book of Genesis we can see the act of Satan recognizing the covering of sin, which highlights salvation or a counterfeit act of offering salvation. How did Satan know about salvation this far back before the Cross of Christ? Satan promoted the fig leaf as a counterfeit in Gen 3:7. But we know that God came on the scene with the first animal sacrifice (pointing ahead to the Cross) and covered their sins with the proper clothing. Again we see analogies pertaining to salvation, reconciliation, and the coming of the work upon the Cross. We know that Satan is the leader and chief protagonist in the conflict, so it would be only just and fair for him to be singled out first for the judgment and punishment after he had refused some form of salvation (Joh 16:11). When the condemnation was put forth, it set into motion the compassion and love that God always offers, which would have been reconciliation. God does not vary or change in His essence nor does He ever first seek to punish or destroy when a negative situation erupts. The heartbeat of our God is always to seek and to save those who are lost. We do have one vague reference to angelic salvation, briefly highlighted in the book of Hebrews.

> "For if the word spoken through angels proved unalterable, and every transgression and disobedience received a just recompense, how shall we escape if we neglect so great a salvation? After it was at the first spoken through the Lord, it was confirmed to us by those who heard, God also bearing witness with them, both by signs and wonders and by various miracles and by gifts of the Holy Spirit according to His own will." (Heb 2:2-4)

This hints at a parallel between angelic salvation and human salvation, but it is still not clear as to every detail of angelic salvation, or about those that came back to receive the title of elect angel. As mentioned earlier in this book there are those lessons that will become apparent and extremely clear in eternity. We know that Satan's mission is to attempt to be the leader and to mimic God. Then we witness his attempt at the fig-leaf cover up. It points out that salvation was not a foreign act to him but something he could try to emulate because he had seen it, or been exposed to it, at some point in his long history.

The only sin that is clearly unpardonable is the rejection of the Gospel which is allotted during a certain period of time. The time between the angelic rebellion and when God stopped the clock on the salvation offer had to have expired, but for all we know the opportunity could have lasted a million years. At some point Satan and one-third of the angels refused reconciliation, probably more than once, and God dropped the gavel and made the judgment. At the moment when Adam and Eve accepted salvation in Genesis chapter 3 we can assume that the salvation offer for fallen angels had expired! There is a verse in Hebrews that is used as an objection toward angelic salvation.

> "For assuredly He does not give help to angels, but He gives help to the descendant of Abraham." (Heb 2:16)

The word 'help' is epilambanw and is a word that is not used for salvation, but for giving of help in a time of distress. The distress is noted in the prior verse (Heb 2:15) referring to death! The Jews had a grave fear of death in the first century. Furthermore, if this verse excluded angels from salvation, it would have also excluded most of the Arab race, Asians, Africans, and Indians, as well as most Europeans, because they were not considered descendants from Abraham.

The Ark of the Covenant illustrates that angels benefit from the work of Christ. Two cherubim are located over the mercy seat of the Ark, these angels are the replacements for Lucifer who abandoned his post. These two are partakers of the work of Christ as pre-figured by the Ark as they hover over and look into these things. Another item is the Veil of Exodus in the temple, which was a reminder of the humanity of Christ (Exo 26:31-35). Part of it was made of fine white linen which references experiential righteousness. It was under a blue veil pointing to the fact that for a while Christ was made lower than angels, while the purple of the veil highlights the royalty of Christ. The scarlet represents the upcoming work on the Cross. This veil was to be made with cherubim on them. The curtain speaks of Christ and His work and the angels were embroidered upon them! The linen curtains of Exo 26:1-6 were also the same color scheme, having angels upon them as well. This weaves the angels into the works and salvation offered by Jesus Christ. Just in case you need more evidence it is interesting to note that angels are often pictured wearing white garments.

In Mar 16:5 the angel at the tomb is said to be in white. The verb is a perfect passive participle indicating that he was clothed in these garments by God at some point in the past, and angels continue to wear them in the present. Luke uses the word esthes for these garments as he also does in Acts 1 with the angels at Christ's final ascension into heaven. The white garment is mentioned for the bride of Christ in Rev 19:8 and this comes in a passive voice as with the angels, pointing out that God clothes all of us in perfect righteousness because of salvation. These white garments are the same garments given to born again believers, putting us all in the same boat, sinners saved by grace.

The simple and plain answer to this is that only Christ is forever holy, blameless, and pure, and no one else could have gone to the Cross but the unblemished Lamb. If angels were perfect creatures who never failed, certainly one of them could have done all the work Jesus Christ did here on earth. But the Bible is clear that Christ was the unique one who never sinned, meaning that all other creatures or beings have failed at some point! Heb 2:9-10 indicates that Christ would taste death for all creation. In 1Ti 5:21 angels are called chosen or elect, which would indicate that there was a time when they were not chosen and not elect, but had a choice to make for or against Jesus Christ. This very well could be another scheme from Satan to keep mankind ignorant of the things of God. It would be fitting for him if even believers were unaware that angels are fallen creatures, in need of divine solutions, much like themselves. Our ignorance of Bible doctrine is his strength in the invisible warfare we know as the Angelic Conflict.

GLOSSARY OF TERMS

AMBASSADORSHIP

An ambassador is a high-ranking minister of state or of royalty sent to another state to represent his sovereign or country. By analogy, we are spiritual aristocracy as members of the royal family of God, and Christ is the King who has sent us into a foreign country, the cosmic world.

ANGELIC CONFLICT

The angelic conflict is the result of prehistoric creatures being in opposition to God, which began with the fall of Satan and continued until all angelic creatures had made a decision for or against God. It refers to the two trials of Satan and fallen angels, one in prehistoric times, the other during human history.

ANGELOLOGY

The study of both elect and fallen angels.

ANTI-SEMITISM

Anti-Semitism is a person, a group, an organization, or a nation who is hostile to the Jews.

ASCENSION AND SESSION

The ascension is that doctrine of Christology pertaining to the transfer of our Lord's true humanity from planet earth to the third heaven in a resurrection body. The session is that doctrine of Christology pertaining to the glorification of our Lord's humanity at the right hand of the Father. These definitions presume your understanding of the Hypostatic Union.

APOSTASY

The falling away from the faith or falling away from the system of belief arrived at through the inculcation of Bible doctrine, 2Th 2:3.

BAPTISM OF THE HOLY SPIRIT

The baptism of the Holy Spirit is one of seven salvation ministries by God the Holy Spirit. In the baptism of the Holy Spirit, the omnipotence of the Holy Spirit enters the believer into union with Christ, making the Church—age believer a part of the royal family of God.

BODY OF CHRIST

The phrase "body of Christ" is used to designate all Church-age believers in their relationship with Jesus Christ. Each person of the Trinity is related to the "body of Christ."

CHRISTIAN DEGENERACY

Degeneracy is the decline to false or inferior standards, accompanied by loss of integrity and sinking into the subnormal status of fragmentation and reversionism. Degeneracy is the process of passing from the higher to the lower; to decline progressively.

CLIENT NATION

A client nation is a national entity under the principle of divine institution number four, and is responsible for custodianship of the Word of God, Bible doctrine.

COSMIC ONE

Cosmic one consists of grieving the Spirit. In Cosmic one the believer becomes involved with sin or preoccupation with self-causing the believer to sin, hence exit the predesigned plan of God (PPOG). Once in cosmic one the believer only need rebound (1Jo 1:9), to get back in fellowship with God.

COSMIC TWO

Cosmic two consists of quenching the Spirit. This is man's exit from the predesigned plan of God by way of antagonism toward God and the plan of God. Cosmic two entails more than sin per se in that it moves into evil. Evil is more than sin; it is a system of thought based on disputes, rejection and contradiction to the Word of God. Evil attempts to frustrate the grace policy of God. This "human viewpoint" takes more than mere rebound to re-enter fellowship with God, it requires recovery as well. Recovery being the cleansing of the mind through consistent inculcation of the accurate teaching of the Word of God.

COSMIC SYSTEM

The phrase the cosmic system involves both cosmic one and cosmic two and entails the over-all objective of Satan in using mankind to prove his superiority over God. The cosmic system is the devil's multifaceted policy for achieving his goal by way of human viewpoint projected through the world system.

DEITY OF JESUS CHRIST

Jesus Christ is eternal God. As a member of the Trinity, He always existed. There never was a time when He did not exist. He is coequal and co-eternal with the Father and the Spirit, Col 1:15. In eternity past, Jesus Christ had the same essence as the Father and Spirit. In time, He still had the same functions of deity, but He also became true humanity. Therefore, He is unique.

DEITY OF THE HOLY SPIRIT

Trinity passages reveal the coequality, co-eternity, and co-infinity of God the Holy Spirit with God the Son and God the Father, 2Co 13:14; Act 5:3-4; Mat 28:19; Act 2:38.

DEMON INFLUENCE

Demon influence is demonization of the soul and personality of the believer or unbeliever living in the cosmic system. There are degrees of demon influence. It depends on how long you reside in the cosmic system without the use of rebound. Demon influence is thought transference of demon doctrine to the believer or unbeliever in the cosmic system.

DEMON POSSESSION

Demon possession is defined as demon invasion of the body of the unbeliever only. Generally, this occurs through the phallic cult or some form of religion. In contrast, demon influence is the demon invasion of the soul with satanic thought. Satanic thought is not expressed in terms of evil but in terms of improving this world, doing nice things for your fellow man, and supporting crusades. It is false thinking comprising the policy and principles by which Satan operates.

DISPENSATIONS

A dispensation is a period of time in human history expressed in terms of divine revelation. The inerrancy of the Word of God is the source for looking at history from the divine viewpoint. Therefore, dispensation is a technical theological term used primarily by the apostle Paul in the presentation of the mystery doctrine of this Church Age. Dispensations are divine categories of human history; therefore, both the divine outline and the divine interpretation of human history. There are many interpretations of history, but the only accurate interpretation is dispensational.

Dispensations are the vehicle by which believers living at a specific time in history can orient to God's will, plan, and purpose for their lives. God's plan is not the same for every dispensation. In fact, the plan is quite different in each dispensation. The most difficult and subtle plan to learn by a believer is the predesigned plan of God for the Church-age. Old Testament believers were under the ritual plan of God. Our Lord Jesus Christ was under the incarnation plan of God. A dispensation is defined traditionally as a period of time during which a particular revelation of God's mind and God's will is operative, and during which man is tested as to his obedience to that specific manifestation of God's will, purpose, and plan. The believer's orientation to both time and to human history is vitally necessary for understanding God's plan and God's purpose.

DIVINE DECREE

The decree of God is His eternal (always existed), holy (perfect integrity), wise (the application of omniscience to creation), and sovereign purpose, comprehending simultaneously all things that ever were or will be in their causes, conditions (status), successions (interaction with others that leads to certain decisions), and relations, and determining their certain futurition.

DIVINE DISCIPLINE

Divine discipline is the sum total of punitive action taken by the justice of God in grace to correct, to punish, to encourage, to train, and to motivate the believer's free will toward the predesigned plan of God for the Church-age. Therefore, divine discipline is distinguished from divine judgment, in that discipline is for believers only, but judgment is directed toward all categories of the human race and angels under certain circumstances.

ELECTION

Election is the expression of the sovereign will of God in eternity past before the universe existed and before mankind lived on the earth. Election is the sovereign right of God over His creation. Election is a Biblical term that is applied to the believer only in the Church Age.

ETERNAL SECURITY

At the moment of salvation God imputes His absolute righteousness to every believer and declares him righteous or justified, Rom 3:21-28. If God excluded from eternal salvation anyone who possesses God's own righteousness, He would have to deny Himself and contradict His own pronouncement of justification. Therefore, our salvation is as strong as the essence of God Himself!

EVIDENCE TESTING

Evidence testing is Satan's cross-examination of every witness presented by God in the historical trial of all fallen angels. In human history, man's thoughts, motives, decisions, and actions are entered as evidence, exhibits, precedents, and arguments in Satan's appeal trial. Every believer who attains maturity is an argument or witness for the Prosecution against Satan. Evidence testing is Satan's cross-examination of every witness presented by God.

EVIL

Evil is the policy of Satan as the ruler of this world. Evil is the modus operandi of Satan from the time of his fall throughout the angelic revolution and down to the point when he became the ruler of the world. Evil is Satan's failure to produce a system of good in mankind and society that would bring in a pseudo-millennium. Evil is Satan's system by which he administers the rulership of this world. Satan cannot restrain sin, and therefore he parlays human good into sin and evil.

FAITH-REST DRILL

The faith-rest drill is one of the ten problem solving devices of the predesigned plan of God for the Church. The ten problem solving devices include: the rebound technique, the filling of the Holy Spirit, the faith-rest drill, grace orientation, doctrinal orientation, a personal sense of destiny, personal love for God the Father, impersonal love for all mankind, sharing the perfect happiness of God, and occupation with the person of Jesus Christ. There are three categories related to the faith-rest drill: faith mechanics, faith functions, and faith execution. The faith-rest drill is that problem-solving device used by believers in all dispensations for carrying and using the shield of faith.

FILLING OF THE HOLY SPIRIT

Spirituality or the filling of the Holy Spirit links salvation adjustment to the justice of God to maturity adjustment to the justice of God. To make it from salvation to spiritual maturity requires the filling of the Holy Spirit and the daily intake of Bible doctrine. We already have perfect righteousness judicially imputed at salvation. At the moment of salvation, the Holy Spirit indwells the body of the believer. Because the body is the headquarters of the old sin nature, the Holy Spirit sets up His headquarters in the body for counteraction. The battlefield is the soul. This counteraction is spearheaded by the filling of the Holy Spirit.

The Fruit of the Spirit is that which God the Holy Spirit produces in the life of the believer. GAL 5:22-23, "But the fruit of the Spirit is love, joy, peace, patience, kindness, goodness, faithfulness, gentleness, self-control; against such things there is no law."

Grace orientation is being oriented to the grace policy of God through the inculcation of Bible doctrine under genuine humility and the teaching ministry of God the Holy Spirit. The grace-orientated believer does not judge others and always offers other believers privacy while minding one's own business! Grace orientation offers to others the very grace that God offers to you!

GREAT WHITE THRONE JUDGMENT

This is the final judgment for unbelievers only. It is here that all their good and evil will be evaluated and receive just condemnation. Condemnation since they rejected the person of the Lord Jesus Christ as their personal savior and judgment because all the "good" deeds they performed were conducted in human power rather than in the power of the Holy Spirit, Rev 20:12-15.

HADES OR SHEOL

The Hebrew word SHEOL originally meant in post-Biblical Hebrew the deep parts of the sea. But both Sheol and the Greek word Hades are used to refer to anything that is subterranean and large. Therefore, they are used for the vast subterranean place of the departed dead of the human race and the abode of certain fallen angels. Both Sheol and Hades are mistranslated "hell" which adds to the confusion. HADES is used from classical times and before for the underworld and the realm of the dead. Sheol is sometimes used for the grave, as in Gen 37:35, 42:38; 1Sa 2:6, and other passages.

HEART

The Biblical nouns for heart always refer to the right lobe of the soul, with the exception of one passage in the Bible. The Hebrew LEBH and the Greek KARDIA are both translated "heart."

HISTORICAL TRENDS

Even though history is the record of man's thoughts, decisions, actions and motivations, it is Jesus Christ who controls history. This is the first dispensation in which Jesus Christ controls history from His Hypostatic Union. There are two sources of judgment in history: the sovereign decisions of the Lord Jesus Christ, and the erroneous decisions of mankind.

HUMAN SPIRIT

The human spirit is the immaterial part of man designed by God to convert, to store, and to utilize spiritual phenomena. The human spirit receives spiritual information that the Holy Spirit converts into gnosis (knowledge).

HYPOSTATIC UNION

In the person of the incarnate Christ are two natures, inseparably united without mixture or loss of separate identity, without loss or transfer of properties or attributes, the union being personal and eternal. Since the incarnation, Jesus Christ is true humanity and undiminished deity in one unique person forever.

Exegesis: The Bible should be studied in the original languages (Hebrew, Aramaic, and Koine Greek), with full context of the selected verse or verses, paying strict attention to grammar, syntax, and the etymology of the words form the original languages!

Idolatry

Anyone or anything which takes a higher position in one's life above one's personal love for God manifested by the intake of His Word. Idolatry points to an inordinate attachment or an extreme devotion to something or someone standing in priority over that of the believer's personal love for God! Exo 20:3-5.

Impersonal love

A virtue love which emphasis the character of the subject (you) rather than the object being loved. Impersonal love emphasizes something in you rather than emphasizing something in the object of your love. A great example of impersonal love comes from God the Father in that when we were all yet sinners He loved us through the giving of His only begotten Son.

IMPECCABILITY OF CHRIST

Impeccability is that doctrine of Christology that recognizes the fact that during the entire course of the dispensation of the hypostatic union and forever, our Lord Jesus Christ did not sin though He was tempted in His humanity and the temptations were real.

IMPUTATION

Imputation is the function of the justice of God directed toward mankind and related to the plan of God for mankind. Imputation functions as an act of condemnation or blessing from the Integrity of God to mankind. Therefore imputation may be defined as the action of the justice of God whereby either condemnation or blessing is assigned, ascribed, attributed, superimposed or super induced to another being; therefore to impute over and above that which already exists. The plan of God advances with each imputation. Every imputation is an advance on a previous imputation.

INVISIBLE ASSETS

Are those divine assets provided by God the Father in eternity past for the execution of the PPOG in the believers life. It is our invisible assets which we need to utilize to make our calling and election sure!

INVISIBLE HERO

The purpose of the great power experiment of the Church Age is to manufacture invisible heroes. The invisible hero is the product of Bible doctrine. The invisible hero advances to spiritual maturity. He executes the predesigned plan of God. He spends enough time inside the plan of God and under the ministry of whoever is his right pastor to learn the principles of the mystery doctrine of the Church Age.

JUDGMENT SEAT OF CHRIST

The Judgment Seat of Christ, the evaluation of all Church Age believers. "Judgment" can mean two things: condemnation and evaluation. In this context, it refers to evaluation. The Judgment Seat of Christ is a technical, theological term used to designate the evaluation of the royal family of God at the end of the Church Age after the rapture or resurrection of the Church. It is the evaluation of what use we made of logistical grace provision, the problem solving devices, and divine power. The evaluation is determined on the basis of the execution of the predesigned plan of God or the failure to do so. The purpose of the evaluation is to determine gain or loss of escrow blessings (reward) for eternity. Gain comes from the exploitation, positive volition, and advance in the predesigned plan of God. Loss comes from cosmic living, from failure to execute the Christian way of life as God's game plan for the Church Age. It also means your escrow blessings remain on deposit forever as a memorial to lost opportunity.

JUSTIFICATION

Justification means an act of vindication. This is a judicial act of vindication, because we are born under condemnation, being spiritually dead. Therefore, justification is an official judicial act which occurs every time anyone believes in Christ. The justice of God acts on our behalf pronouncing us justified, which means, having a relationship with God forever, having the perfect righteousness of God imputed to us. Justification means that God recognizes that He has given us His perfect righteousness. Therefore, this is technically called forensic justification. Justification is the judicial act by God, whereby He recognizes we have His perfect righteousness.

JURISPRUDENCE

Jurisprudence refers to the body or system or laws, or the science of law. A court is defined as a place where justice is administered; a place where the function of jurisprudence is designed to determine innocence or guilt. Under the concept of freedom, a person should be considered innocent until proven guilty.

KENOSIS

During the incarnation, our Lord voluntarily restricted the independent use of His divine attributes, which includes His omnipotence. He did this in compliance with the Father's plan for the strategic victory of the angelic conflict. For the plan for the incarnation not only called for the judgment of our sins, the provision of eternal salvation for all members of the human race, but simultaneously for the strategic victory of the angelic conflict. Therefore, the Lord Jesus Christ voluntarily took on Himself true humanity in order to redeem mankind from sin, in order to propitiate God the Father, and to reconcile mankind to God.

LAKE OF FIRE

The lake of fire is the final destination for both fallen angels and unbelieving mankind. It is both literal and eternal. It was prepared originally for Satan and his angels. Matt 25:41. Unbelievers also go there, and there is no way out, Joh 3:18, 36; Heb 9:27.

LAST JUDGMENT

The Last Judgment is the alternative to salvation. In effect, it is facing God's judgment in eternity because you would not face God's judgment in time. The Last Judgment is the expression of the integrity of God toward those who reject Christ as Savior. It is the culminating judgment of human history in which every unbeliever of the human race is judged and sentenced to the lake of fire. They will stand before Jesus Christ who is the Supreme Court judge of heaven, Joh 5:22.

This is also called the second death or the Great White Throne Judgment, Rev 20:12.

LEGALISM

Man's futile attempt to gain salvation or to continue in God's plan by way of some system of do's and don'ts i.e., human good for the purpose of gaining God's approbation!

LIFE BEYOND GNOSIS

Gnosis being doctrinal information learned but not believed or metabolized. Once the doctrinal information is believed or metabolized it is converted into epignosis in the right lobe of the brain thereby becoming wisdom. And, it is by such wisdom that the "life beyond gnosis" is executed! Hence this life is put into operation by the metabolization of Bible doctrine.

LOGISTICAL GRACE

Logistical grace is defined as divine planning, divine support, divine provision, and divine blessing for the execution of predesigned plan of God by the royal family for the fulfillment of God's will, purpose, and plan for your life.

MEDIATORSHIP

A mediator removes disagreement and estrangement between two parties. Both parties are antagonistic to each other and the mediator brings them to a common goal or unity. The mediator must be agreed to by both parties, for he interposes between two parties as the equal of each. By so doing, reconciliation is established and a contract is made. To accomplish this, God the Father must be propitiated and man must be reconciled to God. Therefore the mediator must redeem man to accomplish this. The Hypostatic Union qualifies Jesus Christ as the mediator between God and man. The mechanics are found in 1 Tim 2:5-6, "For you see, there is one God in essence, one mediator between God and man."

MENTAL ATTITUDE

Mental attitude is the function of human thought. The life of every believer is determined experientially by two principles: what he thinks and what he decides. What you really are as a person is what you really think, not what you appear to be on the surface, not the way you are dressed or groomed, but what goes on inside the invisible you, which is your soul. You are not always what you appear to be on the surface. Some people can hide their thoughts and some cannot. People can hide their thoughts and become adept at the practice of hypocrisy.

MENTORSHIP OF HOLY SPIRIT

This is the doctrine of God the Holy Spirit as the mentor or paraclete-helper of all believers.

MERCY

Mercy is rooted in God and experienced in relation to God, from whom it may be acquired as a Christian virtue and exercised in relation to fellow human beings. These are virtues of lovingkindness, graciousness, and compassion.

METABOLIZED DOCTRINE

This consists of taking the accurate doctrine already perceived in the left lobe and believing it. It is in believing said truth that it is metabolized and brought over to the right lobe as epignosis doctrine ready for application!

METABOLISM, SPIRITUAL

Metabolism is defined as the sum total process in the building up of protoplasm and its destruction incidental to life. In other words, it is the chemical changes in the living cells by which energy is provided for vital processes and activities. New material is assimilated to repair waste material in living cells.

MILLENNIUM

The thousand-year reign of Christ on earth from His second advent to the end of human history, prophesied throughout the Old Testament and in Rev 20.

MOMENTUM TESTING

Momentum testing exercises the believer's spiritual autonomy through people testing, thought testing, system testing and disaster testing.

MORNING STAR

One of the names of the Lord Jesus Christ, Rev 22:16.

MOSAIC LAW

The laws God gave to Moses which are made up of 3 Codices:

1) Codex I—Freedom Code; the Decalogue or Ten Commandments.
2) Codex II—Spiritual Code; which includes the complete shadow presentation of Christ and His saving work.
3) Codex III—Establishment Code; civil statues of Israel.

Codices I and III protected human life, freedom, privacy, and property. Codex II charged individual believers and communicators of God's Word with accurately presenting the Gospel and teaching of Bible doctrine. within the nation.

MYSTERY DOCTRINE

The word "mystery" refers to the doctrine for the great power experiment of the Church Age, called the mystery because it was never revealed in Old Testament times.

NECROMANCY

Necromancy is a system of divination or a device for providing information, generally, future information. Necromancy is that system of divination that allegedly contacts the dead for information. The word is formed by combining the two Greek words, NEKROS meaning dead, and MANTEIA meaning divination, to mean divination by contacting the dead, or seeking information from the spirits of dead persons.

NEGATIVE VOLITION

Negative volition is refusal of Bible doctrine. It is divided into two categories. Primary negative volition is refusal to assemble for Bible teaching, the rejection of your right pastor and his authority. Secondary negative volition is refusal to transfer doctrine from the left lobe to the right lobe. Basically, this is rejection of the message.

NEW SPECIES (NEW CREATION)

The Church came from the perpetuation of the great power experiment of the Hypostatic Union into the Church Age, demanding a new spiritual species for the utilization of all divine power. The new spiritual species originates from regeneration and the mechanics of the baptism of the Holy Spirit.

NEW COVENANT TO THE CHURCH

This New Covenant to the Church is a spiritual legacy to the royal family of God and authorizes the royal priesthood. The New Covenant applies only to those who are born again. Hence, the New Covenant is God's grace disposition to the royal family in time and eternity.

OCCUPATION WITH CHRIST

Occupation with Christ is one of three problem-solving devices related to virtue-love. Occupation with Christ is the maximum function of post-salvation epistemological rehabilitation; i.e., learning doctrine on a daily basis so that you advance to spiritual adulthood. This is the only way to execute God's plan, God's purpose, and God's will for your life. Occupation with Christ is defined as personal love for God the Son caused by post-salvation epistemological rehabilitation, which manifests the fact that the mystery doctrine of the Church Age has been and continues to be the #1 priority in your life.

THE OLD SIN NATURE

Biblical documentation of the sin nature is found in Rom 5:12. "Therefore, just as through one man [Adam], sin [the sin nature] entered into the world, and [spiritual] death through [the] sin [nature], so [spiritual] death spread to the entire human race because all sinned [when Adam sinned]." The old sin nature is Adam's trend after the Fall in action. Immediately after Adam sinned, two things occurred simultaneously. He had a new trend historically. He had spiritual death.

OMNIPOTENCE OF GOD

The Latin term omnipotence is taken from the Greek word PANTOKRATOR, and means all-powerful or almighty. It refers specifically to the power or ability attribute of God. It has the connotation of "ruler of all things;" therefore, the eternal supreme power. Omnipotence is the theological term to describe the unlimited, infinite and eternal power of the three persons of the Trinity.

OMNIPRESENCE OF GOD

Literally means "everywhere present" and describes God's attribute of eternal and simultaneous presence in every place. God is not subject to the limitations of space.

OMNISCIENCE OF GOD

Omniscience means "all-knowing" hence this describes God's attribute of complete knowledge of all things, including His foreknowledge.

OPERATION FOOTSTOOL

The termination of the strategic victory of the angelic conflict by which the Lord Jesus Christ returns to earth to establish His kingdom and to remove Satan and all fallen angels. It constitutes the point at which Satan loses the rulership of the world to TLJC, Psa 110:1; Eph 1:22; Heb 1:13; 10:13.

PERSONAL SENSE OF DESTINY

God's meaning, purpose, and definition for the believer's life which becomes stronger as he progresses through the three stages of spiritual adulthood.

PIVOT

The pivot is defined as the accumulation of mature believers living in a client nation or under civil government in a specific geographical location. While a pivot is composed primarily of mature believers, it may also include those positive believers whose momentum has carried them into spiritual adulthood.
Technically, the pivot may include all believers who have fulfilled the principle of virtue first as their first priority in the plan of God. Believers

in the pivot stand out in contrast to believers living in the cosmic system, whose arrogance from motivational arrogance results in self-righteous, crusader arrogance.

PLEROO

To fill up a deficiency. At salvation we are deficient of doctrine. To fully possess. The believer must be fully possessed by the Holy Spirit and Bible doctrine before he can be fully possessed by the blessings of maturity. To fully influence. The believer is fully influenced by Bible doctrine so that he can have capacity for blessing. To fill with a certain quality. Doctrine is the highest quality with which the believer can be filled.

PLEROMA

Complete in itself. Complete in quota. Complete in quality. Complete in duration.

POSITIONAL TRUTH

Positional truth is equivalent to positional sanctification. It is composed of retroactive positional truth and current positional truth. Positional truth is our relationship with Christ in the Church Age. It refers to the Church Age believer in union with Christ. It is the key to understanding the Church Age and the royal family. It is the basis for distinguishing between Christianity and religion. It is one of God's reasons for interrupting the Age of Israel.

It can be defined as God the Holy Spirit at salvation entering us into union with Christ.

PORTFOLIO OF INVISIBLE ASSETS

The portfolio of invisible assets connotes the grace work of God the Father on your behalf in eternity past. God the Father found the way for His justice to provide perfect fantastic blessing to His righteousness in His without any compromise of His essence. In your portfolio of invisible assets God provided everything necessary for the function in life, dying, eternity, growing in grace, and the execution and fulfillment of the predesigned plan of God. The portfolio of invisible assets provides everything necessary for you to have a fantastic life through receiving your escrow blessings which glorify God. If you do not have a fantastic life, it's your own fault, never God's. All you need is positive volition, and God will direct you to the place where you can get the information.

POSITIONAL TRUTH

The Church age believer in Christ is positionally superior to all angels, including the chief fallen angel, Satan, Heb 1:4,13-14; 2:9-11. It is in our position in Christ that we are to view our selves since that is how God sees us! We are not to dwell on our condition!

PPOG

Pre-designed Plan of God, see "predestination".

PREDESTINATION

Predestination is one of the two computer assets in your portfolio of invisible assets; the other is election. Predestination is the provision of the sovereignty of God for you in eternity past to execute God's plan, purpose, and will for your life. Predestination is the work of God the Father in eternity past on behalf of every Church Age believer to execute God's plan, purpose, and will for his life. Therefore, predestination is the grace provision of God the Father for the royal family. Predestination is the provision of the sovereignty of God for the execution of the predesigned plan of God. Predestination includes equal privilege and equal opportunity for the fulfillment of God's plan and purpose for your life in the Church Age.

PREVENTATIVE SUFFERING

Preventative suffering has two categories: punitive preventative suffering and providential preventative suffering. Preventative suffering is defined as short-termed suffering from the sovereignty of God for the benefit of the believer.

PROPITIATION

Propitiation is the Godward side of the work of Christ in salvation. God the Father is satisfied with the sacrificial ministry of our Lord on the cross. Propitiation is the work of Christ on the cross which deals with the integrity of God. Propitiation means what our Lord satisfied the Father. Hence, in propitiation the justice of God judges our sins and the integrity of God is satisfied with that judgment. Propitiation frees the justice of God to immediately give anyone who believes in Christ one-half of divine integrity, the righteousness of God. This is the down payment on our salvation.

PRIVACY

Privacy is a state of being apart from the observation and company of others. It IS the innate right of the human race to seclusion. It is that principle of freedom whereby an individual of the human race has the right to retire from the company of others, remaining in seclusion from the knowledge or observation of others. Privacy, property, and life are the basic concepts of happiness and freedom.

PROBLEM SOLVING DEVICES

The problem solving devices include the rebound technique, the filling of the Spirit, the faith-rest drill, grace orientation, doctrinal orientation, a personal sense of destiny, personal love for God the Father, impersonal love for all mankind, +H or sharing the happiness of God, and occupation with Christ as the priority solution to life.

PREDESIGNED PLAN OF GOD

God has a plan for your life. The name of that plan is the predesigned plan of God. The policy of that plan is grace. The precedence for the grace policy of God comes from the dispensation of the Hypostatic Union. Protocol is a rigid, long-established code and procedure, prescribing complete deference to superior rank and authority, followed by strict adherence to due order and precedence, coupled with precisely correct procedure.

RAPTURE

While the Rapture is defined as the act of being transported, it is also defined as the state of being rapt or carried out of oneself. However, these definitions don't apply here. "Rapture" is used here in a technical theological sense for the resurrection of the royal family of God.

REBOUND

Rebound is the grace function to the believer which accomplishes the following results.

   a. Restoration to fellowship.
   b. Recovery of the filling of the Holy Spirit.
   c. Reentry into the predesigned plan of God.
   d. Recovery from cosmic influence, i.e., grieving the Holy Spirit in cosmic one, and quenching the Holy Spirit in cosmic two.

RECONCILIATION

Reconciliation is stated as a doctrine in 2 Cor 5:18; Eph 2:16; Col 1:20-21. EIRENE is the Greek word which technically refers to the doctrine of reconciliation. Peace" and "reconciliation" are synonymous terms in such passages as Eph 2:14, 15, 17, 4:3, and 6:15. Part of the salvation work of Jesus Christ on the cross is reconciliation, Eph 2:16, 4:3; Col 1:20. All believers are reconciled to God the moment they believe in Christ, but the work of reconciliation actually took place on the cross.

RECOVERY

After involvement in sin and evil the believer rebounds (1Jn 1:9) and then recovers the spiritual life by way of consistent perception and metabolization of accurate Bible doctrine!

REDEMPTION

Redemption emphasizes the fact that we are sinners, not only by choice or volition, but long before that we were sinners at the point of birth. For we had to be condemned before we could be saved. Redemption is viewed from the standpoint of a ransom paid on the cross for our salvation. Redemption views mankind as born into the slave market of sin through the imputation of Adam's original sin at birth. Redemption is the saving work of Christ on the cross by which He purchases our freedom or salvation. The coin of the realm for this purchase is called the "blood of Christ," Eph 1:7; Col 1:14.

REGENERATION

Regeneration is a theological term. It means a second birth or being born again, as Jesus said in Jn 3:3, "Jesus answered and said to him, `Truly, truly, I say to you, unless a person is born again, he cannot see the kingdom of God.'" Jn 3:7, "Do not marvel that I said to you, `You must be born again.'"

REPENTANCE

The Greek transitive verb METANOEO means to change one's thinking, or to change the mind. The cognate noun METANOIA, Rom 2:4, means a change of mind, a conversion, a turning away. Doctrinal viewpoint changes every bit of human viewpoint you've learned. All of us repented at the moment of salvation. Repentance connotes a decision based on mentality, not emotion. It is rational.

RESURRECTION

Resurrection means a person returns from the dead in a body of incorruption and never dies again. Therefore resurrection is rising again from the dead in a human body, and never again being subject to death.

REVERSIONISM

Reversionism is an act of reversing or turning in the opposite way, or a state of being so turned. As believers we were designed to execute the predesigned plan of God. But in reversionism we turn the other way and cannot be distinguished from our pre-salvation status. We are believers thinking human viewpoint. Reversionism is the act of reverting to a former state, habit, belief, or practice of post-salvation sinning. Reversionism is a reversal of your priorities, your attitudes, your affections, the object of your personal love accompanied by the destruction of your impersonal love, and the change of your modus operandi and personality.

ROYAL FAMILY OF GOD

A royal family is the family of a king, here our Lord. Jesus Christ is divine royalty as God. He is a sovereign king as part of the Trinity, possessing all the attributes of divine essence. The royal family of God is defined as every Church Age believer, regardless of his antecedence, background, race, classification, etc. All distinctions are erased at the point of salvation and reconciliation.

ROYAL FAMILY HONOR CODE

The royal family honor code is a system of spiritual integrity mandated by God and revealed by the mystery doctrine of the Church Age. The royal family honor code relates to personal integrity in relationship to other persons. In that sense, the honor code is a supplement to impersonal love for all believers and other pertinent problem solving devices of the predesigned plan of God.

ROYAL PRIESTHOOD

All believers in the Church age are royal priests and represent themselves before God.

SABBATH

The seventh day of the week (Saturday) in which God ceased from His work of creation and declared the day blessed and holy, Gen 2:1-3. Adhered to in Mosaic Law.

SALVATION

The saving of mankind from the power and effects of sin by way of the finished work of Jesus Christ on the Cross.

SANCTIFICATION

Sanctification is a technical theological term for the status quo of the royal family of God in three phases of the predesigned plan of God. The term means to be set apart to God for a special purpose. We, the royal family of God, are set apart to God in three ways from salvation to the eternal state.

SCAR TISSUE OF THE SOUL

Scar tissue of the soul, also known as hardness of the heart, is the result of prolonged residence and function inside the cosmic system.

SECOND ADVENT

There are two advents of Jesus Christ depicted in the Word of God. The First Advent begins with the virgin birth and concludes with the resurrection, ascension and session. During the First Advent, Jesus Christ in Hypostatic Union accomplishes the strategic victory of the angelic conflict and the salvation of the human race. This strategic victory gives Him battlefield royalty. He must have a royal family to go with this royalty. Therefore, there is the need for the Church. The Second Advent is designed to reveal Him as both battlefield royalty and Jewish royalty. He returns to earth in resurrection body and Hypostatic Union.

SEALING MINISTRY OF THE HOLY SPIRIT

Sealing is the Holy Spirit's signature guarantee of three things.

1. The guarantee of eternal salvation, Eph 4:30.
2. The guarantee of eternal security, Eph 4:30.
3. The guarantee of our portfolio of invisible assets, Eph 1:13; 2 Cor 1:21-22.

SELECTION

Selection is a technical term related to the divine imputation of human life at the point of physical birth. God is the inventor of human life, just as He is the creator. At the moment of physical birth, God imputes human life to the format soul, at which point the individual becomes alive. That is selection.

SHEKINAH GLORY

Jesus Christ, the Shekinah Glory of Israel, lived in the Holy of holies, Ex 25:21-22; Lev 26:11-12; Ps 91:1; Heb 9:5. His presence was manifest by a cloud above the tabernacle by day and a pillar of fire by night, so that the Jews could always tell when Jesus Christ was present in the tabernacle.

SIN UNTO DEATH

The sin unto death is maximum punishment from God. It is fair, painful and terminates in physical death.

SLANDER

The spreading of the public lie, or any form of verbal vilification of the doctrinal communicator or doctrinal believer for the purpose of advancing an evil cause.

SLAVE MENTALITY

Is that mentality which is opposite of that of God's. The slave mentality is interested in security regardless of where it comes from. This type of thinking does not accept the responsibility which comes by way of true spirituality before God. Hence the believer involved in the slave mentality is a prime target for satanic deception!

SPIRITUAL CHAMPION

Is the spiritual mature believer who advances through evidence testing and glorifies God thereby becoming a champion in the spiritual realm!

SPIRITUAL SELF-ESTEEM

Spiritual self-esteem is the foundation for the stability of the Christian life. Therefore, spiritual self-esteem is the believer's dependence on God's grace provision for stabilizing self and integrating self into the predesigned plan of God.

SPIRITUAL AUTONOMY

Spiritual autonomy is a continuation of contentment or +H (sharing the happiness of God) as a major problem solving device.

SPIRITUAL GIFTS

The Greek noun CHARISMA for spiritual gifts is based on the word CHARIS, or grace. All spiritual gifts are a matter of grace! No gift is given based on God's foreknown merit of the believer. CHARISMA is primarily a Pauline expression, though it occurs once in 1 Pet 4:10. Spiritual gifts are sovereignly given by the Holy Spirit to each believer at the point of salvation. Therefore, a spiritual gift is never earned, deserved, or developed through any form of emotional experience.

SPIRITUAL MATURITY

The mature believer is defined as a member of the royal family of God who executes the predesigned plan of God of the Church Age.

SPIRITUAL IQ

Has nothing what at all to do with one's human IQ. At the moment of salvation each believer was given equal privilege and equal opportunity to execute the spiritual life by way of the power of the Holy Spirit. It is the power of the H.S. as our teacher which offers us our spiritual IQ!

SPIRITUAL WARFARE

Our warfare in the Christian life is neither physical nor fleshly; it is invisible and spiritual! We are to use our God-given assets (B.D., filling of the Spirit, etc) to battle the forces and deceit of the great Deceiver, Lucifer. B.D. resident in the believer's soul is the only weapon capable of withstanding the incessant barrage of attacks from our great adversary the devil!

SOUL STRUCTURE

See Edification Complex

SOVEREIGNTY OF GOD

The sovereignty of God is His eternal, infinite, and perfect divine volition. The sovereignty of God is His eternal and infinite will expressed in the divine decrees, manifest in the comprehensive divine interpretation of history called dispensations, and the unique plan regarding the Church Age.

SUBSTITUTIONARY SPIRITUAL DEATH OF JESUS CHRIST

Substitutionary spiritual death, which is separation from God in a state of perfection and impeccability. This applies to Jesus Christ.

SUPERGRACE

Supergrace is the highest adult stage of the spiritual life in the royal family of God. Supergrace is maximum glorification of Jesus Christ. Supergrace is the status of spiritual maturity while ultra-supergrace is maximum growth and blessing attended by maximum suffering, which only intensifies the blessing. Supergrace is where the normal function of the royal priesthood and the production of divine good begin.

SUPREME COURT OF HEAVEN

The appeal trial of Satan and his fallen angels which is taken place in heaven in which we are witnesses for the Prosecution, God the Father!

SURPASSING GRACE

Eph 2:7, "that in the approaching ages, He might demonstrate His surpassing grace riches in generosity toward us in Christ Jesus." Surpassing grace is the optimum in spiritual achievement. It is the maximum place of blessing and reward, and the ultimate in glorifying Jesus Christ. Surpassing connotes something beyond supergrace and beyond time.

THEOPHANY

A theophany is a manifestation of the person and work of Jesus Christ in His preincarnate state. This is a theological category for the appearances of Jesus Christ before the First Advent.

TOTAL DEPRAVITY

There is nothing in fallen man which God can find pleasure in or accept, hence our flesh is totally depraved in God's sight!

TONGUES

The gift of tongues was a temporary spiritual gift; so temporary that it was the first one to be discontinued in August of 70 A.D. when Judah no longer existed as a client nation to God. Tongues was used at the beginning of the Church Age to warn Israel of the approaching fifth cycle of discipline and the end of Jewish client nations until the Second Advent of Christ.

TREE OF LIFE

Is associated with perfect life and environment in the Garden, as well as the perpetuation of right relationship with God in the Garden, Gen 2:9;3:22. The tree of life is not seen again by man until the eternal state, Rev 2:7; 22:2,14. The tree of life is related to doctrine, Pro 3:18. Positive volition is related to the tree of life in Pro 13:12. The tree of life will be located forever in the New Jerusalem, Rev 22:2.

TRINITY

Is the title given to the Godhead which consists of three members each holding a specific function. God the Father as the author of the plan, God the Son and the executor of the plan and God the Holy Spirit as the revealer of the divine plan.

TRIPLE COMPOUND DISCIPLINE

Consists of first of all divine discipline for the sin committed, secondly a double portion of discipline for judging another believer and thirdly the discipline is then compounded to the third degree when the believer also receives the discipline for the other believer's sin that he judged. Hence this nosey believer receives triple the amount of discipline!

TRIUMPHAL PROCESSION

The third heaven was where the triumphal procession of our Lord terminated. Our Lord's triumph proceeded through billions and billions of light years of space in the second heaven or stellar universe. The triumphal procession terminated with the Father's command to "sit down." Only the true humanity of Christ actually sat down.

TYPOLOGY

From the Greek word for form or pattern, which in biblical times denoted both the original model or the prototype and the copy that resulted. In the N.T. the latter was labeled the anti-type, and this was especially used in two decisions: (1) The correspondence between two historical situations like the flood and baptism (1Pe 3:21) or two figures like Adam and Christ (Rom 5:14), (2) The correspondence between the heavenly pattern and its earthly counterpart, e.g., the divine original behind the earthly tent/tabernacle (Act 7:44; Heb 8:5;9:24).

UNCONDITIONAL LOVE

See Impersonal love

ULTRA-SUPERGRACE

Ultra-supergrace is the most advanced stage of spiritual maturity related to time, history, and the angelic conflict. Once the believer breaks the maturity barrier through the daily metabolization of doctrine, he moves into three different spheres of maturity.

UNLIMITED ATONEMENT

Atonement is defined as the saving work of Christ on the cross. The burnt offering of the Old Testament was accepted to make an atonement, Lev 1:4. However, animal sacrifices have no efficacy, Heb 10:4; only the perfect sacrifice of Christ is efficacious, Heb 9:26 and 10:5-10. So atonement is the reconciliation between God and man, accomplished by the efficacious sacrifice of our Lord Jesus Christ on the cross. Hence, unlimited atonement and propitiation remove the barrier between God and man, so that every person in the human race can have eternal salvation.

THE UNPARDONABLE SIN

This is the one sin Jesus Christ could not and did not die for on the cross, Jn 3:18, 36. This sin is the rejection of Christ and His work on the cross.

This sin is related to the convicting ministry of the Holy Spirit, Gen 6:3; Jn 16:7-11; Heb 10:29. Rejection of Christ is called "sin," Jn 16:9.

VIRGIN BIRTH

Since the old sin nature is passed down from the man in copulation, the seed for the formation of the body of TLJC was implanted in virgin Mary by way of the power of the Holy Spirit, hence God is the father of Jesus Christ and Mary was the mother. Mat 1:18,22-25 and Luk 1:26-38 teach us that the birth of Jesus resulted from a miraculous conception.

VIRTUE LOVE

See Impersonal love

VOLITIONAL RESPONSIBILITY

This is the most common and the first cause for human suffering in general, and is also a specific cause for believers. Our emphasis here is on believers only.
Every human being must take the responsibility for his own decisions and his own actions in life. You must understand that you can never blame others for your misery, your unhappiness, and your suffering. You take full responsibility yourself, based on your own wrong decisions related to your associations, your activities, your motives, your functions in life.

WITNESSING

Is the communication of the good news of the Gospel of Jesus Christ to the unbeliever on a personal basis, known as personal evangelism. Witnessing therefore is the responsibility of every believer. But the believer is responsible only to communicate the accurate information concerning the finished work of TLJC on the Cross . . . the believer is not responsible to make anyone accept the information!